Praise for *Magical Faery Plants*

"A well-researched and lovingly crafted guide to the nature spirits. Filled with lovely rhyming chants and magickal verses, it will entice you to build your own faery altar and garden. Through this book you will learn to contact the faeries and travel to the fae realms (and return safely!). The herb spells and prescriptions are filled with power and magick."

—Ellen Evert Hopman, author of *Scottish Herbs and Fairy Lore* and *Once Around the Sun*

"Sandra Kynes has gifted us with an inspiring and incredibly useful work in *Magical Faery Plants*. Her breadth of knowledge, experience, and a clear connection with the faery realm are evident throughout, all backed with research from reputable sources and packed full of practical suggestions you'll be eager to try for yourself. This is a valuable addition to any faery and nature lover's library."

—Emily Carding, author of *Seeking Faery*

MAGICAL FAERY PLANTS

©Jessicaa Weiser

About the Author

Sandra Kynes is a member of the Bards, Ovates and Druids. She likes to develop creative ways to explore the world and integrate them with her spiritual path and everyday life. Her unique views and methods form the basis of her books, which serve as reference material for Pagans, Wiccans, and anyone interested in experiencing their spirituality in a different way.

Sandra has lived in New York City, Europe, England, and now mid-coast Maine, where she lives with her family and cats in a mid-nineteenth-century farmhouse surrounded by meadows and woods. She loves connecting with nature through gardening, hiking, bird-watching, and kayaking. Visit her website at www.kynes.net.

MAGICAL FAERY PLANTS

A GUIDE FOR
WORKING
WITH
FAERIES &
NATURE
SPIRITS

SANDRA KYNES

Llewellyn Publications
Woodbury, Minnesota

First Edition
First Printing, 2022

Book design by Colleen McLaren
Cover art by Leanna TenEycke
Cover design by Shira Atakpu
Interior art by Melani Huggins

Llewellyn Publications is a registered trademark of Llewellyn Worldwide Ltd.

Library of Congress Cataloging-in-Publication Data (Pending)
ISBN: 978-0-7387-7032-1

Llewellyn Worldwide Ltd. does not participate in, endorse, or have any authority or responsibility concerning private business transactions between our authors and the public.

All mail addressed to the author is forwarded, but the publisher cannot, unless specifically instructed by the author, give out an address or phone number.

Any internet references contained in this work are current at publication time, but the publisher cannot guarantee that a specific location will continue to be maintained. Please refer to the publisher's website for links to authors' websites and other sources.

Llewellyn Publications
A Division of Llewellyn Worldwide Ltd.
2143 Wooddale Drive
Woodbury, MN 55125-2989
www.llewellyn.com

Printed in the United States of America

Also by Sandra Kynes

Tree Magic (2021)

Beginner's Guide to Herbal Remedies (2020)

Magical Symbols and Alphabets (2020)

Llewellyn's Complete Book of Essential Oils (2019)

365 Days of Crystal Magic (2018)

Crystal Magic (2017)

Plant Magic (2017)

Bird Magic (2016)

Herb Gardener's Essential Guide (2016)

Star Magic (2015)

Mixing Essential Oils for Magic (2013)

Llewellyn's Complete Book of Correspondences (2013)

Change at Hand (2009)

Sea Magic (2008)

Your Altar (2007)

Whispers from the Woods (2006)

A Year of Ritual (2004)

Gemstone Feng Shui (2002)

This book is dedicated to everyone who believes.

Contents

Contents

Contents

Contents

Contents

Contents

Introduction

Lingering at the edge of our awareness, we sense a fleeting presence of something just beyond our reach, yet a persistent feeling tells us that we can make contact if we open our hearts and minds. We know that what we sense is not something left over from childhood dreams, because many of us believe that there is more to this world than meets the eye. In addition, we know that the natural world is the key to unlock this age-old mystery.

Establishing a connection with nature helps us access different levels of awareness that bring deeper significance to our lives. With this connection comes the self-realization that nature is not out there and separate from us; we are part of it. And when we remove the blinders of our human world, we find the fullness of this planet and the faeries and nature spirits that reside here with us. With their help, we can learn how to abide in concert with the natural world and discover how to make our everyday lives more meaningful and magical.

Before we can connect with them, we need to define who they are because the terms *faery* and *nature spirit* encompass a wide range of spiritual and supernatural beings, with variations in their descriptions that change over time and often differ according to location.

First, there are the two common spellings, *faery* and *fairy*. Although these words have different meanings, *fairy* is frequently used when *faery* is intended. Perhaps by habit, I have been guilty of this.

The word *faery* indicates actual beings and their world that exists close to but separate from our own. These beings are part of the long-standing faery beliefs and traditions as detailed by Scottish scholar and minister Rev. Robert Kirk (1644–1692), American anthropologist and author W. Y. Evans-Wentz (1878–1965), and Scottish author, composer, and teacher R. J. Stewart (b. 1949).[1]

The word *fairy* refers to the imaginary beings and their land in stories of entertainment, not folklore. Characters such as Tinker Bell and the flower fairies of Cicely Mary Barker are examples of storybook fairies. They are cute and enjoyable, but they are not real faeries or nature spirits; they are pretend beings. That said, where the traditional and customary spelling is *fairy* in plant names (such as fairy flax, fairy bells, fairy cups) and other terms (such as fairy ring, fairy horse, fairy path)I have maintained these conventions throughout the book.

Magical Faery Plants is about the faery beings that exist in their own realm and from time to time enter ours. The faery tradition, often referred to as the faery faith, is not only a belief in these beings but a path for developing a relationship and working with them. According to R. J. Stewart, out of all the spiritual and supernatural beings, faeries are the closest to humans.[2] Perhaps this is one reason why we can often sense their presence. Although sometimes regarded as part of an underworld tradition, faeries are frequently described as intermediary spirits for chthonic deities, similar to angels being intermediaries for over-world deities. Whether or not they act as any type of go-between, faeries possess ancient power, magic, and wisdom in their own right.

This book is also about nature spirits, the beings that are closely connected with a place (*genius loci*), a type of plant, or a specific plant. Just like faeries, there is a widespread belief in nature spirits in many cultures, present and past. Nature spirits function as energy movers for the particular area or plant to which

---

1. Kirk had a keen interest in faeries and was said to have attracted their wrath by revealing too many of their secrets in his book, *The Secret Commonwealth of Elves, Fauns and Fairies.* He collapsed and died while walking Doon Hill, a known faery hill, but many believed he was abducted into faeryland. Evans-Wentz painstakingly collected reports of encounters with faeries, and his work *The Fairy-Faith in Celtic Countries* (first published in 1911) is still regarded as scholarly and culturally important. R. J. Stewart has written extensively on the underworld and faery traditions.

2. Stewart, *The Living World of Faery*, xvii.

they are attached. They not only work with the subtle energy of plants, but animals and humans, too. While the terms *devas* and *elementals* are often thrown into the mix when discussing faeries and nature spirits, I have developed a different definition and opinion on this. That discussion follows in chapter 1.

About This Book

Magical Faery Plants has been a long time in the making, at least twenty years, but the roots go back to my childhood. When I was little, maybe three or four years old, I saw things that other people didn't seem to be aware of. Like most kids who mention anything unusual, adults tried to convince me that I had not seen what I described and, oh my, what an active imagination! I didn't argue with them, but I knew what I had seen among the plants at the edge of our back porch and it wasn't my imagination. My mother usually shushed me and told me to go out and play with other kids. I did they just weren't human kids.

While growing up, I read everything I could get my hands on if it related to faeries. Sadly, it was long after my father passed away that I discovered he had had second sight. I don't know why he didn't speak up when I mentioned my special playmates. Perhaps he didn't think I was ready. I have often wondered what I could have learned from him regarding the fae.

During the last twenty years I have attended workshops, shared my experiences with others, and traveled to Ireland on a faery journey with several like-minded people. Although I lived in the countryside in England for several years, my recent move to the wilds of mid-coast Maine has validated my experiences more than ever. Now surrounded by meadows and large tracts of woods, nature spirits and faeries are especially close at hand. That said, during the many years I lived in New York City I found them accessible in Central Park and various small, green spaces tucked away among the canyons of Manhattan.

Since the time of English author Geoffrey Chaucer (c. 1342/43–1400), faeries were said to be in retreat.[3] But were they withdrawing from the world of humans or perhaps temporarily avoiding it? Today, it seems as though more and more people are reporting that faeries are making themselves known. It also seems that nature spirits are reaching out to those who want to tune into

3. Henderson and Cowan, *Scottish Fairy Belief*, 24.

the natural world. Perhaps this is related to the urgency of climate change or maybe we humans are finally ready to have a mature relationship with them because we can differentiate legend from fact. We realize that they are not devilish entities to be feared or placated.

Even though our worlds (human and faery) are separate, both are intertwined and rely on the health of the planet. We can work with faeries and nature spirits to heal the earth as well as ourselves. Because the natural world is integral to our spiritual and magical lives, and the lives of faeries and nature spirits are intimately bound to it, plants offer the perfect path to communicate and work with them.

Part one of this book provides background information on the history and written accounts of faeries and nature spirits. It contains details on where to find them, and how to contact them through methods such as meditation and visualization. Another chapter guides you through my three-step faery attunement process, which makes it easier to connect and work with them. Other chapters cover faery magic, dream work, journeying to faeryland, and instructions for making different types of tools. Information about altars and gardens are also included.

Part two contains profiles for the common plants found throughout faery lore plus some of the obscure ones. It also includes profiles for a number of plants that are not found in the faery folklore, but have become associated with the fae. Whether you are new or experienced in working with faeries and nature spirits, *Magical Faery Plants* provides a fresh, twenty-first century approach that will be an essential go-to reference on your bookshelf.

PART
ONE

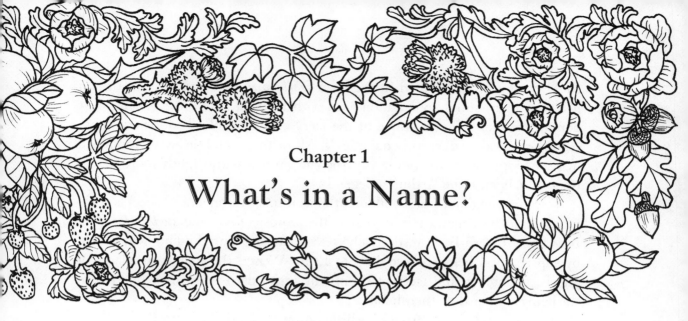

Chapter 1
What's in a Name?

The word *faerie/fairy* has a long, interwoven history from several languages. The modern English word comes from the Middle English *fairie* (also spelled *faierie*), which was applied to the faery people, their homeland, and enchantment. These terms were taken from the Old French *faerie* and *faierie* that had evolved from the earlier forms *fée*, *feie*, and *fayee*.[4] There is a plethora of spellings for these terms scattered throughout many sources. Also derived from Old French, the terms *fey* and *fay* emerged in medieval literary romances such as the thirteen-century *Lancelot du Lac* (author unknown).[5] Throughout this book I have used the words *faery* and *fae* interchangeably.

In the medieval Provençale language of southern France, the term for faery was *fada*; in Italian it was *fata*. The Latin *fata* could refer to a divining woman, enchantress, witch, or the Fates, which were the three Roman goddesses who spun the destiny of humans.[6] According to many sources, both of these terms may have been derived from the Medieval Latin *fatare*, "to enchant," or *fatum*, "fate" or "destiny." Professors Lizanne Henderson (b. 1968) and Edward Cowan (b. 1944) of the University of Glasgow noted that while the word *fay*

---

4. Editorial Staff, *Webster's Third New International Dictionary*, 816.
5. Fowler, *Fowler's Dictionary of Modern English Usage*, 307.
6. Ritson, *Fairy Tales, Legends and Romances*, 14.

could mean enchantress, when the term *faerie/fairy* came into use in Britain it had a supernatural connotation akin with the Old English *faege*, "fated or doomed to die."[7] The mystique of the faery and fey evolved to include "possessing magical or unearthly qualities."[8] All of these qualities were combined in Fata Morgana or Morgan le Fay, the enchantress with slightly more than a tinge of danger in the Arthurian legends.

Found throughout Celtic folklore, the word *sídhe* (pronounced shee) is commonly used by Pagans and Wiccans. The words *síd/síde* and *síodh/sídhe* (Old Irish and Modern Irish, respectively) refer to ancient burial mounds inhabited by supernatural beings. According to Evans-Wentz, the *sídhe* were places of ghosts, phantoms, and faeries.[9] Eventually in Modern Irish, *sídhe* referred to the beings rather than their habitat.

American scholar of Anglo-Irish literature Richard Finneran (1943–2005) noted that the Old Irish words *síde* and *síthe* and the Modern Irish *sídhe* also referred to a blast of air or a whirlwind that was "not necessarily the wind" or not caused by any type of weather condition.[10] We shall explore the relevance of this later.

Devas and Elementals

Although the terms *devas* and *plant devas* have come into popular use, I have come to the conclusion that *nature spirits* is a more straightforward designation that is free from cultural or religious ties. The word *devas* comes from Hinduism and Buddhism, where it refers to a demigod or divine being.[11] According to Hindu mythology, some devas embodied the powers of the natural world. Early twentieth-century Theosophists employed this link between devas and the natural world to describe angel-like beings. Founded in New York City in 1875, the Theosophical Society incorporated Hinduism, Buddhism, esoteric

---

7. Henderson and Cowan, *Scottish Fairy Belief*, 17.
8. Fowler, *Fowler's Dictionary of Modern English Usage*, 307.
9. Evans-Wentz, *The Fairy Faith in Celtic Countries*, 291.
10. Finneran, *The Yeats Reader*, 22.
11. Monier-Williams, *A Sanskrit-English Dictionary*, 430.

Christianity, and spiritualism into a religious philosophy. Scottish scientist and hermetic magician Robert Ogilvie-Crombie (1899–1975), sometimes referred to simply as ROC, was a theosophist known for talking to nature spirits in the botanical gardens of Edinburgh. His ideas were incorporated into Findhorn, a spiritual community in northern Scotland founded in the 1960s that became world-famous for working with plants and nature spirits.[12] In addition to being called *devas*, the nature spirits there are sometimes referred to as the Findhorn fairies.

While faeries and nature spirits may have an affinity with one of the four elements, calling them *elementals* is a misnomer. Elementals are, well, more elemental than faeries and nature spirits. However, this is not to imply that they are a type of simple, little being, because they are complex in their own way. In my opinion, they are a presence and to some extent a force of nature rather than a being in the way faeries and nature spirits are.

During the Middle Ages, there was a belief in the existence of creatures that consisted purely of one element. Despite a popular notion that elementals were devils, alchemists viewed them as semi-material spirits of the elements. Swiss physician and alchemist Theophrastus Bombastus von Hohenheim (1493–1541), who called himself Paracelsus, advanced the concept of elementals and standardized the names for them.[13] He provided descriptions of them in his treatise *A Book on Nymphs, Sylphs, Pygmies and Salamanders and Other Spirits*. Although it has a different connotation today, the term *pygmy* comes from the Greek *pygmaois*, meaning "dwarfish," which was derived from *pygmē*, a unit of measure also known as the cubit.[14] Nowadays, elementals are more commonly referred to as undines (water), sylphs (air), gnomes (earth), and salamanders (fire).

While Paracelsus regarded elementals as anthropomorphic, he believed that they had a parallel evolution to humans and while they inhabited a separate realm from humans, they could also pass into ours. Picking up where Paracelsus left off,

---

12. Stewart, *The Living World of Faery*, xxi.
13. Pogačnik, *Nature Spirits & Elemental Beings*, 59.
14. Barnhart, *The Barnhart Concise Dictionary of Etymology*, 622.

categorizing nature spirits by element and calling them *elementals* came of age in the 1880s through the work of Helena Petrovna Blavatsky (1831–1891).[15] Blavatsky was a Russian émigré, occultist, philosopher, and one of the co-founders of the Theosophical Society. From here, the concept of elementals became intertwined with folklore and literature, and provided a wellspring of new ideas for the Victorian fairy mania. Theosophist ideas and nomenclature also took root in modern Paganism.

According to some theories, elementals are sentient beings, not spirits; others claim the opposite. Regardless of what they may be, their presence can be felt and occasionally seen. In my own experience, I can understand why they have been regarded as tricksters or mischievous sprites. One of my most memorable events with them took place when I was in Ireland. After a stormy night, my friends and I were enjoying a warm, sunny day and tried to perform a ritual in the ruins of an ancient hill fort. Honoring the forces of the weather, Germaine began by saying, "Hail, wind and rain," meaning a salutation of "hail and welcome" to simply acknowledge the rain and wind of the previous night. Before anything further could be said, we were pelted with hail and rain and nearly blown off the hill. As fast as it started, the sky was clear and blue again without a trace of the storm. Coincidence? We didn't think so.

Despite this experience, I do not believe that the elementals were being vindictive or mischievous. Being mostly of one element—comprised of, living in it, or whatever—I think they lack a balanced perspective or understanding and simply delivered what they may have believed we were requesting. Because of this, I think it is very challenging to enlist their aid in magic or ritual. When I sense their presence, I simply acknowledge them and wish them well. The decision to work with elementals is a personal one, of course.

Origin Theories

Through the centuries, there have been a number of theories as to where the faeries came from. One prevalent notion is that they descended from Celtic deities. According to legend, when the Tuatha Dé Danann, people of the God-

---

15. Silver, *Strange and Secret Peoples*, 39.

dess Danu, arrived in Ireland, they conquered the earlier inhabitants, the Fir-bolgs. In turn, the Tuatha Dé Danann later retreated underground into old burial mounds and to magical islands in the west when the Milesians conquered them. A related theory notes that the Dé Danann were not the original faeries, but joined them as a separate class of their own.[16] The original faeries were said to have been the Firbolgs who had migrated to the Western Isles. While these theories relate to Ireland, they do not explain the existence of faeries elsewhere in the world.

Seventeenth-century Puritans believed in faeries and that they were associated with the Devil.[17] Faeries were also reputed to be ghosts and sometimes specifically those of Pagans who were trapped between heaven and earth. A number of other theories linked them with the Pagan dead in one way or another.[18] Faeries also became associated with various forms of the Wild Hunt, a spectral cavalcade of the dead that traveled across the night sky during midwinter, led by either the Norse god Wodan or a powerful huntsman.[19]

In Scotland, a belief persisted in the Highlands that the ancestors dwelled within the faery hills. Elsewhere, faeries were similarly associated with the underworld and the realm of the dead as legends became entangled with ancient mythology. An example found in medieval literature is Chaucer's reference to Pluto, Greek god of the dead, as the king of the faeries.[20] Also, just as Persephone was told not to partake of food in the underworld, eating or drinking in faeryland was a taboo that would prevent a person from returning home. Ancient burial tombs, cairns, and dolmens became associated with the fae and were believed to be entrances to faeryland.

---

16. Mahon, *Ireland's Fairy Lore*, 18.
17. Briggs, *The Fairies in Tradition and Literature*, 66.
18. Henderson and Cowan, *Scottish Fairy Belief*, 19.
19. Briggs, *The Fairies in Tradition and Literature*, 63.
20. Phillpotts, *The Faeryland Companion*, 8.

Ancient dolmens were believed to be entrances to faeryland.

Another common theory was that faeries were an ancient folk memory of pygmy people who had lived in subterranean earthen houses. According to Henderson and Cowan, one such example dates to the writing of German historian Adam of Bremen (flourished eleventh century) concerning the Pictish tribes of northern Scotland. He noted that the Picts were a race of short-statured people who lived underground or in prehistoric burial mounds.[21] This diminishing in size of the Picts is not surprising because Pictish Scotland was one of the last bastions of Paganism in the British Isles. Belittling a people is a way to disparage their importance and worth.

Just as the personalities and actions of many ancient deities served to explain the workings of the world, unusual events, and mysterious phenomena, so too did

21. Henderson and Cowan, *Scottish Fairy Belief*, 21.

faeries. Because of this, it is important to examine the folklore and separate out the things that may have been difficult to accept or understand. Perhaps special-needs infants were easier to rationalize and deal with if they were regarded as faery changelings. This is not to suggest that all incidences can be explained away. However, faeries are not to be feared and placated as once thought, nor should they be overly sentimentalized or viewed as playthings. Like any type of being they deserve respect. Furthermore, through honesty and maturity, we can establish a meaningful connection and relationship with them.

Chapter 2
The Written Trail

Faeries and nature spirits have fascinated people for millennia, and tracing the written accounts of them is a subject that could fill an entire book. This chapter is intended to illustrate the antiquity of their documentation and provide a brief overview of how they have appeared in various cultures.

English antiquarian and author Joseph Ritson (1752–1803) noted that the earliest mention of faeries comes from the *Iliad*, written by Greek poet Homer (ninth or eighth century BCE).[22] However, if we look farther afield we can find older sources. Written in India around 1500–1000 BCE, the Vedas are sacred texts that contain mythological accounts, hymns, and poems.

While the Vedas mention aerial beings called *gandharvas*, which have been likened to faeries, it is the *apsaras* who more closely fit the bill.[23] Also called *spirits of the clouds* and *celestial nymphs*, apsaras were originally associated with water and trees.[24] Later, as they became affiliated with other types of flora, some of their names were the same as the plants with which they were allied. Described as exceptionally beautiful, they enjoyed dancing, singing, and playing. In addition, they could assume other forms and were adept in magic. Like some faeries of Western mythology, they could be terrifying at times. As a form

---

22. Ritson, *Fairy Tales, Legends and Romances*, 11.
23. Dalal, *The Vedas*, 342.
24. Monier-Williams, *A Sanskrit-English Dictionary*, 59.

of magical being in their own right, nature spirits were also mentioned in the Vedas and the later epic poem *Mahabharata*, which was written approximately 400–200 CE.[25]

In China, Hsi Wang Mu, also known as Mother of the West and Queen of the West, was first mentioned in the *Zhuangzi*, one of the older books of Taoism written by philosopher Zhuang Zhou (c. 369–286 BCE).[26] As a goddess revered in several Asian cultures, Hsi Wang Mu is noted as living with her faery legions in the sacred Kunlun Mountains that run along the northern border of what is now Tibet.

Faeries possessing great beauty are featured in a number of Chinese folktales. In these legends, faeryland is often reached by crossing a bridge.[27] The people who eventually return to their homes discover that time has moved at a very different pace. The disparity in the passage of time is also a hallmark of faeryland in Celtic mythology.

To the west of the Kunlun range are the mountains of the Hindu Kush of northern Pakistan. Mountain faeries of this region are noted in folklore as cultivating fields of sesame and coriander.[28] According to ancient and current legends, Tirich Mir, the highest mountain in the Hindu Kush, is referred to as the kingdom of the faeries and the jinn.[29] Local lore tells that the faeries descend from the peak to the high mountain meadows in late autumn. They are known locally as *apsaras* and *peri*, their Sanskrit and Persian names, respectively.

And now, back to Homer and Greece. Some of the heroes in the *Iliad* are described as having nymph/faery lovers, and one passage notes that they enjoy the faery pastime of dancing in a circle. In contrast, the sirens of the *Odyssey* were a treacherous form of fae. Throughout Greek mythology, nymphs are portrayed as possessing some type of supernatural or magical power.[30]

---

25. Dalal, *The Vedas*, 342.
26. Sharma, *Women in World Religions*, 179.
27. Dennys, *The Folklore of China*, 96.
28. Ibid., 95.
29. Witzel, "Kalash Religion," 605.
30. Ritson, *Fairy Tales, Legends and Romances*, 12.

While Greek nymphs may in some respects closely resemble faeries, certain types of nymphs are more clearly nature spirits. Dryads, Greek tree nymphs, were originally associated with the oak but came to represent the spirits of other trees. The name *dryad* comes from the Greek *drys*, meaning "oak."[31] Classified as a type of human-like nymph in Greek mythology, the dryads were believed to be born with, inhabit, and then die with a specific tree. Whereas the dryad came to be regarded as a more general spirit that dwelled among all the woodland trees, the hamadryad took on the role of a spirit who lived and died with a particular tree.

While the *peri* or *pari* of Persian mythology was originally more demon-like, later romantic poetry rehabilitated them into beautiful beings that ranked between angels and humans. As previously noted, the apsaras of the Hindu Kush were also known by the Persian name *peri*. Many Persian stories mention that a great compliment to pay a woman was to say that she was peri-born.[32] According to Ritson, the beautiful and mysterious aurora borealis was associated with the peri and sometimes referred to as "perry dancers."[33] Because they were occasionally depicted with wings, the peri became equated with European faeries.

31. Quattrocchi, *CRC World Dictionary of Plant Names*, 848.
32. Keightley, *The Fairy Mythology*, 15.
33. Ritson, *Fairy Tales, Legends and Romances*, 15.

In legend, the aurora borealis is associated with the peri.

In pre-Islamic Arabian mythology, faeries are found in the form of the jinni (plural jinn). Also called *jinnī* in Arabic, the name was Anglicized to *genie*.[34] The association of jinn with magic made them popular subjects in literature and folklore throughout the Middle East and North Africa. Although in Western culture we know them mainly through the *Arabian Nights* and Aladdin stories as wish-grantors, they have many parallels with the faeries of Europe.[35]

The jinn can change shape, fly, become invisible, and being dual-dimensional, they can move between their world and ours. Also like faeries, jinn were believed to have a fear of iron. Common in Morocco, the practice of placing an iron sickle in a silo to protect grain echoes the tradition of hanging a horseshoe over the door of a house for protection and luck in the British Isles.[36] The jinn reputedly lived in subterranean homes and often moved about in whirls of dust. Just as Arabs believed a whirlwind on the desert could be a flight of jinn, in Ireland a whirlwind of dust was regarded as faeries on a journey: a fairy wind.[37] Likewise, in Wales, small whirls of dust were believed to conceal faeries.[38] This brings us full circle back to the words *síde*, *síthe*, and *sídhe* that can refer to a faery being or a sudden gust or whirlwind that is not the wind, but a method of concealment.

---

34. Encyclpaedia Britannica Online, s.v. "Jinni," accessed June 3, 2020, https://www.britannica.com/topic/jinni.

35. Formally known as *The Thousand and One Nights*, the collection of stories comes from the Middle East and India. It is unknown who wrote them and when.

36. Lebling, *Legends of the Fire Spirits*, 198.

37. Keightley, *The Fairy Mythology*, 26.

38. Rhys, *Celtic Folklore*, 590.

Jinn were said to travel as a desert whirlwind.

The earliest account in England that relates to the faery realm comes from the Anglo-Saxons.[39] The term *Anglo-Saxon* is a collective noun for the Angles, Saxons, Jutes, and Frisians from northern Germany, the North Sea coast of Denmark, and the Netherlands who migrated to Britain around the fifth century. Information relating to the fae is found in two collections of manuscripts containing medical prescriptions and charms for dealing with elf shot, an invisible, magical weapon reputedly used by elves to cause disease.

Although the Anglo-Saxon manuscripts date to the middle of the tenth and eleventh centuries, the information is considered to be much older. One manuscript, *The Leechbook*, is regarded as the Anglo-Saxon doctor's handbook. From the Old English *læccan*, "to heal," the word *læce* or "leech" was used by the Anglo-Saxons to indicate a person who was skilled in medicine.[40] The practice of using worms called leeches for healing did not occur until the nineteenth century.

The other manuscript, *The Lacnunga*, is a collection of miscellany that contains medicinal remedies.[41] Some of the maladies included in the book are sudden stitch (*faerstice*), a sudden pain in the side; elf hiccup (*ælf-sogotha*), possibly a convulsive disorder; and water elf disease (*wæter-ælf-adl*), which may refer to chickenpox.[42]

In Norse and Germanic mythology, the fae are more commonly known as elves, and the source of information about them comes from two thirteenth-century books collectively known as the Eddas.[43] The Prose Edda was written or compiled by Icelandic chieftain Snorri Sturluson (1179–1241), who wanted to preserve Norse mythology.[44] It is also called the Younger Edda and sometimes Snorri's Edda. The other book, the Poetic Edda, contains older stories and poems. Recorded in the late thirteenth century, it is also called the Elder Edda. The author/compiler of the Poetic Edda is unknown.

---

39. Briggs, *The Fairies in Tradition and Literature*, 4.

40. Furdell, ed., *Textual Healing*, 11.

41. Arnovick, *Written Reliquaries*, 22.

42. Storms, *Anglo-Saxon Magic*, 160.

43. Turville-Petre, *Myth and Religion of the North*, 231.

44. Keightley, *The Faery Mythology*, 61.

According to the Eddas, the elves had relationships with humans and sometimes had children with them. Although elves could cause illness, they also had the ability to heal. The Prose Edda makes a distinction between two types of elves: the elves of light and the elves of darkness. The light elves are described as beautiful luminous beings with an almost demigod status. The dark elves lived underground and are described as the opposite of the light elves, especially in their actions.

Nature spirits show up throughout the folklore of Europe. In Germany, the wood folk, also known as the moss people, were like the Greek hamadryads, living and dying with a particular tree. In a number of Germanic areas, faerylike beings called *seliges fräulein* were the guardians of certain plants.[45]

Medieval Literature

With the rise of universities in the twelfth century came an increase in literacy and book production. Early Medieval literature spanned a wide range from folklore and ghost stories to courtly love and romance. Faeries began to show up almost everywhere in all types of literature.

Walter Map (c. 1140–c. 1209), English writer and courtier of King Henry II (1133–1189), is the author of *De Nugis Vurialium, Courtiers' Trifles*. The book contains stories of the supernatural that have origins in oral folklore. One well-known tale from the Welsh borders that Map included in his work concerns Wild Edric and his faery wife.[46] Another writer who may also have been in King Henry's court was Marie de France (flourished c. 1160–1215). She is the earliest-known woman poet, whose work focused on courtly romances with magical themes. According to British author, folklorist, and scholar Katharine Briggs (1898–1980), "Marie de France's thirteenth-century *Sir Lanval* is a true fairy story dressed as a romance."[47]

Although the Victorians are often cited as being the first to portray faeries as diminutive beings, archdeacon and historian Gerald of Wales (c. 1146–c. 1223) relayed a story about tiny, light-haired faeries whose home was in a

---

45. De Cleene and Lejeune, *Compendium of Symbolic and Ritual Plants in Europe*, vol. 2, 304.

46. Phillpotts, *The Faeryland Companion*, 28.

47. Briggs, *The Fairies in Tradition and Literature*, 10.

subterranean world.[48] Gerald's contemporary, English writer Gervase of Til-bury (c. 1150–1227), noted that half-inch-tall faeries were called *Portunes* and in France they were known as *Neptunes*.[49] Written in the early fifteenth century, *Huon of Bordeaux* (author unknown) is a French epic poem that influenced English poet Edmund Spenser (1552/3–1599) and William Shakespeare (1564–1616).[50] Oberon the faery king originated in *Huon of Bordeaux*, lived on in Shakespeare's *A Midsummer Night's Dream*, and continued in other works through the centuries. The faery Ariel in Shakespeare's *The Tempest* is more of a nature spirit.

Interwoven with Folklore

While Shakespeare's faery queen Titania in *A Midsummer Night's Dream* is stately and regal, his Queen Mab, mentioned in *Romeo and Juliet*, is less so and more in line with folk beliefs. Whether she evolved from the French Dame Habundia, a faery/witch queen, or the Celtic warrior Queen Maeve, who was also regarded as a queen of the faeries, Mab is firmly rooted in folklore.[51] In Warwickshire, instead of being pixie-led or led astray by a will-o-the-wisp, a person was said to have been Mab-led.[52]

Mention the term *fairy tale* and the work of the Brothers Grimm, Jacob (1785–1863) and Wilhelm (1786–1859), usually comes to mind. Their classic collection, *Grimm's Fairy Tales: Stories and Tales of Elves, Goblins and Fairies*, was first published in two volumes from 1812–1815. While they were put forth as thrilling stories for children, the Grimms were folklorists and some of their stories were taken from oral tradition. Their work led to the serious study of folklore by scholars such as the previously mentioned W. Y. Evans-Wentz.[53] While Irish writer William Butler Yeats (1865–1939) is most widely known as a poet and playwright, he is also lauded for his work in folklore, much of which

48. Ibid., 7.
49. Keightley, *The Fairy Mythology*, 285.
50. Ibid., 56.
51. Bane, *Encyclopedia of Fairies in World Folklore and Mythology*, 171.
52. Phillpotts, *The Faeryland Companion*, 49.
53. Zipes, *The Oxford Companion to Fairy Tales*, 205.

was rooted in myth and magic. *Celtic Twilight: Faerie and Folklore*, first published in 1893, may be his most famous.

While English poet Alexander Pope (1688–1744) may have been the first to describe faeries with wings, English painter William Blake (1757–1827), who professed to have seen faeries, fitted them with gossamer butterfly-like wings.[54] However, folklore indicates that instead of wings, faeries used magic spells, wore white caps, or turned reeds and other plants into aerial steeds so they could fly.

---

54. Gaffin, *Running with the Fairies*, 10.

Chapter 3
Getting Started

Before contacting faeries and nature spirits it is important to know why you want to meet them. While you may be driven by curiosity—and who wouldn't want to know firsthand that they exist—it's better to have a reason for contacting them. Like meeting another human, it could be somewhat awkward to do otherwise.

Establish Your Purpose

According to Greek philosopher Heraclitus (flourished c. 500 BCE), people considered the human soul to be part of the natural world. In fact, the ancient Greeks believed that a universal soul passed "not only between humans, but also into plants and inanimate objects."[55] While our modern view on this may be different, most of us feel an incredibly strong connection with nature. Many of us find that drawing closer to the natural world enables us to access different levels of energy and awareness. Worldwide, most cultures (past and present) believe that there are unique healing powers in nature. Establishing a meaningful connection with the natural world enables us to develop our own powers of healing. This may be one motivation for contacting faeries and nature spirits.

As previously mentioned, the fae and nature spirits seem to be making their presence known more now than in the past and an important reason may be the

---

55. Moodley and West, eds., *Integrating Traditional Healing Practices*, 125.

health of our planet. Even though our realms are separate, they are intertwined and rely on the integrity of the earth. Climate change is an important matter that humans have been slow to acknowledge and even slower to take action on. Nature spirits and faeries can help us see more clearly what we need to do and by working with them we can begin to heal the damage. Of course, raising awareness and working with energy is one tiny part of the overall work that is needed, but it is something we can all do no matter our abilities or where we live.

A powerful reason that many of us have for establishing a relationship with faeries and nature spirits is that we want to connect with the natural world on a deep, soul level. We are aware of something greater in this world than ourselves and we recognize that we are a part of it. We know that if we can touch another realm our lives will be transformed on many levels, especially spiritual.

In addition, we find that drawing closer to the natural world enhances our health and enables us to find a sense of harmony around us—not only when we are out in nature, but at home too. This grounded sense of being reverberates through us and helps us tap into our true potential. Establishing a relationship with faeries and nature spirits also helps us expand awareness, fine-tune intuition, and develop subtle skills. We begin to live in magic because we associate with the world around us in a new way as our everyday experiences become deeper and more meaningful.

These are just a few general reasons for wanting to contact and work with faeries and nature spirits. The most important point is to be clear about what you hope to achieve in your relationships with them. In addition, it's important to keep in mind that this takes time and patience.

Where to Find Them

Nature spirits can be found almost everywhere, including a public park, your backyard, and sometimes among houseplants. Initially, the fae may be harder to find. Or, more accurately, it may take more time to convince them to make their presence known to you. There is a major difference in the basic attitude of nature spirits and faeries. Without sounding disrespectful, it can seem as different as trying to relate with cats and dogs. Dogs (nature spirits) are friendly and happy to meet you, cats (faeries) are often more reserved and have their own plans that you may or may not fit into. Be patient; keep an open mind and heart.

If you are finding nature spirits, look in the same places for faeries. Also look in transitional spaces that serve as thresholds, such as the edge of a meadow or woods, the areas where suburbs turn into fields, or the scrubland along a beach. A shoreline area with dog roses is almost always a sure bet. Watery places such as springs, marshes, and streams, especially where water sources join together, are liminal thresholds. Also, if you are out on a foggy day, look for a mist gate, a magical gap in the mist or fog that sometimes surrounds a faery place.[56] Occasionally, you may even find a faery in your home.

A solitary tree or small copse of trees can be a faery island in the human world.

Be on the lookout for a solitary tree, a pair of trees, or a small copse of different trees in the middle of a field or meadow. I like to think of these places

---

56. Tongue, *Forgotten Folk-tales of the English Counties*, 74.

as faery islands in the human world. At any rate, if you find several such places in one area, try to determine whether they are aligned in any way and examine the energy between them, as there may be a fairy path connecting them. Like a ley line, a fairy path is a line of energy. It runs along a frequently used trail that connects sites important to the fae.[57] The property I recently purchased has a number of small copses that were left standing by previous owners who had cleared some of the woods around the house several decades ago. I'm still exploring these groups of trees because several seem to have an energetic connection. At first I wondered if the previous owners had been sensitive to it until I discovered that they had constructed a large stone circle. That answered my question.

Making Contact

Descriptions of various types of faeries and what they are called can be found in many books. However, not all faeries that we encounter fit into a particular category or can be found in books. In addition, faeries do not appear the same in all geographical locations. Because of this, it's best to have no expectation of what you may see or experience.

Faeries and nature spirits will check you out first before allowing contact. Being extremely perceptive, they will sense what is in your heart and reflect back what you bring in your soul. You will not receive sincerity or friendship if you are insincere or manipulative.

When reaching out to faeries and nature spirits, you can speak to them aloud or in your mind. Whichever way you choose to communicate, do so clearly. Remember my experience with elementals? They were only giving us what they thought we wanted.

Just as important as expressing yourself clearly, is to pay attention and be sure you understand what is being communicated to you. Ask questions if you are unsure. Non-verbal communication is common, but ask questions if you are not sure what they are trying to convey to you. Even when dealing with other humans, non-verbal communication can be difficult; it can be especially challenging with other beings. Have patience; it takes time to learn how to converse with faeries and nature spirits.

---

57. Stewart, *The Living World of Faery*, 39.

Adding to the challenge is the fact that the method and manner of communication often varies from one individual to another. You may find that some individuals answer your questions and share things directly and others indirectly. Information can be sprinkled like faery dust throughout a conversation, leaving you to connect the dots afterward. Things that are said to you or feelings you received might only become clear after your encounter ends. Writing down a few notes about your experience immediately afterward and meditating on them can help bring clarity. Usually, after working with an individual a couple of times, you will discover a rhythm to their communication style, which will make it easier to converse and learn.

When you sense the presence of a faery or nature spirit, say so and let them know what you are experiencing. Always be respectful and honest. Remember that you are dealing with an intelligent being, not a pet or plaything for your amusement. Never try to command them to do something for you; they will see that you are a false ally and not someone to befriend. Remember the old adage that you have to be a friend to have a friend.

When you start getting close to making contact, you may have a sense of heightened energy. Preceding a few encounters, I felt a tingling rush of energy. One time when I was walking in the woods I felt a circle of energy running through the trees surrounding me. The odd thing, or so it seemed at the time, was that I felt part of that energy. At other times, the energy may be subtle and feel only slightly different than usual. This is why using the faery attunement, which is covered in the next chapter, is especially helpful for working with them.

While you may not see a faery or nature spirit, occasionally you may catch something out of the corner of your eye. You may notice just tiny snips of movement that are gone when you turn to look. It is not unusual to see faint, sparkling energy. At times for me, they have appeared as patches of little blue sparkles or swirls. No pun intended, but pixies have appeared to me several times as blue, shimmery pixelated images. Also, it is not unusual to experience a welling up of emotion the first couple of times you make contact because it can be an extremely moving experience. You sense that something very special is happening to you, something that is life-changing because you will never feel quite the same after connecting with another realm.

Once you start working with faeries and nature spirits, they may randomly appear even when you are not actively seeking contact. I encountered one when I was simply out for a walk. We surprised each other and were both slightly taken aback. The faery quickly vanished, but I felt privileged to have seen her. She appeared to me several times after that incident.

Ending a Relationship

Although it may seem odd to mention severing ties when just getting started, it is important to know how to handle the situation. As when dealing with other humans, we occasionally meet faeries that we are not compatible with or feel uncomfortable about and we need to end the relationship. This is not a failure on your part; it happens. For this reason, never view a liaison with the fae through rose-colored glasses because, like the human world, faeryland is populated with good and bad. However, don't be afraid or suspicious of every encounter; simply stay aware. As with all communication, make it clear that you do not want to continue your association. Be calm and polite.

Because of the belief that faeries fear iron, it is often suggested to visualize a symbolic cutting of your connection with an iron knife. There has been a great deal of debate about why faeries are said fear iron. The jinn are also reputed to have an aversion to it. Reasons range from faeries having been defeated by iron swords in battle to the idea that they reject modernity. It is also explained as a fear that harkens back to Homer's hero Odysseus, whose sword frightened the spirits of the dead. However, Briggs pointed out a paradox in these ideas: how could faeries fear iron if some legends note that they are masters and teachers of metal skills?[58]

At any rate, because this book relates to plants, rue (*Ruta graveolens*) can be used to sever ties. Like faeries, rue has been described as potent against jinn, too. Also known as the herb of grace, rue provides a graceful way to cut connections. If you don't have rue in your garden, the dried herb can be purchased. (Be sure to read the cautions in the profile for rue in part two.) However, because in magic we frequently work with symbols, a picture of the plant can take the place of the real thing.

---

58. Briggs, *The Fairies in Tradition and Literature*, 27.

Place a bowl and dried rue or a picture of the plant on your altar. Light a candle as you recall your last contact with the faery. Tear the picture into tiny pieces or crumble the herb, and then drop them into the bowl as you say:

With this common plant of rue,
I am no longer linked with you.
Never again contact me,
Fare thee well and blessed be.

Repeat the incantation two more times. Sit in front of your altar and visualize a burden being lifted from you. Afterward, bury the herb or pieces of the picture outside in the ground.

Chapter 4
The Faery Attunement

Before contacting faeries and nature spirits, it is important to be mentally and energetically ready. Preparation and contact is accomplished through an attunement process that taps into the power of seven and the techniques of meditation and visualization. The three parts of the faery attunement process include: engaging the breath, activating your energy, and aligning with your surroundings.

Meditation and Visualization

Because of our rush to do everything and be engaged 24/7, we need to learn how to slow down and move inward, which enables us to move outward in a way that is suitable for contacting faeries and nature spirits. Meditation and visualization are important tools because they provide the means to move to a different state of consciousness. These techniques allow us to drop the barriers that separate our everyday state of mind from a deeper level of consciousness. Both meditation and visualization are thresholds where the conscious and unconscious touch.

In meditation, we quiet the mind and come into stillness where we are present in the moment. We observe the energy around us and remain open and receptive to contact. Visualization is the cultivation of mental imagery. It is a technique that involves shifting our view of reality away from mundane thoughts and actions in order to tap into the network of energy that underlies the world of our everyday consciousness. Not only does visualization provide access to a different reality, it also provides a way for us to function in that reality.

While using these techniques, it is important to be mindful that you do not slip into a daydream or fantasy. Don't imagine that the elves of Rivendell are on your doorstep waiting to meet you. It will be obvious to the fae and nature spirits that you are not sincere in contacting them and simply entertaining yourself. Relax, enter with no expectations about what may occur, and allow the experience of visualization to draw you along.

The Power of Seven

Seven is the number that is symbolic of bringing all things into existence and for initiating change. To the ancient Egyptians it was a symbol of eternal life as well as a complete cycle. Seven is a foundation: There are seven days to the week, seven major chakras, seven visible colors in a rainbow, and seven crystalline structures. There are seven tones in an octave and seven musical keys. Rome was built on seven hills. Siddhartha reputedly walked around the Bodhi tree seven times before sitting down to meditate, reaching enlightenment, and becoming Buddha. Seven has been perceived as a lucky number and one that brings gifts.

The faery star embodies the power of seven.

The seven-pointed star is known as the faery star, elven star, witch's star, astrologer's star, and the star of the seven sisters (the Pleiades). In Celtic practices, it represents the four cities and gifts brought by the Tuatha Dé Danann and the three realms of sky, sea, and earth. In other practices, the seven-pointed star encompasses the cardinal directions as well as above, below, and center. It is a melding of the four elements with the three worlds of heaven, earth, and underworld.

Although there are variations in faery practices, the points of the star represent the qualities of honor and unity, truth and knowledge, justice and trust, love and blessings, service and devotion, faith and wisdom, hope and healing. You can empower your magical and spiritual practices by gazing at the symbol of the faery star while meditating on what these qualities mean to you.

As you read through the following details for the faery attunement, it may seem like a lengthy process, but after using it several times you'll find that it is not time-consuming. Whenever you go through the attunement, spend as much time on each of the steps as feels appropriate. Go at your own pace.

Engage the Breath

The first step in the faery attunement is to engage the breath, uniting mind and body and bringing your attention and physical self into balance. Begin with silence. Silence is something that we are generally not used to because of the social pressure to be plugged in, connected, and constantly available. Sitting in silence may take practice, which is why it may be helpful to spend a little time on this each day. As you sit in silence, listen. Listening to silence isn't about emptiness or creating a void; it is about being aware and present with your mind fully engaged. As someone pointed out to me when discussing meditation, the words *listen* and *silent* use the same letters.

Beyond the squawking parrot of our thoughts exists a soft whisper. We must be silent and listen carefully to hear it. This is the voice of the soul, the inner self. Through this voice, wisdom arrives; we need only to sit in silence and let it happen. Through this voice, we can communicate with other worlds, with the realms of faeries and nature spirits. Through this voice we can also find inner peace.

To begin, sit comfortably and focus your attention on long, slow breaths. At the start of an inhalation, slowly count to seven. Stop and hold the breath in for a moment, and then begin to exhale as you slowly count to seven again. Stop and hold the breath out for a moment before beginning the next inhalation and slowly counting to seven. Do this until you feel the stillness within. Eventually you will find the number of breaths that suit you for the preparation process.

Engaging the breath and mind will keep you rooted in the present moment, which will help cultivate awareness of self and surroundings. Once we are able to move inward to that sense of self, we can use that awareness to outwardly sense other beings. After engaging the breath and mind, we activate the chakras in preparation for sensing and working with energy.

Activate Your Energy

According to ancient Hindu texts, humans exist on both a physical level and a subtle level. Chakras are energy fields in the subtle body with corresponding energy centers in the nerve plexuses of the physical body. Seven of these nerve plexuses/energy centers constitute the major chakras that run from the base of the spine to the top of the head. Secondary chakras are located on the palms of the hands and the soles of the feet. In addition to the chakras within the physical body, there are several others that are known as gateway or celestial chakras. Three of these are located above the head and a fourth is within the ground beneath our feet. Called the *earth star chakra*, it resides approximately three feet below the ground, connecting us with the energy of the earth. This chakra is instrumental in working with the natural world and is part of the process of activating the chakras and working with the realms of faeries and nature spirits.

In this second step of the faery attunement process, we activate the chakras, tune into our flow of energy, and then connect it with the earth star. Begin by standing comfortably. Place your left palm on your stomach and your right palm over your heart. The left hand is over the solar plexus chakra, which is the seat of courage and power; the right hand is over the heart chakra, the seat of love and compassion. The heart chakra serves to maintain balance and moderate the energy of the solar plexus, which can be extremely strong and overpowering. With your hands in these positions, feel the energy of these two powerful chakras expanding and merging. Visualize the energy as a soft, white light expanding and surrounding you.

With the energy of your heart and solar plexus chakras (your compassion and willpower), this light rises to the top of your head. After a moment, it moves down along your spine, activating all seven chakras into one gentle flow of energy. Continue to visualize the light and energy moving down your legs as you bring your awareness to the soles of your feet. Sense the power of the earth star keeping you connected with the earth. See the white light extending from your feet down through the earth star and deep into the earth. Feel the stability of the earth and your connection with her. This cord of energy will also connect you to the realms of faeries and nature spirits. When you feel your energy connecting with the earth, allow the image of the white light to fade and dissolve.

Align with Your Surroundings

Focusing attention and integrating your energy with your surroundings helps to expand awareness for finding and communicating with other realms. After establishing your connection with the earth star and earth, the final step is to acknowledge and align with the seven directions. I have adapted this idea from R. J. Stewart for my own work with faeries and nature spirits.[59]

The seven directions are: above, below, within, before, behind, left, and right. If you prefer, you can attune to the cardinal directions by facing east. The direction "before" aligns with east, "behind" with west, "left" with north, and "right" with south.

For this step you can stand or sit. Hold your hands open in front of you, elbows bent at waist height and palms facing up. Speak the following words aloud or silently with your inner voice:

The sky above me, the earth below me, and the spirit within me;
Unite with what lies before me, behind me, to my left, and to my right.
In faith and truth, I acknowledge and honor all that is around me.

---

59. R. J. Stewart, *Earth Light*, 42.

Close your eyes and reach out with your energy. You may choose to meditate on what you feel or to visualize your energy moving outward. As you do this, you may sense a shift in the energy around you or you may feel a presence nearby. You may even hear unfamiliar sounds. Don't try to communicate; simply wait for a faery or nature spirit to acknowledge you.

Even though the goal is to make contact, don't expect anything to happen immediately or even the first several times you go through the faery attunement process and reach out. Making contact takes time, and it doesn't occur every time even after you have done it once or twice. Don't feel disappointed; be patient.

When you feel that your contact session has run its course or if you get distracted, end it. Open your eyes and sit quietly for a few minutes. Take your time to re-cross the threshold into your everyday world.

You may want to use a journal to chart your experiences with faeries and nature spirits. Like dreams, things that occur can disappear in a split second like a gossamer mist that is lost to the conscious mind. I have kept journals on and off for over forty years and whenever I read through them, I'm amazed at how much I have forgotten, but I often find clarity for the present. Reading through them while working on this book was a journey in itself that helped me remember so much and reaffirm my path.

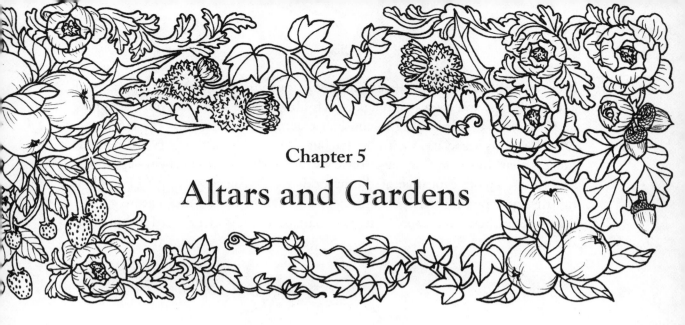

Chapter 5
Altars and Gardens

Whether or not we go out into the woods or meadows to work with faeries and nature spirits, keeping a special place in the home or nearby in a garden helps to build and maintain contact with them. A space that is set aside and made special for these spiritual beings will attract them because it shows your interest and sincerity.

Altars

An altar is not just a thing that holds a collection of objects; it is a place of power. When we use an altar, we step outside the boundaries of everyday life because intention and energy transform it into a space that transcends the mundane world. Because the objects that we place on an altar are often a mix of inspirational and devotional, personal and sacred, the resulting space visibly and energetically links the spiritual and physical worlds. An altar is not a passive space; there is constant interaction because of the energies that converge there.

While a separate table altar may be ideal, a windowsill or shelf can work just as well. Creating an altar is about intention and using whatever works for you. If you choose to use an altar cloth, select colors found in nature or perhaps a botanical print pattern. An altar can be as simple or elaborate as you like. I keep several altars and they are continually morphing. I go through periods of adding things, and then stripping an altar almost bare so it can evolve again.

Of course, the first thing to consider placing on your altar is the faery star, not only for its association with the fae but also because of the faery attunement process that draws on the power of seven. A candle or two is always appropriate; choose colors evocative of the natural world. You may want to include a figurine or a picture that personifies your vision of faeries and nature spirits. Also use an item that represents your particular interest or relationship with them.

A faery altar can be as simple or elaborate as you like.

Of course, plants are especially potent for the altar when working with faeries and nature spirits. A potted plant, vase of flowers, or dried leaves placed on a small plate work well. You can start with whatever you have at hand and change them up as you read about the various plants in this book.

A wreath isn't just for hanging on your door at Yule. A small one can be placed on your altar around the base of a candle or figurine. It can be made from a slender twig or long flower stem by winding it into shape and tying it in place with pieces of ribbon or yarn. I like to think of the little wreaths I put on my altar as faery circles. There is more about making wreaths in chapter 8.

Before adding anything to your altar, read the following section, Prepare and Attune Objects and Tools, for details on how to cleanse and charge things. After an object is prepared and you are ready to place it on your altar, take a moment to hold it and sense its energy to help you decide where it should go. It is important that the things you use and how you arrange them have personal meaning for you. Listen to your inner voice and it will be right for you.

A faery altar is also a place of contact. After lighting a candle and going through the faery attunement, meditate or visualize as you sit in front of your altar. Hold a flower or leaf and invite any nearby faery or nature spirit to join you. Let them know why you have asked them into your home. Occasionally you may experience a surge of energy, but most often it may be a subtle feeling, the sense of a presence. Each encounter is unique.

Once in a while you may hear someone speak to you, and it may not be with your ears. A phrase or a sentence may seem to pop into your head. At times, you may be uncertain whether or not you have had contact, and it's good to be a little skeptical. Your intuition and heart-of-hearts will tell you what is true, but if you are really unsure, then it probably did not happen. When contact is meant to occur, it will.

In addition to an altar, it is common to keep several other special places around the house as well as outside. A little niche in the corner of a room, a shelf, a stair landing—the possibilities are endless, but this doesn't mean you need to fill every available space in your house. Wait until you get a sense that there is something unique about a certain spot. These can change from time to time. Listen and watch for subtle clues or a shift in energy to tell you that it's time for something new.

Prepare and Attune Objects and Tools

Whether you make, purchase, or find an item for your altar, prepare and attune it with your energy and intention before using it. While there are many ways to cleanse an item for magical use, here's a quick and powerful method using your own energy.

Hold the object between your hands and close your eyes. Engage the energy of your chakras as in the faery attunement process. Visualize the energy moving up through your body, and then pausing at your heart center. See, with your mind's eye, and feel it move down your arms surrounding the object. After a moment or two, it moves back up your arms, and then down through your body to the earth, where any unneeded energy from the item will be neutralized.

After cleansing, attune or charge an object by visualizing your energy merging with it as you say:

As above, so below, and within; stir the energy to begin.
Before, behind, left, and right; surround this item with power and light.
For my altar, this I prepare; and so my purpose it will share.

Gardens

Creating a garden that is attractive to faeries and nature spirits is not about setting up an overtly sentimentalized miniature tableau for Tinker Bell. This is not to say that some cute features shouldn't be included, but if you are serious about working with faeries and nature spirits, don't set up a Disney-style faeryland. After all, you are creating a place for touching and communicating with another realm, which makes it a sacred space. Of course, this doesn't mean you can't have fun or romanticize it a little. Finding balance is the key to make it work.

Faeries and nature spirits show us how to live closer to the natural world even if we don't live on acres and acres of land. A garden can consist of a few potted plants on a balcony or windowsill. I have had gardens of all sizes, including in apartments in Manhattan where I lived for a number of years. Nature finds a way to persist anywhere and so can you.

Start with what you like; we all have favorite plants. While my English grandmother was an avid gardener and her preferences influenced mine, I like to experiment with different plants and, whenever possible, include species native to the area where I live. Including native plants in your garden is especially helpful for attuning to local nature spirits. Birds, butterflies, and many other critters will appreciate it, too.

Maintenance is important because a garden can become quickly overgrown. The first summer I moved out to the countryside in Maine, I felt bad about removing plants from the front garden by my door, but I felt reassured because it was to reestablish a healthy garden. Whenever possible, if you have to thin out a garden, relocate the plants somewhere else or give them away. Sometimes it can be a challenge to maintain balance because it's good to leave a little spot that is more natural. As you do things in the garden, talk to any nature spirits or faeries that may be near. Explain and make your intentions clear. Remain sensitive; keep your energy and heart open to receive suggestions.

Position an outdoor altar where you will have privacy. A fence along the side of a yard or an area with tall shrubs can provide this. A flat rock can function as an outdoor altar or use a small table if space allows. Populate it with figurines, lanterns, and natural objects such as stones, acorns, or a potted plant. As with your indoor altar, include the faery star. It can be painted on a fence or on the altar, or you can hang faery star pendants from several trees or shrubs.

Another item to include on your altar is an offering bowl or plate. Offerings can include honeyed tea, fairy mead (milk, honey, and a drop of vanilla extract), or small pieces of bread soaked in honey. You may find that these appear untouched, but remember that faeries inhabit an ethereal realm. While they cannot consume these as we do, they are attracted to them and can absorb the essence of human foods.

On a Porch

If you are locating your faery garden on a porch or balcony, the first thing to do is to create a private area that passersby will not easily see. Use railings or put up lattice supports upon which climbing plants can grow. If climbing plants are not feasible, buy or construct a folding screen that will provide a backdrop to the garden. Placing it in a corner of the porch can create a cozy area that will be conducive for arranging plants and other items for your faery area.

In front of the screen or climbing plants, position a flower box or two for taller plants. Use a bowl to create a water feature that is an appropriate size for your porch arrangement. Place smaller potted plants around the water to create a natural setting. Old china bowls and saucers from a thrift shop make nice drainage pans for smaller flowerpots and add a special touch.

Create a faery garden on a porch or balcony with potted plants.

Wild Areas and Water

As previously mentioned, leave a small area untamed if possible. Even if it's only a corner underneath a bush, the fae and nature spirits will appreciate it. You can create a liminal spot by allowing blackberry or climbing rose canes to arch over, making a small threshold. A liminal threshold can be created on a porch, too, with almost any type of climbing plant.

If you have a big garden or enough space, leave a larger area wild and dedicate it to the faeries and nature spirits. Throughout Europe and the British Isles, setting aside a piece of land from everyday use was a fairly common practice that dates to Roman times. If a sacred site was disturbed, a place nearby was left wild for the genius loci that may have been displaced. In addition, the Romans dedicated part of an outdoor area near the home for the use of household spirits.

Many of these reserved areas contained a well and a special tree. Wells and springs were believed to hold the power of local deities and spirits. According to legend, a spring or well could be an entrance to faeryland.[60] The combination of a tree and sacred well is still regarded as especially potent. The term *well* generally included springs and small pools but on occasion it extended to the water that collects in a hollow created by the forked limbs of a tree.

In addition to leaving a votive offering at these sites, it was common practice to tie a piece of cloth on a branch of a tree while making a wish or praying for something or someone. It was believed that by the time the cloth disintegrated, the healing or request would materialize. This practice was also used to symbolically remove a burden. In the British Isles, these were called *cloutie* or *clootie trees*. The word *cloutie* referred to the strip of cloth.[61] Cloutie trees were most often hawthorn, blackthorn, or ash. In Ireland, a cloutie tree was also regarded as a faery tree and the piece of land that was left wild for the faeries was called *cloutie's croft*.[62]

Christians adapted the practice of petitioning God at a cloutie tree. However, setting aside a piece of land for spirits or faeries evolved into a method

---

60. Phillpotts, *The Faeryland Companion*, 24.
61. McNeill, *The Silver Bough*, 114.
62. Ibid., 58.

of appeasing the Devil. The piece of land became known euphemistically as Goodman's or Gudeman's field, Halyman's rig, and a host of other names.[63] In Ireland, the cloutie croft remained a special place for faeries.

Whether or not you have room for a cloutie croft, designate a special tree as a cloutie tree or add a small water feature such as a decorative bowl or a birdbath. Be sure to keep the water clean and fresh to show the faeries and nature spirits that you care about them. Position rocks and plants around the bowl to make the setting as natural as possible.

Make your garden a peaceful oasis, a place where you want to spend time. Use it to meditate and do ritual, or to just sit and observe. Your energy and intention will attract the faeries and nature spirits, too. In turn, you will probably become more attracted to this special place you have created. Working with faeries and nature spirits and attuning to the seven directions helps us align with the earth and develop deeper mindfulness of her sacredness.

---

63. Henderson and Cowan, *Scottish Fairy Belief*, 362.

Chapter 6
Faery Magic

In addition to working with energy, magic is an attitude toward the world and an awareness of its natural rhythms. It is a way of perceiving and living in the world. It includes the small things that occur in everyday life that act as reminders of who we are and where we fit in the vast web of existence. Magic is intertwined with our connection to the natural world. To me, coincidence is another form of magic that can occur as a major event in life or a very minor incident that can easily go unnoticed. Either way, it usually shepherds us toward or away from something or someone. Magic can be like a guiding hand that provides a gentle nudge or sometimes a shove to get us on the right track. I believe that at least one guiding hand in my life has come from the faery realm.

One reason that faeries have been of great interest to humans is because they are magical beings. While they have powers and can do things we cannot, never ask faeries to do your bidding because they are not servants and it is not appropriate. However, they can help with guidance and support. While nature spirits are not magical in the same sense as faeries, they can show you the energetic nuances of plants that can assist you.

Throughout folklore, faeries have been noted as using spells, many of which included plants.[64] Incorporating plants into spells and rituals is an especially effective way to follow their lead. People have used plants as amulets and charms

---

64. Phillpotts, *The Faeryland Companion*, 35.

for as long as records exist. By using plants, we follow in the footsteps of our ancestors with the help of faeries and nature spirits to guide us in crafting our own magic. Whatever your purpose, give your spell or request for aid careful thought. Be specific and realistic about what you want to achieve.

Spells and Requests

Before a spell is carried out, an incantation sung or recited, or a request made, you need to have a clear purpose in mind. Spells can be simple or elaborate. However, the saying "less is more" is often good advice. The actions and words in a spell are meant to focus the mind and energy for visualizing the outcome. Picturing your desire in your mind is an important part of the process. However, if a spell is too complicated, a lot of energy can be wasted on trying to get it right and it can end up like a performance devoid of feeling and power. Needless to say, it will not be effective.

Objects used during spellwork aid in directing the energy for your purpose. As in ritual, objects used in spells are symbols of the energy we want to move or the things we want to effect. Since we are working with the magical energy of plants, place one that is associated with your request on your altar when asking for aid or guidance from the fae. Part of a plant, a picture of it, or essential oil from it can be used to represent your chosen plant. When burning anything, use a cast-iron cauldron or some other fireproof vessel and place it on a safe, heat-resistant surface. Make sure it is big enough to accommodate anything you burn. Keep in mind that you don't need huge amounts of things for spells because magic works with symbols and intent. Place a plant, flower, or leaves associated with your request on your altar when asking for aid or guidance from the fae.

Assemble the things you need for a spell on your faery altar. Prepare a candle by inscribing it with the faery star. When everything is ready, light the candle and go through the faery attunement of engaging the breath, activating your energy, and aligning with your surroundings.

Use a wand or simply point to cast a circle, or as I like to think of it, a magical faery ring. This is not for protection, but rather to create a neutral space that will act as a cauldron for the energy you raise. By holding and building the energy prior to sending it out, a circle can increase the power of your spell or request.

Call the cardinal directions as you cast your faery ring in a clockwise direction. Visualize the circle as sparkling blue light as you say:

Power of North, East, South, and West,
May this magic by faery be blessed.
From realm to realm, circle round me;
Sacred this space, I now decree.

Go about your spell or request as planned and, before sending out the energy, visualize your desired outcome. Afterward, hold the image for a moment or two, and then let it fade. Thank the fae and nature spirits for their help. Dissolve your faery ring by turning in a counterclockwise direction as you say:

Farewell West, South, East, and North,
As this energy now goes forth.
This work, its purpose has been made,
And now this faery ring will fade.

Take time to ground excess energy by connecting with your earth star. You may want to leave things in place on your altar for a day or two. However, if you burned anything for the purpose of releasing or banishing, dispose of the ashes outside right away.

Some spells may work quickly while others may take time or need repeats. Reevaluate and check that you were clear about what you wanted. Reexamine how you asked for aid and if it didn't seem to work, try a different approach if you feel it is necessary. In the end, if it is not working for you, it could be that what you want is not meant to happen at this particular time. Accept that possibility gracefully and move on.

Dream Work

In the fertility of darkness, dreams open our creative channels and illuminate the areas of our minds that we cannot access during waking hours. It has been my experience that faeries sometimes present themselves in dreams before actually meeting or making contact. Likewise, places that appear in visualizations or meditations may first appear in a dream. It was in a dream that I first heard the sweet sounds of faery music.

Unlike other practices for which we raise energy, in dream work we want to avoid too much active energy that will keep us from reaching a deep level of sleep. The use of a dream pillow or other scented object is often helpful. You can sew a small pillow or use a little organza drawstring bag for this purpose.

Dried leaves or flowers, or essential oil from a plant that corresponds to your purpose, can be used for scent. If you are simply opening the psychic pathways for contact, use lavender or other plants associated with psychic abilities. However, lavender is exceptionally helpful. In addition to being calming for sleep, it enhances awareness and intuition for dream work and all forms of psychic work. Whatever plant(s) you use, place the dream pillow under or beside your bed pillow. If you are using a drawstring bag, it can be hung on a bedpost.

A plant on your bedside table can aid in dream work.

Another way to use plants in dream work is to place one on your bedside table or position plants or pictures of them around your bed. One time when I used multiple pictures for dream work, I woke in the middle of the night to find a circle of energy connecting the photographs I had placed around the room.

Another technique is to write something on a picture of a plant to keep under your pillow. It could contain a few simple keywords for what you are seeking or an invitation for faeries to enter your dreams. Regardless of whether or not you use any type of object to aid in dream work, set your intention before going to sleep by saying:

Now I lay me down to rest;
May a faery be my guest.
In the realm of mind and dream,
Of gentle shadow and soft moonbeam.

When engaging in any type of dream work, keep a journal or other method for recording your experiences at your bedside. It is a common occurrence when wanting to remember a dream only to have it quickly evaporate like a wisp of mist. Before falling asleep, set the intention of waking during the night after you have had a dream. While this doesn't always work, I have been able to wake up long enough to write things down. A couple of times I was surprised in the morning because I did not remember waking up and recording my experiences.

The Faery Journal

As mentioned, recording experiences and dreams over time can provide information about your relationship with faeries and nature spirits as well as events in your life. It's easy to forget how far we have traveled along our paths, and yet, the ability to look back can be a powerful tool for furthering our journeys and bringing the present into focus. When reading through older journal entries, you may find answers to current questions, or you may find clues about things that are important for you to examine. While writing this book, I took the time to go through decades of journals. It was an interesting journey that illuminated some of the recent changes in my life.

Journaling is not to be confused with the "Dear Diary, Today I…" writings of our pre-teen years. There are no hard-and-fast rules to keeping a journal except honesty. Journal entries do not have to be written every day, week, month, or year, for that matter. There are some gaps of a year or more in some of my journals. Regardless of the time between entries, journaling is something that I keep returning to because it is a powerful process for working things out and understanding my life.

A faery journal is just that: a special journal that is written for the purpose of recording your experiences with faeries and nature spirits. However, a faery journal isn't limited to that. Related doodles, symbols, sigils, pressed flowers or leaves, spells, and recipes all have their place within it. Over time, as energy becomes focused in the pages, a faery journal becomes an object of power. When placed on your altar it can boost the energy of spells and rituals. In addition, it can become a signal to the fae that you would like their presence.

As you use your journal, keep in mind that it is not necessary to write well-thought-out or complete sentences; getting your feelings and thoughts on paper, or somewhere digitally, is more important. You can go back and embellish your initial thoughts with follow-up comments. You may also want to consider using a technique called *mind mapping*, which can aid in bringing thoughts and information to the surface by word association. English author Tony Buzan (1942–2019) developed the technique as a tool to free the mind's hidden power. Basically, it's a method of brainstorming that uses word association for organizing thoughts. Where journaling is concerned, mind mapping works for connecting information. After meditation, visualization, or contact with faeries and nature spirits, creating a mind map is a way to draw out details and get them down on paper quickly. You can refer back to it later to write more completely about your experience.

To begin a mind map, start with a keyword or short phrase that relates to your experience, meditation, or dream. It might be a thought, an object, the title of a song, a feeling. Write it in the middle of a piece of paper, and then draw a circle around it. Write down another word or object from your experience and put a circle around it. Draw a line between the circles if you think they are connected. Keep going until you feel that you have remembered everything. You may have a page full of circles and lines that resemble a spider web or a lot of circles that are not connected. I like to think of these as bubbles: thoughts and information bubbling up from the inner self as well as messages from the faery realm.

Sometimes you may have a number of circles with only a few connected by lines and other times you may not realize things are connected until you refer back to the mind map at a later time or sit and meditate with it. For example, three things within a mind map I drew after an experience I had in the woods were: doorway, oaks, a sense of opening. I realized that this referred to two oak trees where a path skirted around them. On my next visit to the woods, I stopped between the trees and put my hands on them. Their energy flowed through me. These became my gateway trees and, each time I entered the woods, I put my hands on them for a moment before continuing on the path. It was like going through a doorway that heightened my energy and awareness and opened the way to many magical experiences in the woods. While not every mind map produces such results, the act of keeping a faery journal provides a foundation for understanding your experiences and gaining insight.

Chapter 7

Journey to Faeryland

Journeying is a method that involves a shift in consciousness to otherworld energies, the network that underlies the world of our ordinary everyday state of mind. Because consciousness and reality are fluid, the journey technique provides access to a different reality as well as a way to function in that reality. It is a naturally occurring state that does not require special equipment or drugs. In fact, drugs and alcohol inhibit rather than enhance the process.

Visualization is crucial to the journey process. It helps to free the mind and open the inner channels to receive images, sensations, and information. During a journey we descend within ourselves to find our interior spiritual realm. It is through this inner place and inner self that we can reach out and connect with other realms. Communication is on a subtle, spiritual level.

Journeying does not require an intermediary because anyone can reach their inner self and work with other realms. While it may take a little practice, the key is in letting go of your ordinary state of consciousness. Like falling asleep, when we let go we are able to dream and perhaps temporarily enter faeryland. Unlike dreaming, journeying is intentional.

A journey cannot be achieved as a guided visualization because you need to connect with your inner self and use your individual energy and experiences to work and communicate with the faery realm in a way that is unique to you.

One size does not fit all because each person's perception and reality is different. A journey bridges the levels of consciousness. How you find your way into and out of the faery realm is part of your reality and will always work for you.

A journey puts us in touch with specific beings and places. What you find and experience in a journey is a result of the fae you meet and any interactions that may occur. Everyone's journey is different and each journey is different.

Although the faeries we encounter in a journey may not appear as we expect, when we first meet them they often take a form that we understand or are familiar with from folklore.[65] Over time your journeys will have their own quality and the imagery will evolve as energies become aligned between your world and the faery realm. You may find that the same being may appear different in subsequent journeys. The faery guide who usually meets me when I enter that realm has several ways of appearing.

The folklore of faeryland is full of stories describing the elasticity of time. In some legends, a night in faeryland was equal to seven years of ordinary consciousness; in others it stretched to several hundred years. When journeying to any different realm, faery or otherwise, the movement of time may seem altered to us. Sometimes our perception of a journey may be that we were there a long time and sometimes we may seem to be there only briefly. To avoid confusion and make it easier to return, determine the amount of time you will spend on your journey beforehand, and then set a clock to sound gentle chimes or music to signal that it is time to leave faeryland. Having a callback signal helps to gradually shift through the levels of consciousness and ease your return to the mundane world.

When preparing for a journey, allow plenty of time without interruption in a place that is private and quiet. If you choose to journey during the day you may want to darken the room. At night you may want to light a candle or use very soft lighting. Background sound during a journey can help to shift your level of consciousness. Some people like to use music; others prefer the sound of drumming or rattling. In the past I have used drumming audio, but I have come to prefer silence or very slow, quiet music. Background sound is something to experiment with to find what works best for you.

---

65. Stewart, *Earth Light*, 30.

Take time to prepare just as you would if you were taking a physical journey. Avoid jumping straight into it because shifting consciousness is not like turning a light switch on and off. Use the time setting up your space as part of the process of slowing down and turning inward.

Wear comfortable clothing so you will not feel restricted or uncomfortable. If the weather is cold, you may want to cover yourself with a light blanket. Decide if you are going to sit up or lie down. If you plan to sit, use a comfortable chair. If you lie on the floor, use a pillow and a blanket or something soft underneath you. Consider these things as you prepare because physical discomfort during a journey can be a distraction. It may even inhibit your ability to remain at a different level of consciousness.

As you set up your space, include your faery journal or other means to document your journey as part of the gear to have close at hand. Like dream work and meditation, the process of recording a journey immediately afterward will aid in remembering things. It also helps the transition back to the everyday world.

During your journey, the most important thing to remember is to do what is comfortable for you. If for any reason you feel uneasy, end the journey by retracing your route to the entrance, or simply visualize yourself standing beside your entry point. You have free will and can do this at any time. No being or other entity can control you or take over your journey. Always remember that you are in control. If you encounter other beings that seem belligerent, be polite, but do not be afraid to speak up and stand your ground. Don't be combative; be respectful and calm. Situations like these are a rare occurrence and you should not go into a journey with fear; just know that you are in control.

Entry Points and Beyond

A tree is often used as an entry point to the faery realm because it is rooted in the dense matter of earth yet extends to the ethereal space above. It is important for you to develop your own entry points because they will have greater significance for you and will be easier for you to attune all of your senses to them.

I don't remember the exact entry point for my first journey (I didn't record it!), but I walked down a spiral stone staircase that was longer and went much deeper than I had expected. I went through a door at the bottom of the stairs that opened

A tree is often used as an entry point to the faery realm.

to an outdoor area, which I had seen in a dream the week before. Even though a journey may take you into the earth and underground, it is not unusual to find outdoor places like meadows, woods, and streams. Also in that first journey, I met a being that I had previously seen in a dream. He led me to a door in the side of a hill at the edge of a riverbank. The passage we entered sloped downward, and then opened out to a balcony overlooking a large banquet hall where there was a gathering of fae.

In later journeys, a tree that I was familiar with from my hikes in the woods became my regular entry point. It grew on the side of a hill with many of its large roots exposed. This journey entrance went straight into the banquet hall that I had previously encountered. In many of my journeys there was no spiral staircase or outdoor area. In addition, I have found that sometimes an entry point does not always lead to the same place in faeryland. It changes from time to time and on some journeys I still encounter the spiral staircase. You may find that landscapes and indoor places vary from time to time or remain the same.

The first faery that you encounter may become your guide, providing information and making introductions to others. You may meet the same beings frequently and others only once or twice. The faeries that you meet will know your name and will give you theirs at their choosing. Don't be offended by this; accept their ways. On some visits, beings or their faces may not appear clearly. I had one experience where a being appeared as a changing shimmer of light. The size and shape of the beings you encounter are often not what you may expect. One time, a cat that had walked with me on a hike through the woods in the mundane world showed up in faeryland.

When You Are Ready to Go

Prepare a candle by inscribing it with the faery star, set up your space, and set a clock or other device for your callback signal. When everything is ready, light the candle and go through the faery attunement of engaging the breath, activating your energy, and aligning with your surroundings. Use a wand or simply point to cast your faery ring and visualize it as sparkling blue light as you say:

As above, so below and now within;
My journey to faeryland is about to begin.
As I enter their realm not so far,
I am guided by the faery star.

Make yourself comfortable and begin your journey. Do not go with any particular expectation about what you will see, learn, or whether you will be met by a guide. Be flexible and accept what you find. You may want to determine your entry point beforehand in a place that is familiar to you, but avoid a great deal of detail. Once your journey begins, your entry point may look like the place you had in mind or it may appear slightly different. Places you encounter in faeryland may seem familiar and almost mundane or be completely new and exciting. Accept what you find. Take your time and allow events to unfold.

When you hear your callback signal, begin your preparation to return. Thank any beings you met and say your goodbyes. Retrace your steps and leave by the same route you entered. If your journey takes you into the faery realm but no one appears, wait a few minutes. Look around, but don't wander too far. If no one appears, return the way you entered. Don't be disappointed; it means that this is not the time for you.

After the journey, when you are conscious of being back in your physical body on the floor or sitting in a chair, take a moment or two before getting up. Use a wand or point with a finger to dissolve your faery ring by saying:

Now I have come back home,
From faeryland where I did roam.
Until the fae again I see,
In magic I live; blessed be.

Afterward

The energy shift of a journey can be powerful, which is why it is important to take your time to transition back to the everyday world. As mentioned, journaling or recording your experience aids in the transition. Even immediately after a journey you may not remember everything. Write down details of what you can recall.

Document what you feel is appropriate. The record of your journey doesn't have to be a play-by-play account of everything that occurred, unless you want it to. However, some key facts that you may want to include are a description of any beings you met, any information they conveyed to you, and the environment that you visited, such as a landscape or building interior. Like dream work, being able to go back and review a journey is a valuable tool for understanding what you experienced. It also aids in deciphering information that initially may not seem significant.

If you feel skeptical about having made contact or about any information shared with you, ask to be given a sign. Confirmation may appear in a dream or everyday life. One time when I had asked for confirmation of a particular experience, the creature I had met started appearing everywhere in my mundane world. At first I thought that it was just because it was on my mind, but sightings in magazines, calendars, T-shirts, and television reached an absurd level until I said *"Enough, I believe"* and it stopped. Thirty years on, I still have a relationship with that wonderful creature and guide.

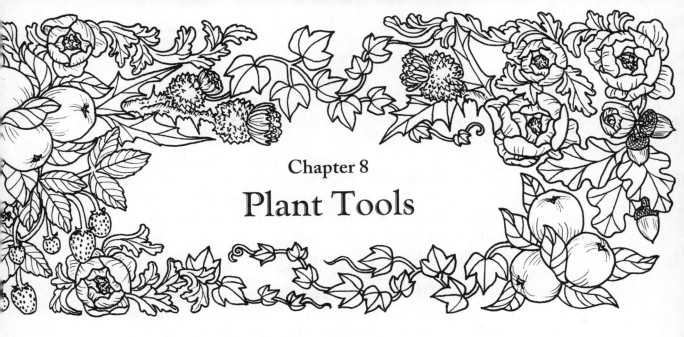

Chapter 8
Plant Tools

Bringing plants into our homes conveys their energy into our personal environments, and when we make them into tools, their energy enhances our work with faeries and nature spirits. The tools that we make with our own hands are imbued with our intentions and function with powerful purpose. While making a tool, you may want to sing, chant, recite poetry, or meditate on the task at hand to begin your magical association with it. When gathering material, only take what is needed to keep in harmony with the natural world. Walk softly and leave no trace.

As previously mentioned, wreaths aren't only for Yule; they can be used in other ways to bring plant energy into your magic and ritual any time of the year. Wands are easy to make and in addition to tree branches, they can be made from any woody shrub or plant. A plant pendulum and diving sticks aid in communicating with nature spirits and faeries. Whether you make, purchase, or are gifted with a tool, cleanse and charge it before use. Refer to the section "Prepare and Attune Objects and Tools" in chapter 5. When not in use, pendulums, divining rods, and wands should be wrapped in a soft cloth and stored with your other magical gear.

Wreath and Circlet

The ancient Greeks used wreaths to wear as chaplets at festivals, to give as awards for special achievement, and to place on statues of deities as offerings. A wreath embodies the power of the circle, which is one of humankind's oldest and most elemental symbols. The circle represents unity, completion, and endlessness. It echoes the turning cycle of life, of the seasons, of time and timelessness. As a circle, whether worn as a circlet or used as a wreath on the altar, it brings a perpetual flow of plant energy into ritual and magic.

While evergreen tree branches are nice to make a winter wreath, bare branches can be used for the base of a wreath that can be decorated according to season or magical intent throughout the year. Look for branches that are slightly curved, and then arrange them in a circle to assess how the wreath may come together. You may need to snip off a few smaller branchlets or secure them to the main branch with yarn or twine. Long, thin willow or birch branches are easily bent into a circle. When working with conifers, arrange them with the needles pointing in the same direction to provide visual continuity and energy flow.

To assemble, use wire, twine, or yarn to attach the tip of one branch to the base of the next or to secure one long branch into shape. Once you have a basic circle, you may want to attach a couple of smaller branches to add volume. A strand of ivy or other type of vine can be wound around it. Experiment, but don't overwork it; allow your wreath to develop organically to hold the integrity of the plant's energy.

Some plants, such as blackberry and rose, have arching branches called *canes*. These are easy to maneuver into shape, but watch out for thorns. A wreath can be placed above or on your altar to draw in the energy of the plant. Depending on the purpose of your wreath, it can be placed anywhere in the home or garden.

Small wreaths can be made from the pliable stems of many types of plants. These can be placed around the base of candles or other objects on your altar. A small wreath can be created for a specific purpose and used in a spell. For an esbat altar, bind a wreath with white yarn or use stems with white flowers so it is evocative of the moon. A group of small wreaths can be used decoratively in your outdoor space to draw the energy of the plant to your home and property.

Wand

A wand can be made for long- or short-term use as well as a specific purpose. Before going for a walk to find a branch, sit quietly, send out your intention, and ask the faeries and nature spirits for blessings and guidance. As for the length of a wand, some sources recommend that it should measure from your elbow to the tip of the middle finger; others say shorter. Follow whatever feels right for you. If you are using a branch from a small plant, you may not have much of a choice for the length; however, a small wand can be just as power-

A small wreath can be placed around the base of a candle or other object on your altar.

ful. Since it's rare to find a branch that is the exact length you need, look for one that is longer and thicker than you envision your finished wand.

If you are using a tree branch, the hard part begins when you get home because you need to set it aside to allow the wood to dry out. Depending on the size of the branch, it can take a couple of months. Remove any small side twigs and thorns, and then lay the branch flat. Turn it every few days to keep it from warping. If you plan to remove the bark, now is the time to do it because it will be easier to do and the wood will dry quicker. Although it may be tempting to use an oven, wood that is dried too quickly has a tendency to crack. Have patience and allow the process to occur naturally. When the wood is seasoned, the color usually fades a little, the weight is lighter, and the wood is a little harder.

While the wood is seasoning, plan how you will decorate your wand. Since it is for faery magic, you may want to carve or paint the faery star on it. If you leave the bark on, anything carved on it will reveal a different-colored inner bark and contrast with the outer layer. While crystals and other objects are often attached to wands, the size of the branch may dictate if this is possible.

You may consider leaving it plain to avoid adding other energy to your work so it will be an exclusive conduit for the plant's energy and yours.

If you want to create a handle for your wand, use strips of ribbon, yarn, or leather to wrap around one end. This may make it more comfortable to hold. The handle should be long enough to accommodate the width of your hand. Instead of wrapping the handle, you can differentiate it by carving a groove to mark where the handle ends or whittle the shaft of the wand to make it narrower than the handle.

After preparing and attuning your wand, sit in front of your altar or in your outdoor space and hold it. Get the feel of it in your hand as you think about the tree or plant that it came from and your purpose for making it.

Pendulum

A pendulum aids in detecting and working with energy. It is frequently used as a tool for divination with questions that have "yes" or "no" answers. Because it functions with subtle vibrations, it is often used to communicate with spirits and can be used when contacting faeries and nature spirits.

Although crystal pendulums are very popular, one made of wood is more appropriate for our purposes since we are working with plants. There are many styles of wooden pendulums on the market. If you have the skill, whittle a piece of wood to a point at one end, attach an eye hook screw to the opposite end, and then tie a six- to eight-inch length of string to the hook. Ideally, the pendulum should measure between one to two inches long.

When working with a specific plant, you can make a temporary pendulum with flowers or leaves. The flowers or leaves will need stems long enough to tie a piece of thread onto. Large or very small flowers and leaves do not work very well, as they are usually too heavy or too light. The plant material needs enough weight to hold the string or threat taut, which means you may need a couple of flowers or leaves. When using such a pendulum, be mindful that its weight is lighter than a wooden one and your breath can interfere with its movement.

When you are ready to work with your pendulum, go through the faery attunement. Next, calibrate the pendulum so responses will be understood.

Hold the end of the pendulum string with the thumb and index finger of your dominant hand and rest your elbow on a table or other flat surface. When the pendulum is completely still, say, *"Show me yes."* Repeat this a few times until the pendulum swings in a definitive pattern, which may be forward and back, right to left, or in a circle. Note which way it swings, and then say, *"Thank you."* When the pendulum is still again, say, *"Show me no."* Again, you may need to ask a few times. Repeat the whole process again to confirm how it will swing for each response.

When you are first getting started, instead of communicating directly with a faery or nature spirit, simply try to detect their presence. Explain what you are doing in case one is nearby, and then ask the pendulum if a faery is present. Ask separately about a nature spirit.

If you receive an affirmative answer, explain to the faery or nature spirit that you would like to communicate with them using the pendulum. Also let them know that it can only accommodate "yes" and "no" answers. Occasionally, the pendulum may become still or swing in a manner that is not clear. Remind the faery or nature spirit that they need to respond with "yes" or "no," and ask if they understand. Be patient. Communicating through a pendulum might be a new experience for the faery or nature spirit. If it's not working, thank them and suggest that you try it another time.

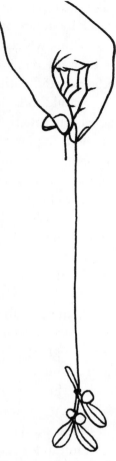

A flower or leaf can be used as a pendulum.

Divining Rods

There are two types of divining rods, which are also known as dowsing rods. The traditional rod is a V- or Y-shaped branch and usually comes from a hazel tree. The other type consists of a pair of copper L-shaped rods known as angle rods and L rods. Used for finding water, a practice that is known as water witching, divining rods are also used to find objects and sense energy. In Germany, they are called *wünschelrute* or "wishing rods."[66] According to legend, wishing rods were especially potent at midnight on May Day to find the luck flower (forget-me-not or cowslip), which could open hidden chambers filled with treasure.

Like the pendulum, a set of divining rods can be used to sense the presence of faeries and nature spirits and to communicate with them. If you purchase a set of angle rods, look for a set with wooden handles, which will aid in keeping in touch with the plant world. If you want to make your own set of rods, start with a pair of wire coat hangers. Simply cut off the hook, cut one end of the hanger bottom so you have a long part, and then bend the shorter part to a right angle. You may need to snip off a little of the shorter part to about five or six inches long. Repeat the process with the second coat hanger.

For handles, look in craft or woodworking shops for wooden spools or pre-drilled dowels. As an alternative, slip wooden beads over the shorter part of the L rod, and then twist the end up with a pair of pliers to keep them from falling off. Whatever you use for handles, the rods need to be able to move back and forth freely. They should feel comfortable to hold.

When using divining rods, hold one in each hand in front of you about eight to ten inches from your body. If you are standing, hold them at waist height or a little higher; when sitting, hold them in front of your chest. Go through the faery attunement, and then calibrate your divining rods so the responses will be clear. Start with the rods in neutral position, pointing straight forward. The rods moving toward each other and crossing or moving away from each other out to the sides distinguish "yes" and "no" answers. Follow the same process as a pendulum for calibrating the rods and working with faeries and nature spirits.

---

66. Grimm, *Teutonic Mythology*, 144.

Chapter 9
Liquid Tools for Magic

The use of oils is intertwined with the history of herbal medicine, which, in turn, has been an integral part of magical practices. In many ancient cultures, people believed that plants were magical and for thousands of years they were used as much for ritual and magic as they were for medicine and food. In addition to the plants themselves, oils made from them were an element of religious practice in cultures worldwide and the anointment with oil was an almost universal practice.

In addition to the tools mentioned in chapter 8, hydrosols and oils are effective tools in their own right. Hydrosols are water-based plant extracts. Just like the plants from which they are made, oils and hydrosols have a wide range of applications for ritual and magic work. The use of hydrosols, essential oils, infused oils, and flower essences provides a way to maintain tradition while giving our practices new depth.

Consecrating candles for ritual and magic with oils and essential oils is a common practice. Hydrosols and flower essences can be used in the same way. Scenting an area with essential oil before and during ritual, magic, or psychic work is another way to harness the vibrational energy of plants. While electronic diffusers and all sorts of gadgets are available, the low-tech tea light candle lamp does the job nicely. Besides, candles enhance the ambiance of ritual and craftwork.

Oils, Hydrosols, and Essences

Let's take a look at these various products. Most cooking and massage oils are made from fruits, nuts, and seeds. Massage oils are also known as carrier oils and base oils. When purchasing them, select one that is classified as "unrefined." Whenever possible, buy oil that is organic. Refined oils are produced as cheaply as possible with the aid of chemical solvents that leech nutrients, aromas, and the life from oils. Unrefined organic oils carry the energy of the plants they came from.

Unrefined oil may be labeled as *cold pressed*, which means that it was not subjected to high temperatures. A similar method called *expeller pressed* employs hydraulic presses. While the friction of a hydraulic press raises the temperature slightly, it does not harm the oil.

Plant material is usually put through a press more than once to obtain as much oil as possible. Oil that is extracted from the first pressing is called *virgin*. The term *extra virgin* means that the oil is of the highest grade. However, when it comes to coconut oil, the unrefined oil is also called *virgin oil* and the refined is called *fractionated oil*.

Essential oils are also known as ethereal oils, volatile oils, and essences. Perhaps it's no coincidence that the word *essence* can mean fragrance or spirit. Derived from the Latin word *esse*, meaning "to be," the word *essence* can refer to the intrinsic nature of something or an extract from a plant: spirit and fragrance.[67] Essential oils are called *volatile* because they are not stable substances and they evaporate at room temperature. The defining factor for what constitutes an essential oil is the method used to extract it from plant material. Essential oils are obtained through the processes of distillation and expression. This differs from aromatic extracts such as concretes and absolutes, which obtain a plant's essential oil by using chemical solvents.

The distillation process uses hot water and steam to obtain essential oil. After the oil is separated from the water, the water itself is an aromatic product called a *hydrosol*. Traditionally known as floral water (e.g., rose water), a hydrosol can be made from other parts of a plant, not just flowers.

---

67. Stevenson, ed., *Oxford Dictionary of English*, 598.

Infused oil is the result of steeping plant material in oil; leaves, seeds, berries, and flowers are most often used. While infused oils are popular for cooking and herbal remedies, they work well for magical applications, too.

The term *flower essence* may cause some confusion because this product is not fragrant and it is not an essential oil. It is simply an infusion of flowers in water that is then mixed with a 50 percent brandy solution, which acts as a preservative. While these are used for various healing purposes, we can attune them to our intentions for magic and use them as we would an oil or hydrosol.

How to Make a Hydrosol

As mentioned, a hydrosol is a by-product of the essential oil distillation process; however, there are three methods for making it at home. These include hot infusion, cold infusion, and steam distillation. All three methods require fresh flowers or leaves.

For the hot infusion method, preheat a large glass jar with hot tap water, which will prevent it from cracking or shattering when boiled water is poured into it. After drying the jar, fill it half to two-thirds with plant material, boil some water, and pour it into the jar. Use at least enough water to cover the plant material. Put the lid on the jar, let it stand for three to four hours, and then strain out the bits of plants. For the cold infusion method, simply place the plant material in the jar and add enough cold water to cover it. Put the lid on and let it stand for about twenty-four hours before straining out the plant material.

The steam distillation method requires a little more work, but it's fun to experiment with. You will need a big stainless-steel pot (a stock pot or lobster pot works well) and two small ceramic or glass bowls. Place one bowl upside down in the middle of the pot to serve as a pedestal for the second bowl. Set that bowl right side up to act as a catch basin for condensation. Add the flowers and leaves and water to the pot. The water level should be below the catch basin (top) bowl so it does not float around in the pot. Place the lid upside down on the pot. This will direct the condensation to the center where it will drip into the catch basin bowl. When the water begins to boil, turn down the heat to a low simmer. To quicken the condensation process, place ice cubes on top of the upside-down lid.

To make the procedure less messy, put the ice cubes in a plastic bag. Place a tea towel on the lid of the pot and the bag of ice cubes on top. The ice cubes may need to be replaced a few times during the process. After thirty or forty minutes, turn off the heat and let the pot cool before removing the lid and retrieving the catch basin. After the catch basin cools, pour the hydrosol into a jar with a tight-fitting lid and store it in the fridge.

Hydrosols made with either infusion method will keep for a few days, even if stored in the refrigerator. When made by the steam method, they can last several months. However, even when stored in the fridge, being mostly water, a hydrosol can go bad. If it becomes cloudy or smells off, throw it away.

How to Make Infused Oil

Infused oil can be made from any plant that you want to work with. St. John's wort is especially fun to make because the flowers and buds turn the oil bright red.

There are two methods for making infused oils: cold and hot. A cold infusion is an easier but slower process. It works best for leaves and flowers, which tend to be more heat-sensitive. The hot-infused method works best with the tougher parts of a plant such as roots, bark, fruit, and seeds. Dried or fresh plant material can be used. Prepare it by crumbling or chopping it into small pieces. The tougher parts of plants should be cut into very small pieces. Choose any cooking or carrier oil for the base.

For the cold infusion method, fill a jar half or two-thirds with the plant material, and then add enough oil to cover it. Gently poke around with a butter knife to release any air pockets. Leave the jar open for several hours to allow any trapped air to bubble up and escape. If most of the oil gets absorbed, add a little more to cover the plant material. After you put the lid on, gently swirl the contents. Place the jar where it will stay at room temperature for four to six weeks. When it is ready, strain the oil into a dark glass bottle for storage at room temperature, out of direct sunlight.

Plant material that sits in oil longer than four to six weeks may turn moldy. When using fresh plants, check for any condensation in the bottle after it is stored. The moisture content of fresh material is released into the oil and can foster bacteria growth.

For the hot infusion method, use a half to two-thirds cup of dried or fresh plant material and one cup of oil. Place them in a double boiler and cover. A double boiler is a set of saucepans that fit together; the larger bottom pan is used to boil water to create steam and warm the smaller upper pan. The upper saucepan has a lid. Instead of a double boiler, a stainless-steel mixing bowl can be placed over a large saucepan of water. You will need a lid to cover the bowl. The bottom of the bowl should not touch the water in the pan because the contents may overheat.

With the heat as low as possible, warm the oil for thirty minutes to an hour. When you remove the pot from the heat, allow the oil to cool completely. Strain it into a dark glass bottle for storage at room temperature, out of direct sunlight.

Before Use and Precautions

Whether you purchase or make a hydrosol, oil, or essence, as with any other type of magical and ritual tool, prepare it prior to use. Refer to the section "Prepare and Attune Objects and Tools" in chapter 5 for details. After preparing a liquid tool, I like to attune it by holding the jar or bottle between my hands and saying:

> *By north, south, east, and west,*
> *May my purpose by fae be blessed.*
> *Above, below, and within;*
> *It's time for magic to begin.*

Essential oils are fabulous to work with, but because they can damage varnish, paint, plastic, and other surfaces, it is important to dilute them in a carrier oil. Since my altar is a wooden table, instead of diluting the essential oil I dab it on the underside of the tabletop and visualize the plant energy giving it magical support. As an alternative to putting oil directly on magic or divination tools, put a few drops on a cotton ball and place it where you store these items. This will allow them to slowly absorb the vibrational energy of the oil without causing damage. You may also want to do this when working with infused oil, as you may not want to apply it directly to clothing or expensive objects.

When using essential oil for anointing, because it is usually placed on the forehead or scalp, review safety guidelines and precautions from the manufacturer. Mix the essential oil with a carrier oil using a dilution ratio of 1 percent or 1 ½ percent at most. This percentage is approximately three to five drops of essential oil in a tablespoon of carrier oil. Essential oil used on other parts of the body can range from 1 to 3 percent ratios. Any blends used on children should not exceed a 1 percent dilution. Because hydrosols are water-based they can be used directly on the body, but check for manufacturer precautions first.

Use your imagination and you will find many uses for these products in your magical practices. Of course, pleasant scents are especially effective for attracting faeries and nature spirits.

PART TWO

The Faery Plants

Throughout folklore, plants used as charms against faeries and their meddling were at other times noted as being used by them. Many of the plants included here are well-known for magical use and some are a bit obscure, and others are not found in faery folklore but have become associated with them. While the reasons certain plants are merely associated with faeries is unknown, my thought is that at some point people may have had experiences with these plants that brought them closer to the faery realm. Perhaps these plants will aid others, too.

Although the spellings of *faery* and *fairy* were differentiated in the introduction, throughout the following plant profiles where the traditional and customary spelling is *fairy* in plant names (such as fairy flax, fairy bells, fairy cups) and other terms (such as fairy ring, fairy horse, fairy path), I have maintaied these conventions.

Also of note is that a number of the plants used for protection from faeries and their meddling deal with cattle and milk. The importance of this may be lost on us in the twenty-first century because we live in a world where few of us are farmers or have a subsistence life on the land. In the past, cows and the food and products produced from them were vitally important to a family's prosperity and basic survival. All means were used to protect them.

While many of these plants have a great deal of history, the following profiles focus on faery folklore and magical use. Each profile also includes information on items that can be purchased when the plant itself is not available. While things that can be purchased may change from time to time, this information is intended as a starting place for what you may find on the market. When purchasing tea, especially flower tea, check whether or not other plants are included. This is fairly common to give a tea more flavor, but is not always compatible with magical use.

Although some plants are well-known and generally safe to consume, such as thyme or rose hip tea, others are sometimes sold as tea or herbs, but may not be safe to ingest. Always err on the side of caution and do not consume anything that may not be safe, especially during pregnancy or if you have a medical condition. Handling and using plants must be done with knowledge, common sense, and safety in mind. While some plants should not be handled, others can be when done so with care. When in doubt about identifying plants in the wild, it is safer to use photographs to represent them.

Plant Symbolism

Whenever possible, coordinate the symbolism of the part of a plant you use for magic with your purpose. While symbolism and purpose may not always align, when they do, it adds an extra boost of energy and depth to magic.

Residing under the earth, roots are the most natural plant part for grounding energy and providing stability to magic work. Roots can aid psychic work and journeying as well as post-ritual grounding. Roots encourage us to hold secrets when bidden.

Sturdy wood and bark provide protective energy for rituals, spells, and charms. Wood and bark gauges growth of a tree and can aid in manifesting your growth on various levels: social, emotional, and spiritual. Within and encircling a plant, wood and bark symbolically provide balance and strength.

From the time they burst forth in the spring until the wind whisks them away in the autumn, leaves enfold the world with aerial enchantment. Personifying energy and growth, leaves give magic and personal endeavors an encouraging boost. Showy or subtle, flowers and catkins are often a crowning glory. They represent beauty with a goal: attraction, sex, and fertility. Using flowers can be especially potent when they add fragrance to magic work. Of course, leaves are often aromatic, too.

With the base word *fruit*, fruition means completion or culmination, and so a piece of fruit symbolizes manifestation and success. Fruit represents an increase in power and energy. The feel and smell of fruit is the personification of abundance and freedom from want. Use fruit to increase what you have and to gain what you seek.

Seeds and nuts represent beginnings and the future. They can be instrumental when encouraging something new in your life. They also represent duality, such as the alternation between life and death, light and dark. Seeds and nuts move between the worlds; blown by a breeze or snuggled into the earth, they represent beginnings, changes, and cycles.

Agrimony

Common Agrimony (Agrimonia eupatoria)
Folk names: Cockleburr, fairy's wand

Agrimony has yellow, five-petaled flowers that grow in clusters on tall spires that reach almost four feet. Its leaves consist of lance-shaped leaflets that are deeply veined and coarsely toothed. Larger leaves form a base rosette, while smaller ones grow up the stems. The whole plant is slightly aromatic. Seed capsules form burrs that get stuck on clothing and animals as they pass by.

Faery Folklore
Regarded as a highly magical plant, agrimony was used to cure elf shot in Scotland.

Magical Workings
Powers and attributes: Balance/harmony, banish, dream work, family and home, healing, hexes (break, protect from), negativity (remove, ward off), protection, purification, release (let go, move on), spirit guides/spirits
Items to purchase when the plant is not available: Flower essence; cut, dried leaves; seeds

To bless a new home before moving in, burn a pinch of dried leaves as you walk through the house. Also do this to dispel any type of negativity. Burn a dried leaf and smudge yourself with the smoke to cleanse your aura. Add an infusion of agrimony to your bathwater to create a personal protective barrier against negativity. To send a hex back to its origin, burn a handful of dried leaves in your cauldron as you say three times:

Agrimony, agrimony,
Herb of strength and great power,
Return this spell to the hexer
Forever and within an hour.

When the ashes are cool, take them outside and bury them in the ground.

Alder
Black Alder, European Alder (Alnus glutinosa)
Red Alder, Oregon Alder (A. rubra)
Folk name: Aller (black alder)

Often sporting multiple trunks, alders have rounded, glossy-green leaves. The black alder leaves are notched at the tip. Slender, drooping male catkins and small pine cone-like female catkins appear on the trees before the leaves develop. Commonly called *cones* and *black knobs*, the female catkins stay on the tree and turn brown.

Faery Folklore

Alder has been regarded as a highly magical tree protected by faeries. According to legend, faeries used the catkins to dye their clothes green. Other stories note that an alder log was often left in place of a person who the fae took away to faeryland.

In Ireland, a solitary alder tree is considered a lone bush that can provide access to the faery realm. (See the profile for Lone Bush.) In Denmark, standing beneath an alder at midnight on Midsummer's Eve enables a person to see the faery king and his entourage on the way to their revels. According to Danish folklore, the fae live under alders or in alder thickets. White fairy horses are noted as especially fond of this tree.

Magical Workings

Powers and attributes: Authority/leadership, banish, changes/transitions, clarity (enhance, foster), divination, dream work, healing, intuition, knowledge (seek, acquire), luck, negativity (remove, ward off), prophecy, protection, renewal, see faeries, spirit guides/spirits, strength

Items to purchase when the tree is not available: Charcoal; wood chips; flower essences are made from the red alder and the green alder (*A. crispa*)

Because fairies are attracted to alders, leave an offering beneath one to signal that you would like to contact them. Hold a branch of alder to enhance your contact with spirit guides. Because of its use in the past for making spinning wheels, alder is especially effective for any form of divination. Hold three leaves between your palms before a session to foster clarity. Use any part of the alder as a charm to strengthen intuition.

To invite prophetic dreams, place a leaf under your bed. Also use alder for meditation and to raise healing energy. Place an alder cone in a decorative bag to take with you on travels or to keep in your car as a protective charm. Gather a handful of male catkins for magic work. Burn a few to aid in banishing rituals and spells.

Angelica

Garden Angelica, European Angelica (Angelica archangelica)
Wild Angelica, Woodland Angelica (A. sylvestris)
Folk names: Masterwort, wild celery

Reaching five to eight feet tall, garden angelica is best described as statuesque. Its hollow stalks are round and purplish with branching stems. The large, bright-green leaflets are lobed and coarsely toothed. Tiny, honey-scented, white or greenish flowers grow in globe or umbrella-shaped clusters. Ribbed on one side, the seeds turn pale brownish yellow when ripe. The yellowish-gray root is long, thick, and fleshy. Wild angelica is shorter than its garden cousin, with smaller flower heads that are more profuse. The leaflets are not lobed and have grooved stalks.

Faery Folklore

Angelica was used to protect cattle from elf shot. For humans, a piece of dried root was worn around the neck for protection from enchantment.

Magical Workings

Powers and attributes: Balance/harmony, banish, bind, challenges/obstacles (overcome), consecrate/bless, courage, defense, divination, dream work, growth, healing, hexes (break, protect from), inspiration, knowledge (seek, acquire), loss/sorrow (ease, recover from), manifest (dreams, desires, will), negativity (remove, ward off), peace, protection, purification, renewal, secrets, security, spirituality, strength, success, support (provide, receive)

Items to purchase when the plant is not available: Two essential oils are made from this plant, one from the roots and the other from the seeds; cut, dried roots

Grow angelica in your garden or place a few flowers or leaves on your outdoor altar to invite faeries and nature spirits to your property. First and foremost, angelica is a protector. Burn pieces of dried root to protect against and break hexes, and to banish all forms of negativity. Angelica also provides psychic protection during dream work and divination.

To aid in grounding energy after ritual or magic work, hold a piece of root in each hand. Smoke from the burning root is ideal for consecrating ritual space. Place a few drops of either essential oil on a cotton ball to store with your ritual and magic tools to keep them energetically ready for use. Angelica also aids in keeping secrets. Place a picture of it on your altar if you are having trouble holding a confidence.

Apple
Common Apple, Orchard Apple (Malus domestica syn. *M. communis)*
Folk name: Silver bough

The common cultivated apple is believed to be a hybrid of several crab apple species. Today, there are hundreds of cultivars. Reaching between fifteen to forty feet tall, most apple trees have distinctive crooked trunks. Apple's pointed, oval leaves range from yellowish green to dark green on top and lighter underneath. Its five-petaled flowers are white to pinkish white and grow in clusters.

Faery Folklore
According to legend, falling asleep under an apple tree left a person vulnerable to being carried off by faeries. In Celtic lore, both apple and crab apple were regarded as the fruit of knowledge, magic, and prophecy. Throughout folklore, eating an apple was a way to open the gateway into other realms, most often to faeryland. Although the cultivated apple is associated with legendary Avalon, the sacred Isle of Apples is often noted as populated with wild crab apple trees.

In Cornwall, England, it was customary to leave a few apples on the trees after the harvest for the pixies in hopes that they would help the trees produce a good crop the following year. In other areas of England, the act of taking leftover apples from an orchard after the harvest was known as "pixy-wording."[68] The colt pixy, an orchard spirit that takes the form of a horse, was said to guard apple trees.

---

68. Wright, *Rustic Speech and Folk-lore*, 208.

Magical Workings

Powers and attributes: Abundance, ancestors, attraction, balance/harmony, bind, consecrate/bless, creativity, divination, dream work, fertility, happiness, healing, knowledge (seek, acquire), love, luck, peace, prophecy, prosperity/money, relationships, renewal, security, sex/sexuality, spirit guides/spirits, strength, success, wisdom

Items to purchase when the tree is not available: Fresh or dried fruit; apple juice or cider; flower essence

Eat an apple before any type of magical practice to enhance your abilities. This is also an aid when working with the faery realm and accessing ancient wisdom. To consecrate candles for raising healing energy, prepare them with a little flower essence. For a fertility spell, wash and clean a few apple seeds, and then make a circle with them around the base of a candle on your altar.

The color of an apple can provide a magical energy boost. Use a red apple for love, passion, and desire; a yellow or golden apple for success; and a green apple for abundance and prosperity. Burn a small piece of apple wood to scent the home and attract abundance. An old form of love divination requires two apples. Carefully peel the skins off in one long strip. Throw one over each shoulder, and then look for initials formed by the peels to indicate your true love.

Ash

Black Ash, Swamp Ash (Fraxinus nigra)
Common Ash, English Ash, European Ash (F. excelsior)
White Ash, American Ash (F. americana)
Folk name: Venus of the woods (common ash)

The name *ash* refers to the color of the bark. The leaves are composed of five to eleven lance-shaped leaflets with serrated edges. The small, greenish flowers produce clusters of seeds that remain on the tree throughout the winter. Also known as keys or samaras, the flat seeds have a straight wing, unlike the curved maple seed wing.

Faery Folklore

Ash was sometimes used as a substitute for rowan for protection against the fae. In Scotland, ash leaves were placed under milk vessels to prevent faeries from meddling with and removing the milk's nutrition. Striking a person with an ash stick was a cure for enchantment. In Somerset, England, an ash gad (pointed stick) was used as an amulet for protection from faeries. To the contrary, in other parts of England, faeries and elves were noted as being protectors of the ash tree. In Ireland and parts of Britain, it was believed that ash, oak, and hawthorn growing in the same place made the invisible world of the faeries visible. Ash was frequently used as a cloutie tree.

Magical Workings

Powers and attributes: Awareness (expand, heighten), balance/harmony, changes/transitions, communication, concentration/focus, creativity, divination, dream work, fertility, growth, healing, hexes (break, protect from), inspiration, intuition, knowledge (seek, acquire), love, luck, negativity (remove, ward off), peace, prophecy, prosperity/money, protection, purification, renewal, see faeries, spirit guides/spirits, strength, wisdom

Items to purchase when the tree is not available: Flower essence is made from the white ash; baskets made of ash twigs

Because ash provides a connection with the faery realm whether dreaming or journeying, keep a small twig nearby to aid you. Before a divination session, rest for a few minutes with a leaf on your third-eye chakra. For dream work, place a leaf on your bedside table to stimulate psychic dreams. Use ash keys or leaves in protection spells and as charms against any form of negativity. Burn a piece of ash wood for protection against or to break a hex.

To boost the energy of spells, make a circle with ash keys around the base of a candle. Burn a dried leaf in love spells; the rare ash leaf with an even number of leaflets is especially effective for love charms. When seeking creative inspiration, inscribe the faery star and the word *ash* on a candle and place it on your desk or workspace. Also prepare a candle this way for raising healing energy. Ash is especially effective for developing intuition and honing communication skills.

Bilberry

Bilberry (Vaccinium myrtillus)
Folk names: Blueberry, heath berry, whortleberry

Bilberry is a low-growing shrub with fruit that is easily mistaken for blueber-ries (*V. corymbosum*) because of its color. However, bilberries are usually darker blue, almost purple when ripe, and smaller than blueberries. Growing only four to fifteen inches tall, bilberry's small, bright-green leaves are egg-shaped with serrated edges. The drooping, globular flowers range from greenish yellow to slightly reddish to rosy with a greenish tinge.

Faery Folklore

As part of the Lughnasadh festivities in County Limerick, Ireland, it was cus-tomary to place an offering of bilberries and flowers on the cairn at the summit of Knockfierna, a well-known faery hill. According to legend, the hill was the home of Donn Fírinne and the cairn, his burial site. Donn Fírinne was one of the Tuatha Dé Danann and a faery prince of Limerick. A cave called *Poll na Bruidhne,* located on the side of the hill, was said to lead to his underground castle.

As with other types of berries, the places where bilberries grew were regarded as liminal thresholds where faeries could be encountered. To prevent being led astray, it was common practice to carry a piece of bread in the pocket while picking bilberries. Allegedly, faeries would keep away because the woman who baked the bread had blessed it.

Magical Workings

Powers and attributes: Dream work, family and home, healing, hexes (break, protect from), love, luck, manifest (desires, dreams, will), prophecy, prosperity/money, protection, success

Items to purchase when the plant is not available: Cut, dried leaves; dried berries; leaf tea; jam

To pay tribute to the faeries, place a few bilberries or a teaspoon of bilberry jam on a plate on your altar when celebrating Lughnasadh. To aid in making a plan or dream come true, write a keyword or two on a picture of bilberry fruit, and then light a candle as you say:

> *Faery bright, faery sprite,*
> *I call on you for help tonight.*
> *With this fruit of deep dark blue,*
> *Help this dream of mine come true.*

Hold the bilberry picture between your hands as you visualize a positive outcome. Afterward, keep the picture on your altar until your goal is attained.

Birch

American White Birch, Paper Birch (Betula papyrifera)
Silver Birch, European White Birch (B. alba syn. B. pendula)
Folk name: Lady of the woods (silver birch)

Both trees have slender, often multiple, trunks with peeling, white or pale bark. The leaves are triangular to heart-shaped with serrated edges. In early spring, birches produce drooping, yellowish-brown male catkins and upright, greenish female catkins. Birch trees are frequently host to fairy butter, jelly fungus (*Tremella mesenterica*).

Faery Folklore

According to Celtic legend, the god Lugh used birch and its related ogham character Beith to protect his wife from faeries. In earlier times in Ireland, birch was reputedly disliked by faeries. In parts of England, branches were wrapped with red and white ribbons and propped against stable doors to keep faeries from borrowing horses. Birch crosses were hung over house doors to guard against faery enchantment. A twig of birch was placed in a baby's cradle to prevent faeries from substituting it with a changeling.

As with many plants, faeries were said to not like birch but also to be fond of it. According to some legends, they especially liked the catkins. Dense tangles of birch branches are called *fairy's brooms*. In Ireland, a solitary birch tree is regarded as a lone bush. (See the profile for Lone Bush.) In Scotland, a spirit known as the Ghillie Dhu was said to live in birch woods, and in Russia a genie or spirit of the forest known as the Lieschi often stayed in the tops of birch trees.

Magical Workings

Powers and attributes: Abundance, awareness (expand, heighten), banish, challenges/obstacles (overcome), changes/transitions, clarity (enhance, foster), concentration/focus, consecrate/bless, creativity, divination, fertility, healing, inspiration, intuition, knowledge (seek, acquire), love, negativity (remove, ward off), protection, purification, release (let go, move on), renewal, spirit guides/spirits, support (provide, receive), wisdom

Items to purchase when the tree is not available: Essential oil is made from the silver birch; flower essence is also made from the silver birch

Crumble and sprinkle pieces of dried birch bark around your property to attract faeries; also place a few catkins on your altar. To symbolically sweep and clear away negative energy before ritual, or to provide protection during magic work, gather several birch branches to use as a broom. For clarity in a divination session, hold a birch leaf between your palms to focus your energy beforehand. This also helps to develop and fine-tune intuition.

Use pieces of bark in a sachet for love spells and place a twig under your bed to aid in fertility. Burn a few small pieces of bark for purification and to bless the beginning of a project, relationship, new home, or when making any type of fresh start.

Blackberry

American Blackberry (Rubus villosus)
European Blackberry (R. fruticosus)
Folk names: Bramble, bramble thorn, brambleberry

Blackberry bushes are sprawling shrubs with woody, arching stems called *canes*. Blackberry leaves consist of three to five coarsely toothed leaflets. Its white, five-petaled flowers grow in clusters at the ends of the stems. Each flower produces a berry, which is technically a cluster of little fruits. The berries change from green to red to black as they ripen. They are fully ripe when dull black, not glossy.

Faery Folklore

In Celtic mythology, the Tuatha Dé Danann brought the bramble with them to Ireland. According to legends elsewhere, blackberry bushes marked an area frequented by elves and was a plant under the protection of faeries. In Scottish superstition, faeries were said to defile blackberries at Michaelmas (September 29th) and Samhain. In Ireland, blackberries were not to be gathered after October 31st because the *pooka* was said to have spat on them. The pooka, or *puca*, is regarded as a type of faery that takes an animal form. In Brittany, France, eating blackberries was avoided because faeries didn't like humans using their magical fruit.

Magical Workings

Powers and attributes: Abundance, awareness (expand, heighten), balance/harmony, challenges/obstacles (overcome), communication, fertility, growth, happiness, healing, intuition, knowledge (seek, acquire), luck, prosperity/money, protection, purification, spirit guides/spirits

Items to purchase when the plant is not available: Blackberries; blackberry juice; blackberry wine; dried leaves; blackberry leaf tea

Grow a blackberry bush on your property to attract faeries, or set out a small bowl of berries as a token of friendship. Eat a handful of blackberries before magic work to reach deeper levels of consciousness, especially when working with the faery realm. Use the berry juice to prepare candles when communicating with spirits.

Blackberries enhance and aid in developing intuition. To attract prosperity, burn a dried leaf as part of a spell. Crumble a handful of dried leaves, and then sprinkle them around your property to attract luck. Blackberries are instrumental for healing; use them on your altar when sending energy to someone who is ill. To stimulate protective energy, make a wreath with several prickly canes and hang it above your altar or on your front door.

Blackthorn
Blackthorn (Prunus spinosa)
Folk names: Blackthorn plum, fairy tree, sloe plum, wishing thorn

Blackthorn is a shrubby tree with dense, spiny branches. Its white, five-petaled flowers bloom in early spring, before the leaves appear, and stand in stark contrast to the dark thorns and bark. Called *sloes*, the blue-black fruit is small and round. Sloes ripen in the autumn after the first hard frost.

Faery Folklore
In Ireland, a solitary blackthorn is regarded as a lone bush and fairy thorn. (See the profile for Lone Bush.) They were never disturbed because fairies were believed to inhabit them. If one grew in the middle of a field, a farmer would plow around it rather than incur the wrath of the faeries. This tree was also believed to be a gateway to the faery realm. Blackthorn was frequently used as a cloutie tree.

Faeries called *Lunantishee* (Luna sídhe, moon faeries) were believed to serve as guardians of the blackthorn in Ireland. According to legend, the Lunantishee would inflict bad luck on a person who dared to cut anything from the tree on or around the dates of May 11th or November 11th. On the old Julian calendar, these were the approximate days of Beltane and Samhain.

This tree's dark, sturdy wood made it the preferred walking stick in Ireland. Although it was useful to ward off any form of danger encountered during an afternoon ramble, it was believed that faeries would not meddle with anyone carrying a blackthorn stick because they held the tree in high regard.

Magical Workings

Powers and attributes: Authority/leadership, banish, challenges/obstacles (overcome), defense, hexes (break, protect from), loyalty/fidelity, negativity (remove, ward off), protection, purification, strength, truth

Items to purchase when the tree is not available: Flower essence; walking stick; dried sloes are often marketed as blackthorn berries; pieces of bark are often marketed as sloe tree bark

In keeping with tradition, avoid taking any anything from a blackthorn around Beltane and Samhain; instead, leave an offering at the base of the tree or in the branches. To purify outdoor space for magic or ritual, strew crumbled, dried blackthorn leaves around the area. This will also boost magical energy and attract faeries.

To honor the fae at your indoor altar, sprinkle a small amount of blackthorn flower essence around it. To strengthen the energy of a spell, crumble and burn a few leaves. Alternatively, use a picture of a blackthorn tree in place of leaves. When incorporated into a spell, the sloes strengthen your energy. They can be dried and used as amulets for protection or to help gain control of a situation.

Bluebell

Common Bluebell, English Bluebell (Hyacinthoides non-scripta)
Folk names: Fairy bells, harebell, wood bells

The fragrant bluebell is famous and beloved for carpeting woodlands in the early spring with a splash of color. The pendulous flowers dangle from slender, arching stems that grow to about twelve inches tall. The flowers are deep, violet blue. They have a smaller, more tubular shape than the harebell (*Campanula rotundifolia*), with which they are often confused because of the shared folk names.

Faery Folklore

Bluebell was reputedly one of the most powerful faery plants. Although the flowers were rung to call the fae together, if a human heard the sound, it meant someone they know would soon die. Nevertheless, these flowers were believed to aid in seeing faeries. According to some legends, stepping on bluebells would result in being led astray by faeries or pixies. Escape was not possible until another human came to the rescue. Other legends warned that picking bluebell flowers would result in a person wandering lost forever.

Because an area where bluebells grew was an indication of faery habitat, children were commonly told to stay out of the woods to avoid trouble. Closely associated with enchantment, some stories indicate that bluebell flowers were used for dark faery magic.

Magical Workings
Powers and attributes: Challenges/obstacles (overcome), love, loyalty/fidelity, manifest (desires, dreams, will), nightmares, renewal, see faeries, truth
Items to purchase when the plant is not available: Flower essence

Growing bluebells in your garden is a way to attract faeries and nature spirits to your property. When you seek contact, hold a sprig of flowers as you visualize the encounter. For help in making your wishes come true, write what you seek on a picture of bluebells, and then burn it in your cauldron. When the ashes cool, scatter them outside as you visualize your desire. The same method can be used for overcoming any type of obstacle in your life. For help in keeping bad dreams at bay, tuck a picture of bluebells or a small organza bag of dried flowers under each corner of your mattress.

Bog Myrtle
Bog Myrtle, Sweet Gale (Myrica gale)
Folk names: Bayberry, candleberry, gale, moor myrtle

Bog myrtle is a bushy shrub that reaches a height of only two to four feet. Its foliage is dark green to grayish green and is sweetly scented. The oval leaves have broad tips that taper at the base; they grow in a spiral around the branches. Upright yellow-orange (male) and red (female) flowers develop into clusters of pointed, egg-shaped seeds.

Caution: Although bog myrtle is sometimes used in tea and food, it is an abortifacient and pregnant women should never ingest it.

Faery Folklore
In many areas of Scotland, this plant was used to keep mischievous faeries away. However, in the formerly Pictish areas of Scotland the faeries reputedly wore badges of bog myrtle sprigs.

Magical Workings

Powers and attributes: Adaptability, concentration/focus, defense, determination/endurance, dream work, inspiration, luck, peace, prosperity/money, protection, purification, relationships

Items to purchase when the plant is not available: Flower essence; essential oil; cut, dried leaves; seeds. Although bog myrtle is also known as bayberry and candleberry, bayberry candles are made from the wax myrtles (*Myrica pensylvanica* and *M. cerifera*).

The wisdom of bog myrtle is to learn how to adapt and cultivate the ability to bend with circumstances rather than break. While this may seem like giving in or surrendering, the lesson is to bide your time, because with determination you can reach your goals. To foster inspiration and insight, diffuse a little essential oil during meditation. Keep a picture of bog myrtle in your work area when you need to focus your attention on a project at hand.

For support in dream work, place a few seeds in a sachet to hang on your bedpost. Bog myrtle will also aid in remembering your dreams. For good luck, carry a picture of bog myrtle in your wallet. Burn a pinch of dried leaves for protection spells to raise defensive energy and purify your space.

Boxwood
Common Box, English Boxwood (Buxus sempervirens)
Folk names: Box, box tree

Boxwood is a multi-branched hedge tree with dense, evergreen foliage that is often used for topiary. It usually grows between fifteen and twenty feet tall and wide. Box has small, oval leaves and rounded clusters of yellowish flowers. The seed capsules have three horn-like protrusions and turn brown when they mature in late summer.

Faery Folklore

In Bavaria, Germany, a piece of boxwood was placed in a baby's cradle to prevent faeries from replacing the infant with a changeling. In other areas of Europe, the holly sprigs used for protection from a range of goblins and malicious faeries in the winter were replaced in the spring with boxwood branches.

Magical Workings

Powers and attributes: Ancestors, defense, divination, fertility, happiness, hexes (break, protect from), love, luck, prophecy, prosperity/money, protection, renewal

Items to purchase when the plant is not available: Seeds; candle rings and door wreaths made from leafy branches; the wood is widely used for figurines

Use a few branches of boxwood to make a wreath for your front door to let faeries and nature spirits know they are welcome. Grow a box tree on your property to invite prosperity and happiness to your family. Leave it unclipped in a natural state to attract faeries and nature spirits.

To break a hex, use a box branch to "comb" your aura with downward strokes as you visualize any negativity being swept away from you. Comb your aura three nights in a row, and then bury the branch in the ground. Store a small branch with your divination gear to support and strengthen the energy of your tools. Place several leaves or a piece of bark in a small pouch to use as a love charm. To honor loved ones who have passed, include a small box branch on your altar at Samhain. As an alternative, use a picture of the tree and write the names of those you want to remember during your ritual.

Bracken
Bracken Fern, Western Bracken Fern (Pteridium aquilinum syn. *Pteris aquilina)*
Folk names: Brake fern, female fern, trows' caird

Reaching about four feet tall, bracken fern has triangular fronds that rise directly from its deep roots. The fronds commonly tilt to an almost horizontal position. Known as sori or fruit dots, the spore cases appear in rows near the margins of the frond leaflets. In the early spring, bracken ferns emerge with multiple fiddleheads on their stalks.

Caution: Bracken fiddleheads should not be eaten.

Faery Folklore

According to legend, fern seeds (spores) were believed to be invisible except when falling from the plant and faeries would try to catch them. Faeries were said to never harm a human who had witnessed seeds falling. Faeries on the

Scottish islands of Orkney and Shetland are known as trows and most ferns are generally called *trows' cairds*. A caird or card is a tool used to prepare wool for spinning.

In Ireland, a faery changeling was said to turn into a clump of ferns or yellow iris when thrown in a river. Pity the family who witnessed the demise of an infant who did not change into a bunch of plants. In the Celtic myth *The Cattle Raid of Cooley*, a fern was used as proof that a person had visited the faery realm. In another tale, faeries turned ferns into pigs. Whenever the bracken was said to ring with laughter, it meant that faeries were cavorting among the ferns.

Magical Workings

Powers and attributes: Abundance, banish, concentration/focus, defense, divination, hexes (break, protect from), love, luck, negativity (remove, ward off), prosperity/money, protection, psychic abilities, purification, release (let go, move on), security, spirit guides/spirits, trust

Items to purchase when the plant is not available: Dried fronds

Its ethereal fronds make the bracken fern a perfect addition to a shaded garden area to attract faeries and nature spirits. Place a leaf on your altar for aid in connecting with their realm. To clear negative energy and banish unwanted spirits, burn a small piece of dried stem. Use leaves in protection spells against hexes. Kiss a fern leaf to seal an oath.

Broom
Common Broom, Scotch Broom (Cytisus scoparius)
Folk names: Besom, broom straw

Broom is a hardy, multi-stemmed evergreen shrub that can reach eight feet tall and wide. Its long, flexible branches served as the original household broom. The yellow flowers are fragrant. The lower leaves consist of three leaflets, while the upper leaves are single. When mature, the gray-green seedpods turn black and snap open with a popping sound to eject the small, black seeds. Broom is easily confused with gorse (*Ulex europaeus*).

Caution: Do not burn broom, as the smoke is toxic.

Faery Folklore

In Ireland, a lone bush of broom was reputedly a dwelling or gathering place of faeries. (See the profile for Lone Bush.) In *Tam Lin*, an old ballad from the Scottish borders, a broom bush was the home of the faery queen. Other versions of the story note that Tam Lin, also known as Thomas the Rhymer, met the faery queen under a hawthorn or yew. See the profile on Yew for more on this story.

Magical Workings

Powers and attributes: Balance/harmony, banish, challenges/obstacles (overcome), communication, concentration/focus, creativity, determination/endurance, divination, family and home, fertility, healing, intuition, negativity (remove, ward off), peace, prophecy, prosperity/money, protection, purification, security, strength, wisdom

Items to purchase when the plant is not available: Flower essence; dried bunches of flowers are marketed as broom bloom

Hang a handful of dried flowers to attract faeries and nature spirits to your home. Use the flower essence to strengthen intuition or sharpen communication skills. Broom can also aid in surmounting obstacles and restoring balance to your life.

When used for ritual, broom prepares a sacred area by removing psychic dross and negative energy. After casting a circle, hold the branches in front of you, and then use a sweeping motion, starting at the center and moving out to the edge of your circle. As you do this, visualize removing anything unwanted from your life. Say three times:

> *Besom broom of power and light,*
> *Cast things out; set them to flight.*
> *Be gone the things that hinder me;*
> *This is my will; so mote it be.*

Burdock and Bitter Dock
Greater Burdock (Arctium lappa)
Bitter Dock, Broad-leaved Dock (Rumex obtusifolius)
Folk names: Billy buttons (burdock), burweed (burdock), docken (bitter dock)

Growing six to eight feet tall, burdock has purplish, grooved stems. Its elongated, heart-shaped leaves are dull green with wavy edges. The purple, thistle-like flowers grow in clusters and develop into round, spiky seedpods. Known as burs, the seedpods turn brown and remain on the plant until they get attached to passing animals or people.

Bitter dock can reach a little over three feet tall. Its large base leaves are oblong and veined, with the central one often a reddish color. Bitter dock has one or more flowering stalks with whorls of drooping, greenish-red flowers. The leaves on the flowering stalks are smaller than the base leaves.

Faery Folklore
In Cornwall, England, pixies were said to ride colts and tangle their manes with burdock burs. These tangles were known as elf locks and elf knots. Bitter dock was used in charms to break faery spells. Other legends note that faeries used the large leaves from both of these plants to shelter from the rain.

Magical Workings
Powers and attributes: Balance/harmony, banish, defense, divination, healing, love, negativity (remove, ward off), peace, protection, purification, release (let go, move on)

Items to purchase when the plant is not available: Cut, dried leaves; cut, dried root; powdered root

To remove something that you no longer want in your life, collect a few burdock burs. Be sure to wear gloves for protection. Meditate on what you want to remove as you roll the burs between your hands to break them up. Throw the pieces to the wind as you say three times:

Be gone, be gone;
From my life be gone.
Never again trouble me;
This is so, blessed be.

To raise protective energy for your home, collect four burs. Keeping them intact, place one at each corner of your house. To purify the energy of your divination tools, store them with a dried root of bitter dock so they will be ready whenever you need them. A picture of bitter dock or a dried root placed on your altar during meditation fosters harmony.

Buttercup
Creeping Buttercup (Ranunculus repens)
Lesser Celandine, Fig Buttercup (R. ficaria)
Meadow Buttercup, Tall Buttercup (R. acris)
Folk names: Elf goblets, fairy basins

Creeping buttercup reaches almost a foot tall. Its leaves are deeply lobed and heavily veined. The meadow buttercup grows from one to three feet tall. Its leaves are similar but with a more feathery appearance. These buttercups have cup-shaped flowers with five rounded, slightly overlapping petals. Lesser celandine is a mat-forming plant that grows in a rosette pattern. It often reaches twelve inches wide. Its oval leaves are irregularly lobed and have wavy edges. The flower is more daisy-like than other buttercups, with seven to twelve petals. The flowers of all these plants are the color of butter.

Caution: Although the sap of these plants can cause skin irritation and blistering, the toxins they contain evaporate as they dry out.

Faery Folklore
Legends note that faeries drink dew from small buttercups and use the larger flowers as basins for washing their hands and faces. Buttercups were traditionally placed on doorsteps and windowsills on May Eve to protect against faery mischief. Because they resemble cow udders, the tuberous roots of lesser celandine were hung in cowsheds to discourage faeries from meddling with the milk.

Magical Workings
Powers and attributes: Abundance, adaptability, divination, dream work, emotions (deal with, support), happiness, love, manifest (desires, dreams, will), prosperity/money, spirituality, success, truth, wisdom

Items to purchase when the plant is not available: Flower essence is made
from the meadow buttercup; dried, pressed flowers

Associated with sunlight and positive thoughts, buttercups can be used in
spells to attract abundance. The flowers are helpful when coping with unsettled
emotions; place a picture of them where you will see it often to aid you. As an
alternative, keep the photo in your pocket. To turn dreams into reality, dry several sprigs of flowers and leaves for use in spells.

To deepen spiritual commitment and open your heart and mind to receive
ancient wisdom, place a bowl of buttercup flowers on your altar while meditating. When fresh flowers are not available, gaze at a picture of them.

Butterwort
Common Butterwort (Pinguicula vulgaris)
Folk names: Bog violet, marsh violet

Butterwort is a carnivorous plant that grows in wet areas such as bogs and fens.
At its base is a star-shaped rosette of fleshy, yellow-green leaves that roll inward
at the edges. A sticky substance on the leaves traps insects. Several stems, four
to eight inches tall, rise from the center of the base rosette. Each curved, leafless stem has one drooping, purple flower. The flower has a three-lobed upper
lip and a slightly longer, two-lobed lower lip.

Faery Folklore
In Scotland, a hoop made with butterwort, dandelion, milkwort, and marigold was placed under a milk pail to protect the contents from faery meddling.
In some areas of the British Isles it was believed that if a cow ate butterwort
it would be safe from elf shot and protected from faery spells. The protection
from spells was passed along to any person who ate cheese made from the milk.

On the Hebride Islands of Scotland, if a pregnant woman ate butter made
from the milk of a cow that ate butterwort her child would always be safe from
faeries. Protection also applied to cheese when butterwort was substituted for
rennet.

Magical Workings

Powers and attributes: Adaptability, awareness (expand, heighten), challenges/obstacles (overcome), determination/endurance, dream work, family and home, healing, hexes (break, protect from), love, luck, negativity (remove, ward off), prophecy, protection, support (receive, provide)

Items to purchase when the plant is not available: Seeds

Keep a few butterwort seeds in your pocket or purse during major transitions in your life to help you move with the changes and to provide a sense of stability. When facing problems, use a picture of butterwort and write a keyword about the situation on each leaf. Hold the picture while you meditate on how to meet the challenges, and then burn it in your cauldron. Scatter the ashes outdoors as you visualize the resolution. To clear negative energy, tie butterwort flowers together like a daisy chain and hang it in your home wherever it is needed.

Cedar
Atlas Cedar, Atlantic Cedar (Cedrus atlantica)
Cedar of Lebanon (C. libani)

Although there are a number of trees called *cedar*, only those of the genus *Cedrus* are true cedars. Both of the cedars included here have cylindrical cones that sit upright on the branches. The Atlas cedar's short needles curve toward the ends of the branches. The needles of the cedar of Lebanon grow in widely spaced clusters that spiral around the branches. The cedar of Lebanon can live up to a thousand years.

Faery Folklore
Cedar is associated with faeries and elves.

Magical Workings
Powers and attributes: Abundance, authority/leadership, balance/harmony, banish, challenges/obstacles (overcome), clarity (enhance, foster), communication, concentration/focus, consecrate/bless, courage, determination/endurance, divination, dream work, emotions (deal with, support), family and home, fertility, growth, healing, hexes (break, protect from), inspiration, justice/legal matters, love, loyalty/fidelity, luck, negativity (remove, ward off), peace, prosperity/money, protection, psychic abilities, purification, release (let go, move on), renewal, security, spirit guides/spirits, spirituality, strength, success, wisdom

Items to purchase when the plant is not available: Incense; cedarwood boxes; figurines and other objects are made from the wood; essential oil is made from the Atlas cedar

Cedar is especially effective for purification. Use a cedar bough to symbolically sweep ritual areas, or store a small sprig with your magic tools to have them ready for use. Burn a small piece of cedarwood or cedar incense to support concentration and clarity for clairvoyance or any type of divination. The aroma also enhances psychic protection for these practices. Use cedar to remove negativity, break hexes, or to eliminate anything unwanted from your life.

The scent of cedarwood stimulates dream work and strengthens psychic abilities. It aids in finding peace of mind and fostering tranquility in the home. Use the foliage in spells to attract love or to encourage a lover to be faithful. Any part of the cedar can be used to facilitate communication with spirits. Use cedar at Imbolc to represent the process of coming into the light from the darkness. Cedar also aids healing and personal growth. Carry an amulet made of cedarwood when seeking justice, especially in legal matters.

Chamomile

German Chamomile (Matricaria recutita syn. *M. chamomilla)*
Roman Chamomile (Chamaemelum nobile syn. *Anthemis nobilis)*

With branching stems, German chamomile stands erect and can reach two or three feet in height. Roman chamomile is a spreading herb with stems that creep along the ground. It is usually less than nine inches tall. Both chamomiles have small, daisy-like flowers with white petals and yellow centers. The flowers grow at the ends of the stems. German chamomile flowers are less fragrant than the apple-scented Roman. Both plants have feathery leaves; however, the leaves of Roman chamomile are a little coarser.

Faery Folklore
Chamomile is associated with faeries.

Magical Workings
Powers and attributes: Abundance, attraction, balance/harmony, challenges/ obstacles (overcome), clarity (enhance, foster), communication, consecrate/ bless, creativity, determination/endurance, divination, dream work, emotions (deal with, support), fertility, growth, healing, hexes (break, protect from), inspiration, intuition, justice/legal matters, love, luck, manifest (desires, dreams, will), negativity (remove, ward off), nightmares, peace, prosperity/money, protection, psychic abilities, purification, sex/sexuality, spirituality, success, wishes

Items to purchase when the plant is not available: Essential oil is made from both types of chamomile; tea; dried flowers; seeds

Well-known for physical and emotional healing, chamomile also brings clarity and success to communication. To enhance dream work, drink a cup of chamomile tea before going to bed. Also drink the tea before divination sessions to hone your intuition. Chamomile aids in grounding energy for psychic work, especially Roman chamomile when channeling. Use essential oil to purify and consecrate altars as well as ritual and magic tools.

To counteract hexes, use two stems of German chamomile to create an X on your altar. Use dried flowers in spells to attract love and luck. Hang a bunch of dried chamomile in the kitchen to attract abundance and prosperity to your home. For emotional balance, place several small jars filled with dried chamomile flowers in places where you will see them often and feel the energy.

Cherry

Sweet Cherry, Wild Cherry (Prunus avium)
European Bird Cherry (P. padus)
Folk names: Bird cherry, merry-tree

The sweet cherry has fragrant, white flowers that grow singly or in clusters and oval, dark green leaves with toothed edges. The fruit is cherry-red and has a large seed also known as a stone. The European bird cherry has white flowers that grow in pendulous clusters. Its dark green leaves are pointed. The fruit is red, but turns black as it ripens.

Faery Folklore
In Serbian lore, the beautiful faeries known as Vila, who live in the forests, are said to enjoy playing and dancing under cherry trees. A type of Finnish tree faery known as the Tuometar is associated with the European bird cherry.

Magical Workings
Powers/attributes: Abundance, attraction, awareness (expand, heighten), balance/harmony, challenges/obstacles (overcome), creativity, divination, fertility, happiness, knowledge (seek, acquire), love, luck, manifest (desires, dreams, will), peace, renewal, spirituality, wisdom

Items to purchase when the tree is not available: Fresh or dried cherries; cherry juice

To heighten awareness during divination sessions, burn a small piece of cherry bark as incense. For help in overcoming a problem, press a cherry blossom in a book, and then keep it in your wallet. When the obstacle or situation is resolved, burn the flower as you affirm your gratitude for the tree's help. To aid in manifesting dreams, take three cherries, and pull the stems off one by one as you visualize what you want to achieve. After eating the three cherries, bury the stones in your garden or a wooded area.

In addition to functioning as a symbol of abundance, the cherry tree also attracts good luck. As part of a spell to stimulate and attract love, place a few blossoms, or a picture of cherry flowers, on your altar. In a bridal bouquet, the flowers foster a long, happy marriage and increase fertility. Just as the flowers are associated with love, so too are the fruit. Use cherry juice to consecrate a red candle for love spells. To attract love, wash two cherry stones, let them dry, and then sew them into a small pouch to carry with you.

Cinquefoil
Creeping Cinquefoil, European Cinquefoil (Potentilla reptans)
Folk name: Five-leaf grass

Cinquefoil reaches four to six inches tall and has yellow, five-petaled flowers that resemble small, wild roses. Stalks with a single flower or leaf rise up from the stems, which grow along the ground. The leaves consist of five or seven oval, coarsely toothed leaflets that grow in a circular pattern around the stalks.

Faery Folklore
Although the fae were said to be fond of the little, rose-like flowers of cinquefoil, both the flowers and leaves were used to break faery spells.

Magical Workings
Powers and attributes: Authority/leadership, challenges/obstacles (overcome), communication, consecrate/bless, defense, divination, dream work, emotions (deal with, support), healing, hexes (break, protect from), inspiration, justice/legal matters, loss/sorrow (ease, recover from), love, luck, manifest (desires, dreams, will), nightmares, prosperity/money, protection, security, spirit guides/spirits, strength, success, wisdom, wishes

Items to purchase when the plant is not available: Dried leaves and roots are marketed as cinquefoil herb

When preparing to step into a leadership position, light a red or orange candle on your altar. Place a small amount of dried, crumbled leaves into a small offering bowl as you visualize the new responsibilities you will be taking on. Once you are comfortably settled in your new role, sprinkle the dried leaves outside as you express gratitude for your success.

To break a hex or any form of negative magic, make an infusion of cinquefoil leaves. Without straining out the plant material, take it outside and pour it on the ground as you say:

This spell that someone tried to cast
Is not to be, it will not last.
With this potion I now pour,
All harm is banished from my door.

When seeking inspiration, place a picture of cinquefoil in your workspace or on your altar. Carry a piece of dried root to aid in sharpening your communication skills.

Also see the profile for Silverweed.

Clover

White Clover (Trifolium repens)
Folk names: Moon clover, shamrock, trefoil

Blooming from March through December, the tiny, white to pale pink clover flowers are clustered into a spherical flower head. Although the leaves usually consist of three leaflets, some plants occasionally produce four or more.

Faery Folklore

A four-leaf clover was believed to enable the finder to see faeries. According to legend, four-leaf clover only grew in areas popular with faeries and elves. Other legends note that they grow only where a faery has stepped and the fae will protect a person who finds one. As a magic talisman, it reputedly enabled the wearer to speak with faeries and to enter the faery realm. However, the four-leaf clover had to be found by chance and not intentionally sought.

In Cornwall, England, special ointment made with a four-leaf clover and applied to the eyelids allowed a person to see the offshore faery islands. Used as a counter charm, a four-leaf clover could break fairy glamour.

Magical Workings

Powers and attributes: Abundance, balance/harmony, banish, dream work, healing, hexes (break, protect from), intuition, love, loyalty/fidelity, luck

(four-leaf clover), prosperity/money, protection, relationships, release (let go, move on), see faeries (four-leaf clover), truth
Items to purchase when the plant is not available: Flower essence; seeds

If you find a four-leaf clover, make a small ring of clover flowers and place it around the special leaf. Faeries will know that you are inviting them to dance. To attract and increase abundance in your life, pick one stem of leaflets, wrap it in a tissue, and press it in a book until it is dry. Keep it in your wallet. Clover flowers and leaves (with any number of leaflets) aid in banishing fear and providing protection from hexes.

Leaving the stems long, pick enough flowers to tie end-to-end and make a crown. Wear this when beginning a spell to attract love, and then place it over your bedpost for three nights. On the following night, burn the crown as you send your energy and intention out to the universe. Also wear a crown of clover when working with faeries and nature spirits to enhance your contact.

Columbine
Garden Columbine, Common Columbine (Aquilegia vulgaris)
Wild Columbine, Red Columbine (A. canadensis)
Folk names: Dancing fairies, rock bells

Columbine has drooping, bell-like flowers with distinctive, backward-pointing spurs. They grow on long, branching stalks that are one to three feet tall. The flowers give way to seeds that look like clusters of small, upright peapods. The wild columbine has red and yellow flowers with long spurs. Garden columbine has violet-blue flowers with short spurs. Columbine's medium-green leaves are rounded and lobed. There are many species of columbine.

Faery Folklore
In parts of England and elsewhere, columbine was called *dancing fairies* because the drooping flowers looked like tiny faeries pirouetting across the landscape. Because of this, the plant has become associated with the fae.

Magical Workings
Powers and attributes: Balance/harmony, consecrate/bless, courage, creativity, emotions (deal with, support), family and home, inspiration, love, negativ-

ity (remove, ward off), peace, purification, release (let go, move on), spirituality, support, trust

Items to purchase when the plant is not available: Flower essence; seeds

Growing columbine in the garden invites blessings to the home. Sprinkle a handful of dried flowers to consecrate ritual space. To bolster courage and balance emotions, tuck a few seeds in your pocket on days when you need support. To keep negative energy from entering your home, scatter dried flowers and leaves across the threshold of your front door. Infuse a few seedpods in olive oil, and then use it to prepare candles for love spells. To deepen your spiritual commitment, place a picture of columbine on your altar to gaze at during contemplation. This will also foster a feeling of peace.

Coriander

Coriander (Coriandrum sativum)
Folk name: Chinese parsley

This plant is known by two names: coriander and cilantro. Coriander refers to the seeds, and cilantro to the lower leaves, which resemble parsley. The upper leaves are delicate and fern-like. With slender, erect stems, this strongly aromatic herb grows about two feet tall. The ball-shaped seeds are golden brown. The small flowers range from white to pink to pale lavender. They have five petals and grow in umbrella-shaped clusters.

Faery Folklore

According to legends in the Hindu Kush region of northern Pakistan, coriander was cultivated by the mountain faeries that were known by their Persian and Sanskrit names of *peri* and *apsaras*, respectively. Coriander seeds dipped in powdered sugar are called *fairy sweets*.

In some areas of Morocco, people fumigate themselves and their homes for protection against malevolent jinn. However, the belief is just the opposite in the area around the city of Fes, where coriander seeds are called *t'effah l-jinn*, "the apples of the jinn."[69]

---

69. Westermarck, *Ritual and Belief in Morocco*, 309.

Magical Workings

Powers and attributes: Balance/harmony, changes/transitions, consecrate/
bless, divination, dream work, emotions (deal with, support), family and
home, fertility, happiness, healing, love, loyalty/fidelity, peace, protection,
psychic abilities, relationships, renewal, secrets, security, sex/sexuality

Items to purchase when the plant is not available: Essential oils are made
from coriander (seeds) and cilantro (leaves); flower essence; seeds, whole
or ground; cut, dried cilantro

To enhance and strengthen your abilities during a divination session, place
a small bowl of seeds on your altar or table. Coriander is also an aid for honing psychic skills, especially clairvoyance. Use either of the essential oils to
consecrate charms and amulets. The seeds are instrumental for raising healing
energy and for well-being, especially emotional balance. Use coriander's power
of protection for the home by sprinkling a handful of crushed seeds in the cardinal directions on your property, as well as scattering them for the directions
above, below, and center.

The scent of coriander used throughout the home fosters peace and security.
Use coriander oil to excite passion with a new lover or to re-ignite the flame
with your longtime partner. Wrap a couple of cilantro leaves in a tissue and tuck
it under your pillow when you want to dream about romance.

Cow Parsley

Cow Parsley, Wild Chervil (Anthriscus sylvestris)
Folk names: Fairy lace, gypsy lace, hedge parsley

Growing three to five feet tall, cow parsley has a ribbed, hairy stalk. Its leaves
are up to two inches long, sharply lobed, and fern-like, giving the plant a delicate airiness. The leaves are dark green and slightly shiny on the upper side.
Reaching up to three inches wide, the white flowers grow in lacy, flat clusters
at the tops of the stems. The flowers are slightly notched, have five petals, and
green centers. The narrow, egg-shaped fruits mature from greenish to yellowish
and eventually black when they split into a pair of seeds.

Caution: Although cow parsley leaves are more feathery and its stalks are ribbed, it is easily confused with hemlock (*Conium maculatum*), which is extremely poisonous.

Faery Folklore

Cow parsley was reputedly used to break faery spells and enchantment. Although it was noted to be effective, it was often blamed for provoking subsequent episodes.

Magical Workings

Powers and attributes: Balance/harmony, courage, emotions (deal with, support), family and home, healing, hexes (break, protect from), love, negativity (remove, ward off), peace, protection, strength

Items to purchase when the plant is not available: Flower essence is marketed as wild chervil; seeds

Grow cow parsley in your garden to attract faeries and nature spirits. Because of its height, it can be used to create a natural screen for your outdoor altar. Give lunar magic a boost by placing a cluster of flowers on your esbat altar. To enhance feelings of peace and bring your energy into alignment, put a dab of flower essence on your third-eye chakra before meditation. For support when you need courage, draw the faery star on a small piece of orange or green cloth and wrap it around three dried leaves. Keep it with you when you need help. To raise healing energy, make an infusion with the leaves and use it to prepare candles for ritual.

Cowslip
Common Cowslip, English Cowslip (Primula veris)
Folk names: Candle of the woods, fairy basins, fairy bells, fairy cups, fairy flower, key flower, luck flower

Cowslip has drooping clusters of funnel-shaped flowers on an erect stem that rises above a rosette of base leaves. The leaves are oval-shaped and wrinkly. The honey-scented flowers are lemon yellow with a reddish spot at the base of each petal. The red spots are called *fairy rubies*.

Faery Folklore

Legends note that the reddish spot on the petals marked where an elf had touched them. Faeries were said to take shelter in cowslips at night, during stormy weather, or whenever passing clouds blocked the moonlight. The music of their soft, sweet voices could be heard from inside the flowers. Faeries reputedly made cowslip wine for their revels on Midsummer's Eve.

As with other bell-shaped flowers, cowslip blossoms were rung by faeries to announce gatherings. Like its cousin the primrose, the cowslip was known as a key flower and luck flower in Germany, and it was believed to be capable of unlocking an enchanted castle, a secret place, or faery treasure.

Magical Workings

Powers and attributes: Divination, healing, love, peace, prosperity/money, protection, secrets, spirit guides/spirits, strength, trust

Items to purchase when the plant is not available: Flower essence; dried flowers; seeds

On May Eve or Beltane day, tie flower stalks along a ribbon and string it across a window as a special decoration for faeries and nature spirits. To foster peace and tranquility, place several cut flowers in a vase before meditation. To enhance communication with spirit guides, dry a couple of leaves, and then burn them in your cauldron as you call for their presence.

For love divination when you are interested in two people, make a tisty-tosty or tissy ball. Choose flower heads where all the flowers are open, and then cut the stalks close to the flowers. Tie the flower heads close together along a length of yarn, and then pull the ends of the yarn together to make a ball. Hold it between your hands and say:

> *Tisty-tosty tell me do;*
> *Who will love me truly true.*

Say the name of one person each time you toss the ball into the air and catch it. When the ball falls apart or lands on the floor, that's the name of your true love.

Crab Apple

American Crab Apple, Sweet Crab Apple (Malus coronaria syn. *Pyrus coronaria)*
European Crab Apple, Wild Apple (M. sylvestris)
Folk name: Applethorn

The crab apple is a small tree with a short, crooked trunk, but what it may lack in height it makes up for with a showy display of fragrant flowers that can range from white to pink to almost rosy. This tree has oval leaves and its small branches have short thorns. By early summer, the little green crab apples become notice-able, and in the autumn, they turn dark red as they ripen.

Faery Folklore

Although the cultivated apple is also associated with the legendary Avalon, Isle of Apples, according to lore it was a place populated with wild crab apple trees. Similarly, in Celtic mythology, Eamhain Abhlach, the Region of Apples, is an otherworld home to faeries as well as Mannanán Mac Lir, sea god and mem-ber of the Tuatha Dé Danann. In Celtic legends, crab apple and apple were regarded as the fruit of knowledge, magic, and prophecy.

Magical Workings

Powers and attributes: Abundance, ancestors, divination, fertility, happiness, healing, knowledge (seek, acquire), love, prophecy, prosperity/money, pro-tection, spirit guides/spirits, wisdom

Items to purchase when the tree is not available: Fresh or dried crab apples; flower essence is made from the European crab apple

Use a crab apple branch or wand to help open the way to the faery realm. It is also an aid when contacting nature spirits. When seeking knowledge for making an important decision, light a candle and meditate as you sit in front of your altar, holding a crab apple leaf in each hand. Hang a wand or branch over your altar while working on a protection spell. Use crab apple blossoms in spells to invite abundance and prosperity into your home. Before performing a spell to attract a lover, prepare yourself with a bath by sprinkling a handful of flower petals in the water. When you are finished bathing, collect the petals and place them in a bowl on your altar.

Associated with Beltane, crab apple blossoms are a traditional and symbolic flower to place on the altar. If your tree blooms too early for the sabbat, place a few flowers in a container in the freezer, and then bring them out just before your ritual. For Samhain, place a circle of crab apples on your altar to honor your ancestors.

Crocus
Saffron Crocus, Autumn Crocus (Crocus sativus)
Wild Crocus, Snow Crocus (C. chrysanthus)
Woodland Crocus, Early Crocus (C. tommasinianus)

Crocus is well-known for its colorful, chalice-shaped flowers. Resembling blades of grass, the long, thin leaves are dark green with a central white or silvery stripe. The woodland crocus flower ranges from pale lavender to reddish purple with a white throat. The wild crocus flower is yellowish orange and sometimes it has maroon markings. These two crocuses are only three to four inches tall. The saffron crocus grows up to six inches tall. Its flower is lilac purple with reddish orange in the center.

Faery Folklore
According to legend, it was generally considered okay to pick the yellow crocus flowers but not the purplish ones because the faeries preferred those. However, regardless of color, no crocus was to be picked in late winter or early spring in case a faery might need it to take shelter on a cold night. Faeries especially enjoy eating milk sops (pieces of bread soaked in milk) that are sprinkled with saffron. In Morocco, saffron was used as an amulet to ward off malevolent jinn.

Magical Workings
Powers and attributes: Banish, divination, dream work, emotions (deal with, support), family and home, fertility, happiness, healing, love, manifest (desires, dreams, will), nightmares, peace, prosperity/money, protection, psychic abilities, relationships, sex/sexuality, skills, strength

Items to purchase when the plant is not available: Flower essence is made from the woodland crocus and marketed as purple crocus; dried stigmas (interior of the flower) from the saffron crocus are marketed as saffron threads; powdered saffron

Because crocus flowers do not last long after picking, it is usually easier to use dried ones. Hang the flowers upside down in a cool, dark place for a week or two until they are dry and slightly brittle. Leaves can be prepared the same way. Place a dried flower or two in a small sachet to use in a charm to attract love, or place the sachet under your pillow at night to banish nightmares. To bless your home and promote peace within, crumble dried flowers and leaves into a powder and sprinkle it at the corners of your house.

To enhance psychic abilities, especially clairvoyance, sprinkle a tiny pinch of powdered leaves on an incense charcoal before divination sessions. As it burns, say three times:

Spring flower, gentle crocus,
Share your power, help me focus.

Cypress
Common Cypress, Italian Cypress (Cupressus sempervirens)

The cypress is an evergreen that grows in narrow, columnar form. Its dense, scale-like, gray-green foliage is strongly aromatic when crushed. Its round, knobby cones grow in clusters. After opening in early autumn to shed seeds, the cones stay on the tree for several years.

Faery Folklore
According to legends in the Middle East, the jinn often lived in cypress trees. In Europe, elves and faeries were also said to make their homes in this tree.

Magical Workings
Powers and attributes: Ancestors, awareness (expand, heighten), banish, bind, changes/transitions, clarity (enhance, foster), concentration/focus, consecrate/bless, defense, divination, emotions (deal with, support), growth, healing, justice/legal matters, knowledge (seek, acquire), loss/sorrow (ease, recover from), peace, protection, release (let go, move on), renewal, security, strength, wisdom

Items to purchase when the plant is not available: Essential oil is made from the needles and twigs; boxes and other small items are made from cypress wood

Cypress is a powerful ally to provide comfort and healing, especially when dealing with emotional trauma and loss. Use cypress essential oil to prepare a candle or place the oil in a diffuser to scent meditation space. At Samhain, place a sprig of cypress on your altar for remembrance to honor ancestors and other loved ones who have passed beyond the veil. Burning a piece of wood is effective for centering and grounding energy before and after ritual. It is also an aid for focusing the mind.

To consecrate and bless ritual objects or in spells for defensive magic, burn a little piece of foliage or use the essential oil to prepare a candle. Hold a branch during ritual or meditation when seeking truth and knowledge and to stimulate growth and renewal. Holding a couple of cypress cones fosters awareness and clarity for divination and channeling. Place a small branch on your altar for strength and wisdom when seeking justice. Hang one over your front door for protection.

Daffodil

Common Daffodil, Wild Daffodil (Narcissus pseudonarcissus)
Folk names: Daffidowndilly, wild jonquil

Forming clumps that often carpet the ground, the daffodil reaches up to fourteen inches tall. It has narrow, gray-green leaves that grow from the base of the stem. The flower consists of pale yellow petals that create a corona around the darker-yellow trumpet. The two shades of yellow is an easy way to distinguish the wild daffodil from its garden cousins.

Faery Folklore

Wherever they grow wild, daffodils were said to indicate a magical place. Legends note that one had to walk carefully among daffodils to avoid trampling a flower in case a faery was sleeping inside. Faeries were said to play hide-and-seek among the thick clusters of daffodils at woodland edges.

Magical Workings

Powers and attributes: Clarity (enhance, foster), consecrate/bless, family and home, love, luck, negativity (remove, ward off), nightmares, peace, protection, relationships, renewal, security, spirit guides/spirits

Items to purchase when the plant is not available: Flower essence; dried flowers

Plant a ring of daffodil bulbs in the autumn to provide a special place for faeries to dance in the spring. Leave offerings for them in the center of the ring. Use a little flower essence when meditating for clarity when making important decisions.

Daffodils growing in several places around the garden bring protection to the home and clear away negative energy from the property. For extra help, cut a daffodil stem, dip the flower in a bowl of water, and then sprinkle it around the outside of your home as you say:

> *Daffodil, daffodil, hear my call;*
> *Against negativity, build a wall.*
> *Keep this home safe and sound;*
> *May only good things come around.*

Carry the bowl with you so you can continue sprinkling water as you recite the incantation.

Daisy

Common Daisy, English Daisy (Bellis perennis)
Folk names: Bairnwort, day's eye, wild daisy

The common daisy has a small flower with a yellow center disk from which white petals radiate. The flowers are about an inch wide and grow on stems that are three to six inches tall. Its dark green, rounded leaves grow in rosettes at the base of the stems. This daisy is a sprawling plant that can be found in lawns and meadows.

Faery Folklore

Although daisy chains and crowns were placed on children in England to protect them from faeries, it was also a flower used when seeking blessings from the fae. In Ireland, daisy chains were also known as fairy chains. In Scotland, daisies were called *bairnwort* and used to bless babies. The word *bairn* refers to a child.[70]

According to legends, faeries use the flowers in spells and charms. In some areas of England it was believed that daisy roots mixed with cream, or the roots boiled in milk, was a dish prescribed by faeries to keep children small and more faery-like.

Magical Workings

Powers and attributes: Attraction, authority/leadership, awareness (expand, heighten), balance/ harmony, challenges/obstacles (overcome), communication, consecrate/bless, creativity, divination, dream work, family and home, fertility, healing, love, loyalty/fidelity, luck, protection, skills, strength, truth

Items to purchase when the plant is not available: Flower essence; dried flowers; seeds

Grow daisies in your garden to invite faeries to your property as well as to communicate with them. The traditional way to make a daisy chain is to slit the lower part of a flower stem with your thumbnail, and then thread another stem through it. Make a small daisy chain and hang it over your child's bed and ask for the faeries' blessings. When not in a relationship, place a daisy chain over your own bed if you want to attract love.

---

70. Kear, *Flower Wisdom*, 7.

Weave a daisy chain to wear as a bracelet during divination sessions to aid in heightening your senses. Dry a few flowers, and then place them in a sachet on your bedside table to enhance dreams and aid in interpreting messages received during sleep. Scatter a few flowers on your doorstep to invite harmony into your home.

Dandelion

Common Dandelion (Taraxacum officinale)
Folk names: Fairy clocks, golden sun, wishes

The bane of those who want a perfect lawn, dandelion's yellow flower spreads out like a little sun, and then develops into a seed head that is white and round as the moon. Deeply toothed leaves form a rosette base from which the flower stem rises.

Faery Folklore

According to legend, faeries could tell time with the flowers or the seed heads. When the flowers opened in the morning it was five o'clock and when they closed in the evening it was eight o'clock. There were two ways of telling time with the seed head: After blowing on it, the number of seeds left indicated the hour of the day. Or, the hour could be determined by how many puffs it took to blow away all of the seeds. Each puff equaled an hour.

In parts of England, seeds floating on the air were called *fairies* and it was considered lucky to catch one. In Scotland, blowing on a seed head was said to release faeries from capture. It was customary when a seed was seen on the wind to catch it, make a wish, and then let it go. A hoop made with dandelion, butterwort, milkwort, and marigold was commonly placed under a milk pail to protect the contents from faery meddling.

Magical Workings

Powers and attributes: Authority/leadership, awareness (expand, heighten), balance/harmony, clarity (enhance, foster), communication, divination, dream work, emotions (deal with, support), healing, love, luck, manifest (desires, dreams, will), negativity (remove, ward off), peace, prophecy, prosperity/money, protection, psychic abilities, purification, skills, spirit guides/spirits, spirituality, wishes

Items to purchase when the plant is not available: Flower essence; dried
flowers; dandelion leaf tea; dried roots

To prepare candles for divination or any type of psychic work, use oil infused
with dandelion leaves. Use dandelion wine or tea as a libation for ritual. Burn
a dried leaf to enhance communication with spirit guides. When dealing with
emotional issues, hold a flower in your open palms during meditation. Keep a
picture of a dandelion in your workspace when you are developing new skills or
when taking on a leadership role.

To make a wish, pick a seed head on a moonlit night so you will have the
power of Luna to aid you. Before blowing on it, say:

Dandelion, round and white,
Bring the wish I make this night,
Underneath the glowing moon;
Dandelion, may it please come soon.

Dill
Garden Dill (Anethum graveolens)
Folk names: Dill weed, dilly

Reaching three feet tall, dill has an erect, hollow stem. The leaves are ferny,
thread-like, and bluish green. Dill has large, flat, umbrella-like clusters of yellow flowers that bloom mid- to late summer. The tiny, oval seeds are flat and
ribbed.

Faery Folklore
To gain second sight and the ability to see faeries, the juice of dill, St. John's
wort, and vervain were made into an ointment and applied to the eyelids for
three days.

Magical Workings
Powers and attributes: Abundance, balance/harmony, challenges/obstacles
(overcome), changes/transitions, creativity, defense, divination, family and
home, growth, hexes (break, protect from), justice/legal matters, knowl-

edge (seek, acquire), love, luck, nightmares, peace, prophecy, prosperity/ money, protection, purification, renewal, security, see faeries, spirit guides/ spirits, success, support (provide, receive), wisdom

Items to purchase when the plant is not available: Essential oil; flower essence; seeds; cut, dried leaves

With a history of use in love potions, dill also helps to overcome hexes related to love and jealousy. It is a powerful plant for protection and purification. Burning a couple of leaves purifies a space for ritual and magic, as does sweeping the area with long dill stalks. Employ it for success in legal matters and any time defense is needed. Dill can help attract money, prosperity, and security. Use the essential oil to boost creativity and support divination. Hang a bundle of dried dill in your kitchen to invite abundance. Place a couple of flower heads in your workspace to boost creativity and on your altar to support divination.

Elder

European Elder, Black Elderberry (Sambucus nigra)
American Elderberry (S. canadensis)
Folk names: Elderberry, ellhorn (European), fairy tree
(European), Lady Elder (European)

Elder is a large shrub that often grows as wide as it does tall. The leaves are oval and the small, white flowers grow in large, umbrella-like clusters that can reach up to ten inches across. The flowers give way to large pendulous clusters of bluish-black berries. The flowers of the American elderberry have a lemon-like scent; the European elder flowers have a musky odor.

Faery Folklore

In Denmark, it was believed that standing beside an elder tree on Midsummer's Eve allowed a person to see the faery king and his entourage pass by on the way to their revels. Likewise, in England, adding elderflowers to the Midsummer's Eve bonfire allowed people to see the fae. Growing this shrub in the garden served as an invitation to faeries and nature spirits who were said to like swinging and playing among the branches. If branches were seen moving when there was little or no wind, it was said that faeries were riding them like hobbyhorses.

On the Isle of Man, most houses had at least one elder tree to please the fae. It was unlucky to cut down an elder or burn the wood. If one were cut down, the faeries would leave the property and grieve.

While elder was believed to provide protection from faeries, legends note that it also protected good ones from bad ones. At Beltane, woven crowns of elder twigs were worn to foster second sight. In Scotland, standing under an elder near a faery hill after applying the juice of the inner bark to the eyelids enabled a person to witness the fairy rade (procession). In Ireland, a solitary elder is regarded as a lone bush and fairy bush. (See the profile for Lone Bush.)

Magical Workings

Powers and attributes: Abundance, banish, challenges/obstacles (overcome), changes/transitions, consecrate/bless, creativity, defense, dream work, healing, hexes (break, protect from), knowledge (seek, acquire), love, loyalty/fidelity, prosperity/money, protection, purification, release (let go, move on), renewal, security, see faeries, spirituality, success, wisdom

Items to use when the tree is not available: Elderberry juice/syrup; dried elderberries; elderberry seed oil is made from the European elder; flower essence is made from the European elder; cut, dried flowers; elderflower tea (When purchasing flower tea, check that other plants have not been included.)

Grow an elder on your property to attract faeries and nature spirits or leave an offering of elderberry juice for them. Use elderflowers to add power to spells. If you are concerned about hexes or dark magic, hang elderflowers over your altar for protection. Make a hydrosol with the flowers and sprinkle it to cleanse an area before ritual or magic work. As an alternative, use the flower essence or burn a dried leaf to smudge the area.

Elderberries add potent energy to love charms and to spells that foster fidelity. For healing circles, place a handful of berries on your altar to support and boost the energy. The flower essence or a little elderberry juice can be used to consecrate candles. Use crumbled, dried berries in a sachet to enhance dream work.

Elecampane

Elecampane (Inula helenium)
Folk names: Elf dock, elfwort, sun flower

With long, lance-shaped leaves, elecampane's erect stem grows three to six feet tall. The base leaves can grow up to three feet long. Its bright flowers have tangled rays of petals, making them look like scraggly, yellow daisies or wild, overgrown dandelions. The flowers are slightly aromatic.

Faery Folklore
According to legend, elecampane roots were used by faeries in various rituals. They also reputedly used the flowers to make garlands. The Anglo-Saxons used elecampane to treat elf shot, especially when a man's virility was at stake.

Magical Workings
Powers and attributes: Communication, divination, happiness, healing, intuition, love, luck, peace, protection, psychic abilities, purification, relationships, secrets, sex/sexuality, spirit guides/spirits, truth
Items to purchase when the plant is not available: Flower essence; essential oil; dried roots; dried flowers; root extract

When grown in the garden, elecampane attracts faeries and nature spirits. As an alternative, place a few dried roots on your outdoor altar or other space where you work with them. Strew flower petals on your doorstep to invite them inside your home or place a picture of elecampane flowers on your altar. Before ritual or magic work outdoors, sprinkle any part of the dried plant to purify the area and create a protective circle as you say:

> *Elecampane, elecampane,*
> *May your power never wane.*
> *Keep this circle round me spun*
> *Until my magic work is done.*

Made from elecampane roots, the essential oil is instrumental for grounding energy after ritual and magic work. As an alternative, hold a dried root between your hands. Use elecampane flower essence or make a hydrosol to prepare candles for a healing circle. To aid in resolving sexual issues, use the essential oil or infused oil from the root to anoint an object in your bedroom. For aid when dealing with relationship problems, keep a small sachet of dried flowers with you.

Burning dried leaves as incense before a divination session enhances psychic abilities. It also helps to cultivate and enhance intuition. To aid in contacting and communicating with spirit guides, roll up a leaf, tie it with a piece of ribbon or yarn, and then place it on your altar.

Elm

American Elm, White Elm (Ulmus Americana syn. U. floridana)
English Elm, Common Elm (U. procera syn. U. campestris)
Wych Elm, Scots Elm (U. glabra)
Folk names: Ellum, elven (English elm, wych elm)

The American elm produces hanging clusters of tiny, reddish-green flowers that appear in the early spring before the slightly oval leaves emerge. Also appearing before the leaves, the English elm's small flowers hang in tassel-like clusters.

The wych elm can be difficult to distinguish from the English elm; however, its flowers and seeds are larger. From Old English, the word *wych* means "to bend" and was applied to this tree because of its pliant branches.[71] Elm seeds, also called *samaras*, are encased in a papery covering.

Faery Folklore

This tree was called *elven* because elves and faeries were noted to be fond of it and frequently chose to live in the branches. Elms were believed to mark the entrance to the otherworld and faery realm. In Scotland, a twig of wych elm was kept beside or in a butter churn to prevent faeries from making off with the butter.

Magical Workings

Powers and attributes: Attraction, changes/transitions, determination/endurance, divination, dream work, healing, intuition, justice/legal matters, love, loyalty/fidelity, manifest (desires, dreams, will), negativity (remove, ward off), prophecy, protection, psychic abilities, renewal, wisdom, wishes

Items to purchase when the tree is not available: Flower essence is made from the English elm

Elm is a good ally for dream work. Before bedtime, hold a picture of an elm tree between your hands as you ground and center your energy and clear your mind. Place the picture on your bedside table. When you wake up in the morning, write down everything you can remember from your dreams. When seeking justice, write your goal on a picture of an elm. Safely burn it as you visualize the energy manifesting into reality. When the ashes are cool, scatter them outside.

Use an elm leaf as a love charm to invite romance into your life. To boost protective energy, place a twig near your front door or in the attic and visualize the energy of the elm surrounding your home. To enhance divination and psychic work, prepare a white candle by carving the word *elm* on it along with the faery star. Also use the candle during dark moon rituals. To raise healing energy, use a green candle.

---

71. Martin, *The Folklore of Trees & Shrubs*, 207.

Evening Primrose

Common Evening Primrose (Oenothera biennis)
Folk names: Evening star, night light, night willow herb

This prairie wildflower has a rosette of large base leaves and an erect stem that can reach three to six feet tall. Lance-shaped leaves with wavy edges grow on the same stems as the flowers. At dusk, the shiny, yellow flowers unfurl to perfume the night air. They close by noon the following day. Blooming a few at a time, these four-petaled flowers are two inches wide and last only one night. The slight phosphorescence of the blossoms emits a faint light, which is visible on dark nights. The flowers give way to clusters of oblong seed capsules.

Faery Folklore

Evening primrose is associated with faeries.

Magical Workings

Powers and attributes: Balance/harmony, banish, changes/transitions, creativity, family and home, healing, nightmares, protection, purification, security, success, truth

Items to purchase when the plant is not available: Oil; dried leaves; seeds; evening primrose herb tea is made from the flowers and roots

The sweet scent of evening primrose will attract faeries to your garden. To boost the energy of spells, place a couple of flowers on your altar. Cut a stalk, let it dry, and then use it as a wand for banishing spells. Place a dried stalk in the attic or some area high in your house to invite protection and foster a sense of safety. Hold a leaf between your palms for help in finding truth while you meditate on a situation. As a healer, evening primrose provides balance during times of change. To commemorate any type of new beginning, burn a dried leaf in your cauldron.

Fairy Circles and Fairy Rings

See the profiles for Grass and Mushroom.

Fairy Flax

Fairy Flax, White Flax (Linum catharticum)
Folk names: Fairy lint, fairy woman's flax

With delicate stems and growing two to three inches tall, fairy flax hides among meadow grasses. Starting as a drooping bud, the slightly bell-shaped flower has five white petals that are veined. The center of the flower is yellow. The leaves are narrow and oval to lance-shaped.

Faery Folklore

According to legend, because this type of flax is extremely delicate yet strong, it was chosen by the faeries to spin, and then weave linen cloth to make their garments. In Germany, the *seliges fräulein*, faeries who watch over certain plants, would sometimes help people spin flax. Throughout Europe, many types of fae aided humans with spinning. Because of their slight bell shape, this plant's flowers were said to make music that humans cannot hear.

Magical Workings

Powers and attributes: Abundance, awareness (expand, heighten), balance/harmony, bind, changes/transitions, divination, family and home, prosperity/money, protection, psychic abilities, renewal, secrets, sex/sexuality, skills, strength

Items to purchase when the plant is not available: Dried stalks with flowers; seeds

Transforming plant fibers into thread that can be turned into cloth, the act of spinning has long been regarded as a magical art, and flax is one of the earliest plants to have been spun. Because spinning can mesmerize and produce a trance-like state, both the process and flax are associated with divination and psychic work. If you can find fairy flax, place it on your altar while engaging in these activities; otherwise, use a picture.

Fairy flax brings strength to esbat rituals, aids during major transitions, and is helpful for issues relating to sexuality. Use it in spells to bind or in charms to attract abundance, money, and prosperity. This plant is instrumental in keeping secrets; place a picture of fairy flax where you will see it often to remind you to hold a confidence. Keep a picture with you when learning new skills.

Fairy Wand
Fairy Wand (Chamaelirium luteum)
Folk names: False unicorn root, starwort

Fairy wand has small, white flowers that look like tiny starbursts. Growing in tight clusters, the flowers form on spikes between four and eight inches long at the top of the stems. Produced on separate plants, male flowers are white and female flowers are slightly greenish. The male flower spike is larger, with a downward-curving tip. The dark green base leaves are spoon-shaped; the stem leaves are smaller and lance-shaped. The plant is usually two to three feet tall.

Caution: This plant is classified as endangered or threatened in some areas; check before gathering in the wild.

Faery Folklore

Fairy wand is associated with faeries.

Magical Workings

Powers and attributes: Banish, consecrate/bless, emotions (deal with, support), fertility, healing, inspiration, loss/sorrow (ease, recover from), love, loyalty/fidelity, protection, purification, sex/sexuality, support (provide, receive), wishes

Items to purchase when the plant is not available: Flower essence; cut, dried roots; powdered root (As noted, this plant is endangered in the wild in some areas; check vendors' sources.)

Fairy wand is helpful when requesting aid from the fae. Write what you are seeking on a picture and place it on your altar. To raise energy for a spell, use a flower spike as a wand. Sprinkle a little flower essence to cast a circle for ritual or to consecrate a special area. When dealing with the loss of a loved one, hold a cup of powdered root between your hands in a private ritual to say goodbye, and then scatter it to the wind or across the person's grave.

Fern

See the profiles for Bracken, Maidenhair Fern, and Moonwort.

Fir

Balsam Fir, Eastern Fir (Abies balsamea)
European Silver Fir (A. alba)
White Fir (A. concolor)

The balsam fir has a narrow, spire-like crown with upper branches that grow at right angles from the trunk; the lower branches droop. Its curved needles are dark green, and its cylindrical cones are grayish green with a slight purple tinge. The European silver fir has a pyramid shape, but with age its crown becomes flattened. The grooved needles are dark green, and the cylindrical cones turn reddish brown as they mature. The white fir has a narrow, conical shape with a spire-like crown that also becomes flattened with age. It has blue-green needles and barrel-shaped cones that turn brownish purple.

Faery Folklore

It was customary in Germany to take boughs of fir into the house to celebrate Yule and to provide comfort for visiting elves. In the Tyrol of Austria, the genie of the forest reputedly preferred to live in a fir tree.

Magical Workings

Powers and attributes: Awareness (expand, heighten), balance/harmony, changes/transitions, clarity (enhance, foster), communication, creativity, defense, divination, emotions (deal with, support), growth, happiness, healing, hexes (break, protect from), inspiration, loss/sorrow (ease, recover from), peace, prosperity/money, protection, psychic abilities, purification, renewal, security, spirit guides/spirits, spirituality, strength, support (provide, receive)

Items to purchase when the plant is not available: Essential oil is made from the European silver fir

Burn a few dried needles to purify an area before ritual or magic work and afterward to aid in grounding energy. Hold a cluster of needles or a cone during meditation to foster clear communication and creative expression. To kindle inspiration, place a few needles or a couple of cones in your workspace. As an all-purpose purifier, fir provides protection and helps to overcome and remove hexes.

The scent of fir heightens awareness for divination and spiritual work and is especially effective for connecting with forest spirits. Use a small branch or a couple of cones for prosperity spells and for support during channeling. The scent of fir also aids in focusing energy inward to restore memories. Through the most trying circumstances, this tree helps to foster hope, happiness, and peace.

Fly Agaric

Fly Agaric (Amanita muscaria)
Folk names: Fairy tables, pixie stools, red cap

Fly agaric is the classic toadstool with a red or sometimes orange cap studded with white flakes. The cap can measure four to eight inches in diameter. The stalk is off-white and has a slightly bulbous base. The prominent ring on the stalk just below the cap is the remnant of a veil that encased the toadstool when it was young. Growing in dense groups and occasionally rings, fly agaric is mostly found in forests, especially near birch trees. Scientifically, there is no difference between toadstools and mushrooms. The term *toadstool* is applied in common speech to poisonous fungi.

Caution: Fly agaric is toxic; it should never be ingested and it is usually recommended to avoid touching it.

Faery Folklore

According to legend, these toadstools are found wherever there are faeries. Also associated with elves, they mark an entrance to their magical realm. In Germanic areas of Europe, fly agaric was said to serve as houses for gnomes. The association of faeries with this toadstool may have something to do with a common description of the fae wearing red caps. When growing in rings, fly agaric was known as pixie stools. This toadstool also marked places favored by the Lieschi, a Russian faerie or genie of the forest.

Magical Workings

Powers and attributes: Awareness (expand, heighten), banish, creativity, divination, dream work, fertility, knowledge (seek, acquire), luck, prophecy, protection, psychic abilities, renewal, secrets, spirit guides/spirits

Items to purchase when the plant is not available: Figurine; lawn ornament

Because fly agaric is poisonous, it is best to use it symbolically with pictures and other items. When you want to remove something or someone from your life, write a few keywords on a picture of this toadstool, and then hold it between your hands as you visualize banishing it/them and moving on. Burn the picture in your cauldron and when the ashes are cool, scatter them outside as you repeat the visualization.

To enhance your flow of creative energy, place a picture of fly agaric in your work area. When contacting spirit guides or other spirits, place a picture or figurine of fly agaric on your altar. Paint a couple of toadstool lawn ornaments the color of fly agaric and place them in your faery garden to emphasize its link with the fae and nature spirits.

Also see the profiles for Jelly Fungus and Mushroom.

Forget-Me-Not

Forget–Me–Not, True Forget–Me–Not (Myosotis scorpioides)
Woodland Forget–Me–Not (M. sylvatica)
Folk names: Luck flower, mouse ear

Forget-me-not is beloved for its sky-blue flowers that can sometimes be pink or white. With five petals shaped like mouse ears, the flowers have yellow centers. They grow in clusters that curve downward on stems that are between six to twelve inches tall. The oblong leaves are medium green with a prominent center vein. Although both species of forget-me-nots look similar, they differ slightly in growing conditions and flowering time.

Faery Folklore

Forget-me-not was often used for protection from faery mischief. Similar to the cowslip and primrose, in Germany the forget-me-not was regarded as a lucky talisman for finding hidden treasure, especially if it was guarded by the fae. It is also associated with the Hollen, faery-like spirits that provide help to humans when called upon.

Magical Workings

Powers and attributes: Adaptability, awareness (expand, heighten), balance/ harmony, bind, clarity (enhance, foster), communication, concentration/ focus, loss/sorrow (ease, recover from), love, loyalty/fidelity, luck, protection, relationships, secrets, strength, success

Items to purchase when the plant is not available: Flower essence; dried flowers; seeds

Forget-me-not is an aid for attuning your energy to faeries and nature spirits. Grow it in your garden or place a picture of the flowers on your altar during visualizations to work with them. As an alternative, hold a flower or photograph between your hands as you say:

Sky-blue flower with ring of gold,
May your secrets now unfold.
With your help to open the way,
I welcome faeries here this day.

As part of a ritual with your lover, pick a bouquet of flowers and pass them one by one back and forth as you each pledge your faith and support to one another. When dealing with loss, especially the breakup of a relationship, write a keyword or a person's name on a picture of forget-me-not flowers. Over the top of that, write an affirmation about your strengths. Carry it with you and gaze at it when needed as a reminder that, while you will never forget the person or situation, you are capable of moving on and enjoying life on your own terms.

Forsythia
Border Forsythia (Forsythia x intermedia)
Folk name: Golden bells

Forsythia is a rambling shrub that can reach eight feet tall and ten feet wide. Beloved by gardeners, its sweeping, arching branches are a hallmark of this plant. The yellow flowers grow in clusters, making the branches look like golden sprays of sunshine. When the flowers fade, oval-shaped leaves with serrated edges fill in the branches, creating a rounded thicket.

Faery Folklore
A shrub of garden origin, forsythia does not appear in folklore but has come to be associated with faeries.

Magical Workings
Powers and attributes: Balance/harmony, changes/transitions, courage, emotions (deal with, support), family and home, fertility, growth, happiness, healing, spirituality

Items to purchase when the plant is not available: Flower essence

It is no surprise that forsythia has become associated with faeries. Its wildly spreading branches and bright flowers that burst onto the scene in early spring would seem a perfect place for them to hold their revels. To foster harmony and happiness in your home, put several cut branches in a vase of water and place it in an area where your family gathers. Use the flowers in charms to increase fertility, or if already pregnant, place them on your altar as an offering of gratitude. A branch of flowers or a picture of forsythia on the altar during meditation aids in deepening your spiritual connection with nature.

Foxglove

Common Foxglove (Digitalis purpurea)
White-flowered Foxglove (D. purpurea var. *alba)*
Folk names: Elf gloves, fairy bells, fairy caps, fairy petticoats,
fairy woman's plant, folk's glove, fox bells, goblin's gloves

Foxglove is a woodland plant that has become a beloved addition to the garden. It has downward-pointing, tubular flowers that are usually purplish pink or white. The interior of the flower has a lace-like pattern. In its first year, the plant consists of a base rosette of leaves. The second year of growth produces tall spires of flowers that can reach three to five feet high.

Caution: Foxglove is toxic and should never be ingested.

Faery Folklore

In many legends, faeries are noted as being especially delighted by foxglove. While there are a number of theories for the word *fox* in its name, the most agreed-upon one is that it is a corruption of the name *folk's glove.* This is a reference to the faery folk wearing the flowers as gloves. Another popular take on this story is that faeries made gloves for foxes so they could move about without a sound.

When flower stalks are bent over, it is reputedly a sign that faeries or pixies are inside the blossoms or that faeries are passing nearby. The spots on the interior of the flowers were said to be where elves had touched them. As bells, the flowers were said to create a magical sound. Children were warned not to pick the flowers; otherwise, they could be carried off by the fae. Contrary to most folklore, in County Leitrim, Ireland, foxglove was believed to be dangerous to faeries and used in charms against them.

Foxglove was used to detect a changeling. The suspect infant was bathed in the juice from foxglove or the plant was placed underneath the cradle. Although it is not explained exactly how it worked, this act forced the faeries to return the missing child and take back the changeling.

Magical Workings

Powers and attributes: Awareness (expand, heighten), balance/ harmony, challenges/obstacles (overcome), communication, creativity, emotions (deal with, support), healing, intuition, peace, protection, relationships, release (let go, move on), truth

Items to purchase when the plant is not available: Flower essence; dried flower stalks, seeds

Because foxglove is a favored plant among the fae, include it in your garden as an invitation for them. Foxglove is also helpful for making contact with nature spirits. Hold a leaf between your hands without removing it from the plant as you whisper a greeting to the spirits. Alternatively, place a picture of the plant on your altar for help in befriending them.

When facing a challenge, keep a picture of foxglove with you or somewhere at home where you will see it often. A picture of foxglove can invite harmony to the workplace. As part of a protection spell or to symbolically release something from your life, crumble a dried leaf and scatter it outdoors.

Geranium
Common Geranium (Pelargonium x *hortorum)*
Rose Geranium (P. roseum)

The flowers and foliage of the common geranium come in a range of colors. The rounded leaves are veined, have shallow lobes, and often have distinct bands or zones of color. The flowers can have single or double blooms in pink, white, red, or salmon. They grow in rounded clusters. Rose geranium is not the familiar garden plant. Its grayish, silvery leaves are deeply lobed and have wavy edges. The small, pink flowers do not form large flower heads like common geranium. It is loved and widely used for its rose-like scent.

Faery Folklore
Geraniums are associated with faeries.

Magical Workings
Powers and attributes: Balance/harmony, communication, concentration/ focus, courage, creativity, emotions (deal with, support), fertility, growth, hexes (break, protect from), loss/sorrow (ease, recover from), love, protection, psychic abilities, relationships, sex/sexuality, spirituality, strength, success, wisdom

Items to purchase when the plant is not available: Essential oil is made from rose geranium; dried petals

Geraniums are vigorous plants that stir energy and foster growth. Tuck a leaf into your pocket to enhance psychic energy. For protection, place a couple of red geraniums on a windowsill in the direction from which you feel a threat. Since they are also associated with focus and success, position one of these plants on or near your desk or wherever you work on anything of a creative or financial nature. Burn a couple of dried leaves or flowers to aid in breaking hexes.

Globeflower
Common Globeflower, European Globeflower (Trollius europaeus)
Folk names: Goblin flower, troll flower

A single, two-inch wide flower rises about two feet above the foliage, which is on the lower part of the stem. Resembling a small, yellow cabbage, the ball-shaped flower remains closed or mostly closed. The dark green leaves have three to five deep lobes. Globeflower inhibits growth of nearby plants.

Caution: Do not ingest, the plant is mildly poisonous; it may cause skin irritation and burns.

Faery Folklore

According to legend in the Netherlands, elves used globeflowers as cups to prepare poison. In Scandinavia, because of the plant's poisonous qualities trolls were said to have meddled with the flowers.

Magical Workings

Powers and attributes: Defense, hexes (break, protect from), negativity (remove, ward off), secrets

Items to purchase when the plant is not available: Seeds

Globeflower's reputation may come from the plant being somewhat toxic or at least very unpleasant for humans and livestock. However, because of its taste, animals usually shun it. Except for breaking hexes, globeflower has not been widely used for magical purposes.

Given its background, it functions easily when magical defense or warding off negative energy is needed. Place a picture of the globeflower on your altar and gaze at it for a few minutes. When the image is firmly fixed in your mind, close your eyes and visualize a globe of soft yellow light encircling you. Feel it hugging you closely, supporting you, and keeping you safe. Bask in the golden glow for a moment, and then let the image fade. Whenever you feel in need of help, bring the image and sensation into your mind.

For aid in keeping a secret, write a keyword that only you understand on a picture of a globeflower. Visualize holding the information close to your heart, and then tuck the picture away in a secure place.

Gooseberry

European Gooseberry (Ribes uva-crispa syn. R. grossularia)
American Gooseberry (R. hirtellum)
Folk names: Dog berry, fayberry, goosegogs

Gooseberry is a wide, spiny shrub that produces small, dangling clusters of bell-shaped flowers. The European gooseberry produces pinkish-yellow flowers and bristly fruit that look like striped, fuzzy grapes. It has a thorn at the base of each leaf stem. The American plant has greenish-white flowers and round, green berries that ripen to a purplish color. It has two or more thorns at the base of the leaf stems. The leaves of both shrubs are lobed and dark green.

Faery Folklore

My English grandmother pronounced this plant's name *gooz-berry* and said that the faeries were fond of the fruit. In Scotland and northern England, children were told to stay away from gooseberry bushes to avoid being kidnapped by Awd Goggie, the faery that guards the unripe berries. On the Isle of Wight, a faery known as the Gooseberry Wife, who usually appears as a huge hairy caterpillar, protects the plant.

Magical Workings

Powers and attributes: Abundance, challenges/obstacles (overcome), fertility, healing, peace, success

Items to purchase when the plant is not available: Fresh or dried fruit; jam

Place a picture of a gooseberry bush in your kitchen to attract abundance. Alternatively, use gooseberry jam. Light a candle on your altar as you hold the jar between your hands and visualize how abundance will enter your life. Take a spoonful of jam and hold it in your mouth for a moment to savor the feeling.

To bring peace of mind, place a sprig of leaves on your altar during meditation. When faced with a challenging situation, purchase dried fruit and wrap three of them in parchment or wax paper (they can be sticky). As you do this, say three times:

> *Gooseberry, gooseberry, one, two, three,*
> *From this trouble, make me free.*
> *Gooseberry, gooseberry, three, two, one,*
> *Blessed be; may it soon be done.*

Continue by placing the gooseberries in a kitchen cupboard for three weeks, and then repeat the incantation as you dispose of them.

Gorse

Common Gorse (Ulex europaeus)
Folk names: Broom, furze, prickly bloom, whin

Gorse is a scruffy, evergreen shrub that is usually as wide as it is tall. Its branches are densely packed with prickly, half-inch long spines that grow among the leaves. The gray-green leaves resemble spruce needles. Although gorse produces a profusion of bright-yellow flowers in the spring and early summer, it often blooms throughout the year. It is frequently host to fairy butter, jelly fungus (*Tremella mesenterica*), especially on the roots. Gorse is easily confused with broom (*Cytisus scoparius*).

Faery Folklore

In Ireland, a solitary gorse shrub is regarded as a lone bush. (See the profile for Lone Bush.) In some parts of the British Isles, sprigs of flowers were placed around milk vessels and butter churns during the month of May to protect them from faery mischief. According to Welsh legend, faeries cannot get through a hedge of gorse due to the plant's magical power rather than its spiny, little thorns. To the contrary, another story notes that a faery helped the gorse by casting a spell so it would grow thorns to protect its flowers. The flowers were sometimes called *fairy gold*.

Magical Workings

Powers and attributes: Abundance, banish, defense, determination/endurance, divination, family and home, fertility, hexes (break, protect from), inspiration, love, negativity (remove, ward off), prosperity/money, protection, purification, renewal

Items to purchase when the tree is not available: Flower essence

For protection spells, carve the faery star on a yellow candle and place a circle of gorse spines around the base of it. For the home, bury a sprig of gorse in the front yard, and then visualize a shield of protective energy rising and surrounding the house. To remove hexes or for defense against dark magic, place gorse spines at each corner of your altar during a banishing spell.

Use the flowers in love sachets or scatter a few in your bathwater to increase personal power for magic. Burn a few dried leaves and spines for help in getting out of a rut. Place a sprig or two in any area of your home where you want to get energy moving. Use a branch to symbolically sweep your altar and ritual area to purify it before magic work.

Grape

Common Grape, European Wine Grape (Vitis vinifera)
Fox Grape, Wild Grape (V. labrusca)

Grapevines have thick, woody base stems and climb with the aid of tendrils. The leaves are deeply lobed and measure five to nine inches across. Spikes of small, greenish-white flowers grow in dense clusters along the stem. The fruit grows in inverted pyramidal clusters and ripens in early autumn. The fruit of the common grape is green; the fox grape is blue-black and ripens to dark purple.

Faery Folklore

Grape is associated with faeries.

Magical Workings

Powers and attributes: Abundance, balance/harmony, bind, changes/transitions, consecrate/bless, creativity, divination, fertility, growth, happiness, healing, inspiration, love, prophecy, prosperity/money, psychic abilities, sex/sexuality

Items to purchase when the plant is not available: Fresh fruit; raisins; grape juice; wine; grapeseed oil

Eat three grapes before divination or any type of psychic work to bring clarity to your session. Use a bunch of grapes in spells to attract abundance and prosperity. To boost the effectiveness of a binding spell, include a short length of vine or several tendrils. Prepare a candle with grapeseed oil for spells to kindle romance or heighten sexual attraction.

Use grape juice or wine as a libation for healing rituals. Meditate with a piece of vine or leaves for inspiration and to help find your best mode for creative expression. When dealing with changes in your life, write your desired outcome on a picture of a grapevine. Keep it in a safe place until your goal has been achieved. Grapes are instrumental for attracting happiness.

Grass

Blue Moor Grass, Elf Grass (Sesleria caerulea syn. *Cynosurus caeruleus)*
Common Quaking Grass, Fairy Grass (Briza media)
Folk names: Fairy circle, fairy ring

Blue moor grass grows in loose tufts six to twelve inches tall. Its twisting, green leaves have a bluish tinge. In late spring it produces narrow spikes of dark, purplish flowers. Common quaking grass forms dense clumps of narrow, green leaves that grow two to three feet tall. Its dangling seed heads resemble oats and tremble in the slightest breeze. Both grasses form circles.

Faery Folklore

Grass growing in a ring was said to be where elves or faeries danced. In Devonshire, England, the rings were reputedly formed by faeries riding colts around in a circle. In other parts of England, a faery ring was considered a lucky place to stand and make a wish. Some stories note that it is okay to walk through or stand in a grass circle but it is unlucky to walk or run around the perimeter because that is a fairy path, which is only for them to use. According to others, running around a fairy ring on the first night of a full moon makes the subterranean revels of the faeries and elves audible.

In Scotland, it was regarded as unlucky to sleep in or to be found in a faery ring after sunset because a grass ring had the power to make contact with supernatural beings. In Germany, setting foot in a fairy ring put a person under the power of the fae. In Scandinavia, standing in a ring that had no grass in the middle at midnight allowed a person to see elves. Grass from a fairy circle was one of the ingredients in a recipe that not only made faeries visible, but also aided in conjuring a certain faery named Elaby Gathon. See the profile on Hollyhock for further details.

Magical Workings

Powers and attributes: Abundance, challenges/obstacles (overcome), communication, happiness, hexes (break, protect from), luck, manifest (desires, dreams, will), negativity (remove, ward off), protection, psychic abilities, see faeries, spirit guides/spirits

Items to purchase when the plant is not available: Dried stalks of common quaking grass with seed heads; seeds from both grasses; flower essence is made from greater quaking grass (*B. maxima*)

If you have space on your property, plant a ring of elf or fairy grass; if not, plant just one or two clumps. Elf grass grows well in pots, too. When the grass is long, carefully pull out a few strands to braid into a ring. Hang the ring in your kitchen to attract abundance. Wear the ring on your wrist or finger as you meditate, and then make a wish. Also wear it to enhance your psychic abilities. To remove hexes or any type of negativity in your life, dry a handful of grass, and then burn a little of it in your cauldron. Long strands of grass can be used for knot magic.

Harebell

Harebell (Campanula rotundifolia)
Folk names: Bellflower, bluebell, fairy bells, fairy caps, fairy ringers,
fairy thimble, hare's bells, tinkle bell, wood bells

This plant has blue-violet, bell-shaped flowers that hang singly or in clusters from slender stems that can reach fifteen inches tall. It blooms in the summer and autumn. While the harebell is frequently confused with the common bluebell (*Hyacinthoides non-scripta*), its flowers are wider and rounder than the bluebell.

Faery Folklore

The shape of the harebell flower provided an association with bells, caps, and cups for faeries. The flowers were reputedly used as drinking cups by faeries that danced around wells. In some legends, if a soft chiming sound was heard, it was usually the faeries ringing the harebell flowers. When heard at midnight, it was to call faeries and elves for nighttime revelry. Other lore reports that hares rang the bells to warn of foxes and other dangers, and faeries rang them to warn of nearby hares. The reason for faeries to send out a warning about hares is unknown.

Magical Workings

Powers and attributes: Abundance, balance/harmony, challenges/obstacles (overcome), clarity (enhance, foster), loss/sorrow (ease, recover from), love, loyalty/fidelity, negativity (remove, ward off), peace, see faeries, spirit guides/spirits, truth

Items to purchase when the plant is not available: Flower essence; seeds

Gently shake a couple of stems with flowers as though you are ringing the bells to call faeries and nature spirits to your property. Associated with shape shifting, dried leaves can be used in spells when an illusion (fairy glamour) is necessary, such as the need for protection. However, never use this plant to deceive.

As an aid for crossing the boundary between realms, keep a picture of the plant with you when journeying to faeryland. Worn by faithful lovers, the flowers are especially suitable for handfasting and personal pledges. Although the drooping flowers are associated with grief, they are an aid for dealing with sorrow. Burn a dried leaf to remove negativity or in a spell to help overcome a problem.

Hawthorn

Common Hawthorn (Crataegus monogyna)
English Hawthorn, Woodland Hawthorn (C. laevigata syn. C. oxyacantha)
Folk names: Haw bush, fairy thorn, Maybush, quickthorn, whitethorn, wishing tree

The hawthorn has shiny leaves with rounded lobes and small thorns that grow along the branches. The five-petaled flowers grow in clusters and are white, often with a blush of pink or with a slight purplish tint. Usually called *haws*, its oval, red fruit is also known as pixie paws and pixie pears.

Faery Folklore

Believed to mark a threshold to the otherworld, hawthorn is part of the triad of powerful faery trees along with oak and ash. Hawthorn is also regarded as a lone bush and fairy bush. (See the profile for Lone Bush.) Like all thorn trees, hawthorns are a meeting place for faeries, and a solitary hawthorn often marked the entrance to a faery hill. Instead of removing a hawthorn that stands in the middle of a field, a farmer usually plows around it rather than disturb the fae. While many legends warn of the dire consequences that occur when this practice is not heeded, others tell of rewards to those who are mindful.

Garlands of hawthorn flowers were hung around doorways of homes and barns to celebrate Beltane and to please the fae. In Brittany, France, solitary hawthorns that grew on the moors were reputed to be trysting places for faeries. In Ireland, faeries were said to dance and make love under hawthorns. Hawthorn was frequently a cloutie tree and it was believed dangerous to take a leaf from one. Thomas the Rhymer was said to have met the faery queen under a hawthorn. Other versions of the story note that he met her under a yew or broom bush. See the profile on Yew for more about Thomas the Rhymer.

Magical Workings
Powers and attributes: Ancestors, challenges/obstacles (overcome), changes/transitions, consecrate/bless, creativity, defense, emotions (deal with, support), family and home, fertility, growth, happiness, love, luck, manifest (desires, dreams, will), negativity (remove, ward off), peace, prosperity/money, protection, purification, relationships, security, see faeries, sex/sexuality, success, wisdom, wishes

Items to purchase when the tree is not available: Dried berries from the common hawthorn, whole or powdered; dried leaves and flowers from the English hawthorn

Wear a sprig of flowers or leaves to aid in contacting faeries and nature spirits. Planting a hawthorn in your garden is a sign of welcome to them. Place a few haws on your outdoor altar along with a little food to invite them near.

As a sign of respect, have a hawthorn wand or simply a branch with you when journeying to faeryland.

Use hawthorn leaves or flowers for protection spells. Also carry one in your pocket or purse. Burn a couple of dried leaves to consecrate and prepare space for magic work. Dry a few haws, and then string them together to make an amulet. Line a kitchen windowsill with haws to attract prosperity. The flowers are effective in charms for attracting love.

Hazel

American Hazelnut (Corylus americana)
Common Hazel, European Hazelnut (C. avellana)

Hazels are shrubby, multi-trunked trees that produce prominent, yellow-brown male catkins and less obvious, reddish female catkins in late winter and early spring. The rounded, heavily veined leaves have serrated edges and a small point at the end. Hazel is frequently host to fairy butter, jelly fungus (*Tremella mesenterica*).

Faery Folklore
According to legend, the hazel was a tree held in high esteem by the Tuatha Dé Danann and was sometimes referred to as *bilé ratha*, "the venerated tree of the rath."[72] Faeries are closely associated with these ancient hilltop ring forts, and reputedly often made their homes in them. In Ireland, a solitary hazel is regarded as a lone bush. (See the profile for Lone Bush.) When it grows with apple and hawthorn, it is said to mark the boundary of a very magical place.

Even though staffs and magic wands used by the fae were often made from this tree, carrying a hazel stick was believed to provide protection against faeries and other spirits. Twigs provided protection against magic in other ways, too, and stirring jam with one was believed to prevent faeries from stealing it. A piece of hazel attached to a horse was said to prevent faeries from borrowing it. A hazel stick was believed necessary to rescue someone who had been abducted by faeries.

---

72. Mac Coitir, *Ireland's Trees: Myths, Legends and Folklore*, 79.

Well-known for its use as a divining rod to find water and treasure, holding a forked hazel branch reputedly enabled a person to see faeries. Hazel buds were one of the ingredients in a recipe that not only made faeries visible, but also aided in conjuring a certain faery named Elaby Gathon. See the profile on Hollyhock for further details.

Magical Workings

Powers and attributes: Abundance, awareness (expand, heighten), balance/harmony, banish, challenges/obstacles (overcome), changes/transitions, communication, creativity, defense, divination, fertility, healing, inspiration, intuition, knowledge (seek, acquire), loss/sorrow (ease, recover from), luck, manifest (desires, dreams, will), prosperity/money, protection, psychic abilities, release (let go, move on), secrets, security, see faeries, strength, support (provide, receive), truth, wisdom, wishes

Items to purchase when the tree is not available: Hazelnuts; hazelnut oil is made from the common hazel; flower essence is made from the common hazel

For aid in contacting faeries, place a few leaves or a small twig on your altar during meditation. Use a hazel stick to draw a faery ring for magic work. In place of a stick, use a brown candle prepared with hazelnut oil and carved with the faery star. Plait a short length of three pliable twigs and carry it for luck. To stimulate creativity, place a handful of dried leaves or a few hazelnuts on your desk or in your workspace.

Eat a few hazelnuts before magic or psychic work to enhance your energy. The leaves and nuts are an aid when initiating changes, and provide support for all forms of communication. A hazel twig can amplify the energy of dark moon rituals.

Heather and Heath
Common Heather (Calluna vulgaris)
Heath, Winter Heath (Erica carnea syn. *E. herbacea)*
Folk names: Hedder, ling

Although heath and heather are nearly identical and their names are often used interchangeably, there is a simple way to tell them apart. Heath has needle-like foliage similar to a spruce tree, while heather has scale-like foliage similar to a cedar. The bell-shaped flowers range from white, pink, lilac, and purple, to reddish.

Faery Folklore

According to legend, faeries feasted on stalks of heather and enjoyed living on the moors, where they would be undisturbed by human activity. Because white heather is associated more closely with faeries and it is relatively rare in the wild, finding it is considered very lucky. In Scotland, white heather was said to grow where faeries had rested. Some fae were thought to be small enough to use the flower bells as caps. In Wales, they were said to dance and play across the tops of heather.

Magical Workings

Powers and attributes: Adaptability, authority/leadership, awareness (expand, heighten), changes/transitions, clarity (enhance, foster), defense, divination, dream work, family and home, growth, healing, knowledge (seek, acquire), love, luck, manifest (desires, dreams, will), peace, protection, psychic abilities, purification, spirit guides/spirits, spirituality, trust

Items to purchase when the plant is not available: Flower essence is made from common heather; dried heather flowers and plants

Growing heather or heath in your garden provides protective energy around your home and will attract faeries. Gazing at a picture of either plant before meditation instills a deep sense of peace and aids in contacting nature spirits. Make a sachet using white flowers for a good luck charm. Carry it with you or place it in a location where you will see it often. To strengthen love spells, place white and pink flowers on your altar for three days. To help foster a deeper connection with your spirit guides, use a sprig of purple flowers on your altar when you contact them.

Burn a few dried sprigs of heather or heath to bring clarity and awareness while developing psychic abilities. Burning the leaves also supports spiritual healing and personal growth. A sprig hung on a bedpost or placed on a night-stand enhances dream work and helps to interpret any messages that you may receive. To foster stability, keep a photograph of heather or heath in your pocket or purse during major transitions in your life.

Hemlock
Hemlock, Poison Hemlock (Conium maculatum)
Folk name: Cowbane

Hemlock has a hollow stem that is marked with purple blotches. The leaves are delicate and fern-like with toothed edges. It has white flowers that grow in small, erect clusters. Each flower develops into a green, deeply ridged fruit that contains several seeds. At maturity, the fruit turns grayish brown.

Hemlock has a white taproot that is easily mistaken for wild parsnip (*Pastinaca sativa*). It can also be mistaken for Queen Anne's lace (*Daucus carota*). Hemlock has a smooth stem with purple spots and streaks; it has no purple spot in the middle of the flower head. The stem of Queen Anne's lace is hairy and all green and its flower head has a purple spot in the center. A crushed leaf of hemlock will have an unpleasant, musty odor.

Caution: All parts of hemlock are poisonous, even dead stems; toxins can be absorbed through the skin; fatal if ingested.

Faery Folklore
According to legend in Scotland, this plant was so poisonous that faeries dipped their arrows in the dew that formed on the leaves to deal a deadly blow to enemies.

Magical Workings
Powers and attributes: Banish, defense, hexes (break, protect from), negativity (remove, ward off), protection, purification, release (let go, move on)

Items to purchase when the plant is not available: Although it is sometimes recommended for purifying ritual tools, especially knives, hemlock is a plant best used symbolically.

To purify ritual and magical tools, wrap a picture of hemlock around them as you say:

Hemlock, hemlock, power strong,
May this cleansing last so long.
With the beauty of your flower,
Give these tools a special power.

Store the picture with your tools, and then just before using them, burn the picture in your cauldron. When you feel the need to boost your defenses, write what you want protection from on a picture of hemlock. Keep it on your altar until the need has passed.

Hogweed
Common Hogweed (Heracleum sphondylium)
Folk names: Cow parsnip, eltrot

Reaching between four and six feet tall, hogweed has ridged stems covered with small, bristly hairs. The stem color ranges from dark green to brownish purple. The leaves are hairy and serrated, with three to five lobes. The umbrella-like flower heads have larger petals around the outside edges of each cluster. The white flowers often have a pinkish hue. The seeds are flat, green disks with reddish markings. They become papery when dried.

Caution: The clear sap is phototoxic and may make the skin more sensitive to ultraviolet light, causing redness, irritation, and sometimes blisters. Wear gloves to handle this plant. Its bigger cousin, giant hogweed (*H. mantegazzianum*) is extremely phototoxic and causes more severe reactions. No part of giant hogweed is safe to touch.

Faery Folklore
Hogweed was used to break faery spells, especially the enchantment of a child. It was also deemed effective for warding off faery mischief.

Magical Workings
Powers and attributes: Fertility, healing, hexes (break, protect from), negativity (remove, ward off), renewal, sex/sexuality, strength
Items to purchase when the plant is not available: Seeds

Despite its name, it seems natural that faeries would like this plant because of its lofty clouds of flowers. Place a cluster of flowers or a photograph of them on your altar when working with faeries or during esbat rituals to heighten lunar magic.

During the most fertile time of your cycle when planning a pregnancy, cut out a picture of the flowers or use a couple of dried seeds and attach it/them to a picture of a baby cradle. Light a red candle on your altar and place the picture next to it as you say:

> *Two join together as one;*
> *May this desire be done.*
> *Two soon becomes three,*
> *Creating new life; so mote it be.*

Keep the picture on your altar for three days, and then place it under your bed.

Holly
American Holly (Ilex opaca)
English Holly, European Holly (I. aquifolium)

Holly leaves have wavy margins and sharp spines. English holly has glossy, dark green leaves; the leaves of the American holly are matte green. Small, white flowers grow in clusters. Holly produces male and female flowers on separate trees; berries occur only on the female tree.

Faery Folklore

Like rowan, holly's red berries made it a plant favored by faeries. In Ireland, holly was regarded as a lone bush and fairy bush. (See the profile for Lone Bush.) In Scotland, houses were decorated with holly on New Year's Eve for protection, especially from faeries. Even though Yule festival greens are traditionally burned at Imbolc, a small sprig of holly was sometimes kept for luck throughout the year. This sprig was used to protect against elf and faery mischief and in the Scottish Highlands it was traditionally hung over the door of the cowshed.

In parts of England, holly was often used for the clavy, a small piece of wood attached to the wall above a kitchen fireplace mantel for the purpose of holding keys. At an inn in Somerset, the clavy was the preferred sitting spot for a hobgoblin known as Charlie.

Magical Workings

Powers and attributes: Balance/harmony, banish, consecrate/bless, courage, defense, divination, dream work, family and home, healing, hexes (break, protect from), intuition, luck, manifest (desires, dreams, will), protection, renewal, security, spirit guides/spirits, spirituality, strength, support (provide, receive), wishes

Items to purchase when the tree is not available: Flower essence is made from English holly

To acknowledge local faeries, place a sprig of holly on your outdoor altar. For good luck, tuck a leaf into your purse or wallet. With sharp spines, holly leaves are the epitome of protection. To enhance the defense of your home, place three leaves under the front door mat. The leaves can also be used in spells for protection against hostile magic.

To enhance dream work, especially divination through dreams, dry several clusters of flowers or use a picture of holly flowers. Sew the flowers or picture into a sachet and place it under your pillow. For spiritual guidance, put holly flowers on your altar and contemplate what you seek.

Hollyhock

Common Hollyhock (Alcea rosea syn. *Althaea rosea)*
Folk name: Rose mallow

Sprouting on towering stalks up to eight feet tall, hollyhock flowers grow individually or in small clusters. The five overlapping petals create a bowl-shaped flower that can measure up to five inches wide. Ranging from white to pink to purplish red, the flowers nod sideways from the stems. The large, heart-shaped leaves have three to seven lobes and grow up to eight inches long. They become progressively smaller toward the top of the stalk.

Faery Folklore

In a recipe from the seventeenth century, hollyhock was used to make fairy oil, which, when anointed to the eyes, made the usually invisible elves visible. Using an elaborate ritual, the ingredients included the buds of hollyhock, marigold flowers, hazel buds, the flower tops of thyme that had been gathered from a hill where faeries had been, and grass from a fairy circle. With the proper incantations, this recipe also enabled a human to conjure the faery named Elaby Gathon or Gathen. This faery was commonly called upon by nannies to watch over and protect babies as they slept, mostly to keep bad faeries from substituting a changeling. Although the word *lullaby* has a different source, it was occasionally attributed to a corruption of L'Elaby.

Magical Workings

Powers and attributes: Abundance, banish, changes/transitions, emotions (deal with, support), family and home, happiness, prosperity/money, release (let go, move on), see faeries, success

Items to purchase when the plant is not available: Flower essence is marketed by flower color; dried flowers; seeds

Grow these quintessential cottage-garden flowers to attract faeries and nature spirits to your property. The white and pink flowers are reputedly their favorites. Hold a flower between your hands or sprinkle your palms with the flower essence to aid in connecting with the faery realm. When going through major transitions in your life, keep a photograph of hollyhocks with you to help smooth the way. After moving to a new house, crumble a handful of dried flowers, and then sprinkle them around, inside and out, to help you and your family feel at home.

Honeysuckle

Common Honeysuckle, European Honeysuckle (Lonicera periclymenum)
Italian Honeysuckle, Italian Woodbine (L. caprifolium)
Folk names: Fairy trumpet, woodbine

Honeysuckle is a twining, climbing vine with woody stems that can grow ten to twenty feet in length. It has rounded leaves and whorls of thin, tubular flowers at the end of the stems. Common honeysuckle flowers are pale to medium yellow and its leaves are dull gray to bluish green. It produces dark red berries in the autumn. Italian honeysuckle has pale yellow to pinkish or purplish tinged flowers and produces orange-red berries in the autumn. Its leaves are dark green above and bluish green underneath.

Faery Folklore

Legends note that honeysuckle marks a faery place where they like to gather and sometimes live. Faeries are also said to enjoy sipping the sweet nectar from the flowers.

Magical Workings

Powers and attributes: Abundance, adaptability, attraction, authority/leadership, awareness (expand, heighten), bind, changes/transitions, clarity (enhance, foster), concentration/focus, creativity, divination, dream work, happiness, healing, hexes (break, protect from), inspiration, intuition, justice/legal matters, love, loyalty/fidelity, luck, peace, prosperity/money, protection, psychic abilities, release (let go, move on), renewal, secrets, skills, strength, wishes

Items to purchase when the plant is not available: Flower essence is made from Italian honeysuckle; dried flowers from the Japanese honeysuckle (*L. japonica*); seeds

Grow honeysuckle in your garden; the scent will attract faeries and nature spirits. A honeysuckle vine growing near the house brings luck. To aid in magic work or to increase psychic powers, especially clairvoyance, place a handful of flowers and leaves on your altar to help you tune into the energy.

To aid in dream work, place fresh honeysuckle flowers on your bedside table. Also do this to encourage dreams of love and passion. For a love token, make a small wreath with the vine to give to your lover. Dried flowers and leaves in a sachet hung over the bed fosters fidelity and affection between partners.

Horse Chestnut

Horse Chestnut (Aesculus hippocastanum)
Folk name: Candle tree

Horse chestnut flowers grow in showy, upright clusters. They are white with a reddish or yellow tinge at the base. The dark green leaflets are arranged in a fan shape. The nuts grow in spiny, round husks.

Caution: The nuts from this tree, which are commonly called *conkers*, are not edible.

Faery Folklore

According to legend, the horse chestnut would light its spires of flowers like candles so faeries would not have to travel in the dark when returning home after a night of dancing and revelry.

Magical Workings

Powers and attributes: Abundance, banish, consecrate/bless, divination, family and home, healing, hexes (break, protect from), justice/legal matters, love, luck, peace, prosperity/money, protection, strength, wishes

Items to purchase when the plant is not available: Flower essence is marketed as white chestnut; nuts

To prepare candles for spells that attract abundance and prosperity, use oil infused with chestnut flowers. Also use this oil to prepare candles for meditation, especially when seeking peace of mind. To build protective energy against a potential hex, break a spiny husk in half and paint your initials on the inside. Carefully hold it between your hands as you sit in front of your altar. Visualize energy from the husk surrounding you. When a picture is clear in your mind, end the visualization but recall the image when you need it for support. Keep the husk on your altar until you feel that the threat is gone.

For general good luck, carry a chestnut in your pocket or purse. For banishing spells, write a few keywords about what you want to remove from your life on a picture of a horse chestnut tree in bloom. To finish your spell, burn the picture in your cauldron and scatter the ashes to the wind. Chestnut is instrumental when seeking justice, especially in legal matters. Write an affirmation on a picture of the tree and carry it with you when meeting with your attorney.

Hyssop
Hyssop (Hyssopus officinalis)
Folk name: Hedge hyssop

Hyssop has upright, angular stems and grows about two feet tall. Like other members of the mint family, its stems are square. Its lance-shaped leaves are dark green and its tiny, purple-blue flowers grow in whorls at the ends of the stems. They bloom from midsummer to early autumn. The stems, leaves, and flowers are aromatic.

Faery Folklore
Hyssop is associated with faeries.

Magical Workings
Powers and attributes: Changes/transitions, clarity (enhance, foster), consecrate/bless, creativity, divination, fertility, growth, healing, hexes (break, protect from), manifest (desires, dreams, will), negativity (remove, ward off), peace, prosperity/money, protection, psychic abilities, purification, sex/sexuality, spirit guides/spirits, spirituality

Items to purchase when the plant is not available: Essential oil; flower essence; cut, dried leaves

Because of its long history of use in cleansing sacred spaces, hyssop is perfect for purifying areas for ritual as well as consecrating altars. Infuse hyssop sprigs in olive oil and use it to anoint participants in ritual. To remove negativity, make a cup of tea with leaves and flowers and sprinkle it around the area or on objects. Also add the tea to a pre-ritual bath or for a healing soak.

To remove hexes and to provide protection against enchantment, dip a stem of hyssop in a bowl of fresh water and sprinkle it around your home and property. Use several stems like a broom to remove negative energy and to encourage unwanted spirits to move on. Place a sprig under your bed to aid in fertility or to help deal with any sexual issue. Burning a couple of leaves raises spiritual vibrations.

Ivy

Common Ivy (Hedera helix)
Folk names: English ivy, ground ivy, true ivy

Ivy is a familiar evergreen vine with woody stems and leaves that have three to five lobes. There are hundreds of cultivars based on leaf shape, size, and variegation. Ivy grows as a climbing vine or a trailing ground cover. It has two stages: In the juvenile stage, it climbs and spreads. In the adult stage, it becomes more shrub-like and produces clusters of greenish-white flowers that develop into blue-black berries.

Faery Folklore
Ivy is associated with faeries.

Magical Workings
Powers and attributes: Attraction, balance/harmony, bind, challenges/obstacles (overcome), divination, fertility, growth, healing, inspiration, knowledge (seek, acquire), love, loyalty/fidelity, luck, negativity (remove, ward off), prophecy, protection, renewal, secrets, security, spirituality

Items to purchase when the plant is not available: Dried leaves; flower essence

Grow ivy on your property or place it as a houseplant in a front window to guard against negative energy. This placement will also attract luck. Make a small wreath of ivy and position it around the base of a candle as part of a binding spell. Include a couple of sprigs on your altar for spiritual journeys that take you inward as well as guide you back out into everyday life. Ivy is instrumental when seeking personal and spiritual growth. Incorporate white ivy leaves into your esbat ritual, as they are associated with the moon.

To represent the balance of light and dark, place ivy on your Mabon altar. Ivy is associated with the Goddess because it grows in a spiral, which is one of her symbols. Create a spiral on your altar with a strand of ivy or draw a spiral on a picture of ivy to symbolize your spiritual journey through the Wheel of the Year.

Jasmine
Common Jasmine (Jasminum officinale)

Jasmine is a climbing shrub that is adored for the fragrance of its star-shaped flowers. The flowers are white to pale pink and grow in clusters of three to five. A healthy jasmine plant produces large amounts of flowers. The leaves consist of five to seven pointed, bright-green leaflets. The vine can spread up to fifteen feet long.

Faery Folklore
Jasmine is associated with faeries.

Magical Workings

Powers and attributes: Abundance, attraction, balance/harmony, bind, challenges/obstacles (overcome), changes/transitions, clarity (enhance, foster), communication, consecrate/bless, creativity, defense, divination, dream work, fertility, growth, happiness, healing, inspiration, intuition, justice/ legal matters, love, luck, peace, prosperity/money, protection, psychic abilities, purification, relationships, sex/sexuality, spirit guides/spirits, spirituality, support (provide, receive)

Items to purchase when the plant is not available: Essential oil; flower essence; dried flowers

Use jasmine flowers to boost defensive magic, enhance divination, and aid in contact with the spirit realm. Make a sachet of dried flowers for protection during dream work. The flowers will also enhance the depth of your dreams. Drape several trailing branches over your altar to help manifest your heart's desire. Place a small bowl or cup of dried flowers in your work area to stimulate ideas.

The scent of jasmine enhances intuition and brings inspiration for creative endeavors and clarity for communication. Burn dried flowers in spells to attract luck and prosperity as well as to bind a pledge. Place a ring of flowers around the base of a yellow candle on your altar to increase psychic skills. Burning a few flowers or a small twig aids in releasing fears. A jasmine bush on your property will attract abundance and peace.

Jelly Fungus

Common Jelly Fungus (Tremella mesenterica syn. *T. albida)*
Folk names: Fairy butter

Ranging from two to five inches in diameter, fairy butter is a type of fungus that sometimes looks like a clump of ribbons but mostly like glossy, golden-yellow or orange-yellow blobs. Resembling butter, it is gelatinous when damp but becomes slightly brittle when dry. It is found on dead trees, fallen branches, and decayed wood. Jelly fungus frequently grows on birch, gorse, and hazel.

Caution: Although jelly fungus is edible, as with any type of fungus, never eat it unless a qualified expert has identified it.

Faery Folklore

According to legend, this yellow fungus is butter that faeries make from the roots of old trees. Other stories note that faeries make it at night and scatter it around. In some parts of the British Isles it was considered lucky to find fairy butter on a house or front gate, even though it may have been flung there by the fae for amusement. In some areas, jelly fungus found on or near the door of a cowshed meant that faeries put a spell on the cows in retaliation for an offense. As a result, the farmer would not have butter for a year.

Magical Workings

Powers and attributes: Balance/harmony, healing, hexes (break, protect from), luck, negativity (remove, ward off), peace, spirit guides/spirits, support (provide, receive)

Items to purchase when the plant is not available: Dried fungus (the color may be dark yellow or orange)

If you find fairy butter, place a little on your altar for the fae. Draw the faery star on a picture of it or hold a piece of the real thing during meditation to foster peace and balance. Also use fairy butter when contacting spirits.

To counteract a hex or any negative magic, write a few keywords on a picture of fairy butter. Burn it in your cauldron as you say:

> *Fairy butter, bright and yellow,*
> *Make this situation mellow.*
> *Any wickedness sent my way*
> *Is neutralized and kept at bay.*

When the ashes are cool, take them outside and scatter in a circle. Take a handful of dirt and scatter it over the ashes.

Also see the profiles for Fly Agaric and Mushroom.

Juniper

Common Juniper (Juniperus communis)
Folk name: Fairy circles

Juniper is a spreading evergreen with multiple trunks and brown to reddish-brown bark. While young plants have needle-like leaves, mature ones develop scale-like foliage. Like holly, juniper has male and female flowers on separate plants, and you need one of each type if you want berries. The round berries come from the female flowers, which are technically cones. Taking about two years to mature, the berries turn from green to blue-black and usually have a powdery, white coating.

Faery Folklore

In Germany, faery-like spirits known as Hollen are associated with the juniper. They provide help to humans when called upon. In England, old junipers were called *fairy circles* because, as new trunks sprout outward from the roots and the center trunks die, the living shrub forms a circle. Juniper was used during childbirth to prevent faeries from substituting a changeling for the infant.

Magical Workings

Powers and attributes: Abundance, balance/harmony, banish, challenges/obstacles (overcome), defense, divination, dream work, emotions (deal with, support), family and home, fertility, growth, happiness, healing, hexes (break, protect from), knowledge (seek, acquire), love, manifest (desires, dreams, will), negativity (remove, ward off), prosperity/money, protection, psychic abilities, purification, release (let go, move on), secrets, security, spirit guides/spirits, spirituality, strength, success, wishes

Items to purchase when the plant is not available: Dried berries; essential oil is made from the berries

To purify a large outdoor space, burn dried juniper needles as incense. To dispel the energy of negative people, burn a few needles and then scatter the ashes. Diffuse a little essential oil to release something you no longer want in your life. Use any part of the juniper to build defensive energy; juniper is especially effective against black magic, hexes, and dealing with unwanted spirits. A juniper bush on your property will aid in manifesting abundance and prosperity.

String berries together into a circlet, let them dry completely, and then use it as a charm to attract a lover. Use dried berries in a sachet to enhance divination and dream work. The berries also help increase psychic abilities. Burning any part of a juniper provides psychic protection and keeps energy grounded in the physical world. As an offering, tie three small, dark blue ribbons within the thick foliage of a juniper. This tree is also helpful in fostering happiness and emotional healing.

Lady's Mantle

Common Lady's Mantle (Alchemilla vulgaris)
Soft Lady's Mantle (A. mollis)
Folk name: Dew cup

The rounded leaves of these plants have shallow lobes and a pleated appearance. Their slightly cupped structure gives them the distinctive ability to hold beads of rain or dew. Lady's mantle grows in spreading mounds that can be a foot or more wide. The small flowers grow in clusters atop branching stems. Soft lady's mantle has gray-green leaves with tiny hairs, which gives them a soft texture. Its flowers are yellowish green and grow on stems that are about eighteen inches tall. Common lady's mantle has fewer hairs on its leaves and green flowers. It is a smaller plant, with flower stems reaching only about twelve to fifteen inches tall.

Faery Folklore

In Ireland and Scotland, lady's mantle was used to remove faery enchantment from humans and animals. In Ireland, juice from the plant was put in drinking water for cows to counteract elf shot. According to other legends, faeries arranged drops of dew on the leaves to reflect the morning sun. They were also said to wash themselves with the dew.

Magical Workings

Powers and attributes: Awareness (expand, heighten), balance/harmony, challenges/obstacles (overcome), changes/transitions, concentration/focus, courage, divination, fertility, happiness, healing, love, luck, peace, purification, relationships, spirituality

Items to purchase when the plant is not available: Cut, dried leaves; flower essence is made from common lady's mantle; seeds

Lady's mantle quite happily grows underneath bushes, which will delight the faeries and nature spirits in your garden. To raise energy for full moon rituals and healing circles, place a bouquet of flowers on your altar. Use dried flowers and leaves in sachets for love spells and to increase romantic passion. Tuck a leaf in your pocket when you need to bolster courage. Lady's mantle also boosts the power of spells. Before divination sessions, hold a leaf between your hands to help focus your attention and energy.

Lady's Smock

Lady's Smock, Bittercress, Meadow Cress (Cardamine pratensis)
Folk names: Cuckoo flower, milkmaids

Growing in clumps up to eighteen inches tall and a foot wide, lady's smock has a rosette of round base leaves and long, narrow leaves on the upper stems. Loose clusters of flowers grow on slender stalks at the tip of the stem. Pinkish-mauve or occasionally white, the flowers have four rounded petals that are broader above the middle and sometimes slightly notched at the tip.

Faery Folklore

Looking like little smocks hung out to dry, the flowers were said to be dresses sewn by elves. This plant was believed to grow in places special to faeries.

Regarded as a sacred faery flower, lady's smock was not included in May Day garlands to avoid offending the fae. In some parts of England, legends note that wearing the flower on May Day would result in the wearer being hauled off by the faeries for the offense. While lady's smock was used in May Day garlands in Oxfordshire, England, it was not allowed in the home because a faery might take the liberty of entering with the flowers.

Magical Workings
Powers and attributes: Divination, fertility, healing, love, sex/sexuality
Items to purchase when the plant is not available: Seeds

Grow lady's smock or sprinkle the seeds around your property to attract faeries. For aid in healing, place a picture of lady's smock flowers on your altar inscribed with the name of the person to whom you want to send energy. For guidance during divination sessions, place a picture or sachet of dried flowers on your altar or table. Place a circle of seeds around the base of a green candle for fertility spells; use a red candle when dealing with issues related to sex. As part of a love charm or spell, carefully drip a little bit of red candle wax on a picture of lady's smock flowers, and then draw the faery star in the wax before it hardens.

Larch
American Larch, Eastern Larch, Tamarack (Larix laricina)
European Larch, Common Larch (L. decidua syn. *L. europaea)*

Larch trees grow high on rocky mountain slopes in conditions where other conifers cannot survive. They have tufts of gray-green needles that grow in tight, spiraling clusters around the branches. Larch is the only coniferous tree that is deciduous; the needles turn golden yellow in the autumn before they drop. The cones are small and round.

Faery Folklore
According to the Tyrolean folklore of Austria, a type of forest spirit or faery dressed in white called *Salgfraulien* often sat underneath old larch trees, singing. These faeries were known to provide aid to humans. Some legends note that they made their homes under the rocks around the roots of larch trees. In

other areas of Europe, they were more like nature spirits and known as the *seliges fräulein* who watched over certain plants.

Magical Workings
Powers and attributes: Healing, intuition, justice/legal matters, knowledge (seek, acquire), luck, protection, spirituality, success

Items to purchase when the plant is not available: Flower essence is made from the European larch; essential oil is obtained from the American larch and sometimes marketed as tamarack oil

Sprinkle a circle of larch needles in your garden as a gift for the faeries and nature spirits. When you need a boost in confidence, place a few needles in a small pouch to carry with you or keep it in your workplace. Use a small piece of wood or a twig as an amulet for good luck. Use the essential oil to aromatically enhance spiritual meditation or journeys to faeryland. Also use the essential oil as an offering to deities. As part of a spell to bring success, prepare a candle with the flower essence.

Write the name of someone to whom you want to send healing energy on a small piece of paper, and then wrap it around three larch needles. Hold it between your hands as you visualize the healing energy making an arch from you to the other person. Afterward, bury the bundle outside.

Laurel
Bay Laurel (Laurus nobilis)
Folk names: Bay tree, true laurel

Laurel is an evergreen that can grow up to fifty feet tall, but it is often kept pruned as a shrub. It may be most familiar as a small, potted tree cut into pom-poms or other topiary shapes. Growing on short stems, the dark green, leathery leaves are sharply pointed. They are commonly known as bay leaves. Blooming in early spring, the small flowers are greenish yellow and grow in clusters. The oval berries are small and turn bluish black when ripe.

Faery Folklore
Laurel is associated with faeries and elves.

Magical Workings

Powers and attributes: Abundance, awareness (expand, heighten), banish, challenges/obstacles (overcome), clarity (enhance, foster), courage, creativity, defense, determination/endurance, divination, dream work, family and home, healing, hexes (break, protect from), inspiration, intuition, justice/legal matters, loyalty/fidelity, manifest (desires, dreams, will), negativity (remove, ward off), peace, prophecy, prosperity/money, protection, psychic abilities, purification, release (let go, move on), spirituality, strength, success, wisdom, wishes

Items to purchase when the plant is not available: Dried bay leaves, whole or powdered; essential oil is obtained from the leaves; hydrosol

Laurel aids in prophetic dreaming, divination, and clairvoyance. Burn a leaf before psychic work to boost skills. Its purification properties also provide protection during this work. Prepare a candle for divination sessions with the essential oil, or make your own hydrosol with the leaves. Laurel also clears and protects the home from negativity; sprinkle powdered leaves around the exterior. Hang a sprig of bay leaves in the kitchen to invite abundance. Burn a dried leaf to enhance defensive magic and remove hexes. To release something that you no longer want in your life, write a keyword on a bay leaf and burn it. Carry a leaf to ward off any type of negative energy, especially when dealing with legal issues.

At Yule, hold a bay leaf as you visualize your wishes and desires for the coming year, and then throw it on the sabbat bonfire or burn it in your cauldron. The scent of bay complements the other aromas of the winter holiday season; add some leaves to a door wreath, as well as your Yule altar.

Lavender
English Lavender, True Lavender (Lavandula angustifolia syn. L. officinalis)
Folk names: Elf leaf

Lavender is a bushy, evergreen shrub that reaches two to three feet tall and spreads about two feet wide. The lower stems turn dense and woody with age.

Small, purplish-lavender flowers grow in whorls atop leafless stems and bloom from midsummer to early autumn. The slightly fuzzy, needle-like leaves are grayish green or silvery green.

Faery Folklore

A mainstay of medieval gardens, lavender was believed to attract elves with its delightful fragrance and silvery leaves. It was used in potions that reputedly enabled a person to see them. Wearing a circlet of lavender flowers and tossing a few sprigs into the Midsummer's Eve bonfire was also said to aid in seeing elves and faeries.

Magical Workings

Powers and attributes: Attraction, awareness (expand, heighten), balance/harmony, challenges/obstacles (overcome), clarity (enhance, foster), communication, concentration/focus, courage, creativity, divination, dream work, emotions (deal with, support), healing, inspiration, intuition, loss/sorrow (ease, recover from), love, loyalty/fidelity, luck, manifest (desires, dreams, will), negativity (remove, ward off), peace, protection, psychic abilities, purification, relationships, release (let go, move on), see faeries, spirit guides/spirits, spirituality, support (provide, receive), wishes

Items to purchase when the plant is not available: Essential oil; flower essence; tea; dried flower buds; dried bunches of flowering stems; leaves

Grow lavender in your garden or place a potted plant beside your altar as a treat for faeries and nature spirits. The scent of lavender enhances awareness and intuition for dream work and all forms of psychic work, especially clairvoyance. Place fresh or dried flowers and leaves wherever you engage in these activities, or place a few drops of lavender essential oil in the melted wax of a pillar candle. Lavender's fragrance also fosters concentration for divination and aids in contacting spirit guides.

With well-known powers of purification, dried leaves or flowers can be burned as incense to consecrate sacred space, release negativity, or to provide protection. Carry a dried flower spike in a sachet to attract love, or to promote fidelity and renewal in a relationship. A bouquet of lavender flowers on your altar helps to deepen spirituality. Save a few bundles of lavender leaves and flowers to toss on a winter fire to scent a room or ritual space.

Lilac

Common Lilac, French Lilac (Syringa vulgaris)
Fairy Tale Series Cultivars:
Tinkerbelle Lilac (S. x 'bailbelle')
Fairy Dust (S. x 'baildust')
Sugar Plum Fairy (S. x 'bailsugar')

Lilac is a multi-stemmed shrub that is beloved for the fragrance of its four-lobed, tubular flowers that hang in inverted pyramidal clusters. They range from white, to lilac, to purple. The pointed heart-shaped leaves range from gray-green to blue-green.

The fairy tale series cultivars are a cross between the Korean lilac (*S. meyeri*) and the little leaf lilac (*S. pubescens* subsp. *microphylla*). The flowers of the Tinkerbelle are deep pink, Fairy Dust flowers are pink and very fragrant, and the Sugar Plum Fairy has rosy-lilac flowers. The compact size of the fairy tale lilacs makes them just right for small gardens. I had a Tinkerbelle lilac at a previous house and it bloomed several times per season.

Faery Folklore

It is no surprise that the sweetly ethereal scent of lilac is associated with the fae and attracts them to the garden. A white lilac flower with five petals instead of four is called a *luck lilac* and is said to be a gift from the fae.

Magical Workings

Powers and attributes: Adaptability, attraction, banish, challenges/obstacles (overcome), concentration/focus, creativity, defense, divination, dream work, emotions (deal with, support), family and home, happiness, hexes (break, protect from), inspiration, love, luck, negativity (remove, ward off), peace, prophecy, protection, psychic abilities, purification, release (let go, move on), renewal, security, spirit guides/spirits, spirituality, wisdom

Items to purchase when the tree is not available: Flower essence is made from the common lilac

Although it was once customary to plant lilacs in front of a house, growing it anywhere on your property will invite nature spirits and faeries to take up residence. Lilac supports divination and psychic work, especially clairvoyance.

Dry a few leaves and burn one before engaging in these practices. A vase of fresh-cut lilac flowers in the bedroom encourages prophetic dreams. The scent is especially helpful for focusing the mind.

To help foster inspiration and increase creativity, place a twig on your desk or somewhere in your workspace. Dry a cluster or two of flowers to use as a charm to attract love. Use the flower essence or make a hydrosol to prepare a candle for a love spell. Dried leaves or flowers can be burned for defensive magic and to break hexes. In addition to repelling negative energy, the smoke aids in banishing unwanted spirits. Burn a few dried leaves to clear ritual space. Carry a piece of bark or part of a twig as a good luck charm or protective amulet.

Lily

Guernsey Lily, Jersey Lily (Nerine sarniensis)
White Globe Lily (Calochortus albus)
Folk name: Fairy lantern (white globe lily)

Growing atop two-foot tall stems, the Guernsey lily produces clusters of large red to orange-red, trumpet-shaped flowers. The wavy-edged petals have an iridescent sheen that makes them look as though they have been sprinkled with glitter. The strap-like leaves emerge after the flowers bloom. The white globe lily is a woodland flower with arching stems that grow from six to twelve inches tall. It has grass-like leaves. The delicate, nodding flowers have overlapping petals that form a closed orb. The flowers are white, often with a pinkish blush. The flower produces a three-lobed seedpod.

Faery Folklore

According to a Guernsey Island legend, a faery king fell in love with a mortal who agreed to go to faeryland with him, but she worried about how it would sadden her family. The king gave her a bulb to plant and when the young woman's mother looked for her, she found the beautiful red flower sprinkled with faery gold. In other legends, faeries used the white globe lilies as lanterns, with fireflies as light bulbs. Lilies in general attract faeries who reputedly like to use them for pillows.

Magical Workings

Powers and attributes: Balance/harmony, changes/transitions, communication, consecrate/bless, creativity, emotion (deal with, support), happiness, love, manifest (desires, dreams, will), negativity (remove, ward off), peace, prosperity/money, protection, relationships, renewal, secrets, spirit guides/ spirits, strength

Items to purchase when the plant is not available: Flower essence is made from the white globe lily; seeds of the white globe lily; bulbs of the Guernsey lily

Place three white globe lily flowers on your altar during full or new moon rituals to call on the beauty and power of Luna. Dry several flowers and use them in a sachet for a love charm. To consecrate and purify ritual space, hold a flower as you circle the area three times. Like most lilies, these are flowers of renewal, especially because they arise from the ground on their own, unaccompanied by leaves. Place a vase of lilies on your altar to aid in transitions or to help initiate a new chapter in your life.

Lily of the Valley

Lily of the Valley (Convallaria majalis)
Folk names: Fairy cups, fairy ladder, May bells, May lily

This tiny flower is famous and beloved for its powerful scent. Its white, bell-shaped flowers are suspended in a row from one side of an arching stem. Two or three broad, lance-shaped leaves grow from the base of the plant. It produces red berries in the autumn.

Caution: Lily of the valley is toxic and can be fatal if ingested.

Faery Folklore

In France, lily of the valley was known as *goblets des fées* (fairy cups) from an old story about the origin of the plant. It told of the fae gathering dew and hanging their cups on blades of grass while they stopped to dance. Having danced and played too long, their cups became stuck to the grass. In Ireland, the plant was known as fairy ladders because the fae were said to like climbing up and down the flowers. In Germany, lily of the valley was a plant watched over by fae known as the *seliges fräulein*.

Magical Workings

Powers and attributes: Balance/harmony, challenges/obstacles (overcome), clarity (enhance, foster), consecrate/bless, courage, defense, emotions (deal with, support), happiness, healing, inspiration, love, luck, peace, protection, skills, spirituality, success

Items to purchase when the plant is not available: Flower essence; dried flowers; lily of the valley herb (cut, dried leaves and flowers)

Leave an offering for faeries underneath lily of the valley in your garden. Include the flowers on your Beltane altar and keep a bouquet on hand for magic work. Use lily of the valley flower essence to prepare candles for healing rituals. When grown in the garden, these flowers invite happiness to a home. Dry a few of the rhizomes (roots) and grind them into a powder. Use a pinch of the powder in charms to overcome challenges and reach goals. Use dried flowers in spells to heal any rift with a lover or friend. Crumble the dried flowers into your cauldron as you say:

> *Sweet-scented flower, small as a bee,*
> *Return this person close to me.*
> *Heal the feelings that pulled us apart;*
> *Help us gain a fresh, new start.*

Linden

Common Linden, European Linden, (Tilia x europaea syn. T. x vulgaris)
Folk name: Lime tree

Lindens are stately trees with a mainly rounded shape and peaked crown. The dark green, heart-shaped leaves are heavily veined and pointed at the tips. Lindens are most notable for their delicate, creamy white flowers that hang in clusters and sweetly scent the summer air. A pale-green bract (a type of modified leaf) protects each cluster of pea-sized nutlets.

Faery Folklore

In parts of Europe, faeries were believed to hide in the bark of lindens and elves were said to live in them. In Scandinavia, a linden was regarded as a favorite place for elves that would try to enchant anyone sitting under the tree after dark.

Magical Workings

Powers and attributes: Attraction, changes/transitions, communication, defense, divination, dream work, happiness, justice/legal matters, love, loyalty/fidelity, luck, negativity (remove, ward off), peace, prophecy, protection, strength, support (provide, receive)

Items to purchase when the tree is not available: Dried leaves and flowers; flower essence

To enhance dream work and foster prophetic dreaming, place a leaf or a picture of the tree in an organza bag on your bedside table. Use the flower essence to prepare candles for divination sessions. When seeking justice, write a few keywords on a picture of the tree and carry it with you when going to court or when meeting with your lawyer. Also carry a picture with you for general good luck.

Linden is an aid for initiating changes in your life and developing strength. Use the flowers in a spell to attract love and romance. Incorporate a few leaves or a picture of a linden in your handfasting ritual to support your vows. Use linden in charms to enhance fidelity in a relationship. The flowers foster a peaceful frame of mind and aid in sharpening communication skills. Burn a dried leaf in your cauldron and waft the smoke in an area where you need to remove negative energy; also do this as part of a protection spell.

Lone Bush and Fairy Bush

Folk names: Gentle thorn, gentry thorn, lonely bush

A solitary hawthorn is often called a *lone bush* and both the hawthorn and blackthorn are known as fairy thorns. In Ireland a lone bush is not limited to hawthorn; alder, birch, blackthorn, broom, elder, gorse, hazel, holly, oak, pussy willow, and rowan also have that distinction. Similarly, a fairy bush, which could be an elder, hawthorn, holly, or rowan, is a tree or shrub that grows on a fairy path or fairy rade trail.

Faery Folklore

Lone bushes were regarded mainly as meeting places of the faeries, but they could also be stopover places. In County Wicklow, Ireland, it was considered unlucky to touch a lone bush that grew in or beside a rath, an ancient ring fort. Because lone bushes where held in great veneration by the faeries, fallen branches were never removed from the site to avoid offending the fae. Some stories tell of hatchets breaking when trying to cut one down, and when a lone bush was plowed up, all the vitality was drained from the surrounding land. According to other legends, if a fairy bush were used for firewood, the result would be heavy sparks and fumes that would make the person who cut the wood gravely ill. After lingering in sickness, they would die.

It was common knowledge that a person should not sit too long under a lone bush and certainly never sleep there. Occasionally, lights were reputedly seen in the vicinity of lone bushes. In County Armagh, a lone bush was never cut down out of respect for the faeries that most likely lived underneath it. In many parts of Ireland it was customary to leave food and drink for the fae under a lone bush on May Eve.

Magical Workings

If you find a lone bush or a small copse that includes one of the fairy thorns, determine if they align with other features in the landscape, such as large rocks or other lone bushes. Use a pendulum or divining rods to examine the area around the tree or copse for a line of energy that may run between it and another feature, as there may be a fairy path in the area. Similar to a ley line, a fairy path is a frequently used trail that connects sites important to the fae. Whether or not you find a fairy path, use the faery attunement and spend time in meditation nearby to make contact.

Maidenhair Fern

Common Maidenhair Fern, Southern Maidenhair Fern (Adiantum capillus-veneris)
Northern Maidenhair Fern (A. pedatum)
Folk name: Fairy fern

Among the most loved ferns, the maidenhair is popular for its delicate fronds with black or dark purple stems that resemble strands of hair. Often grown as a houseplant, the common maidenhair has small, slightly lobed, fan-shaped leaflets. It grows twelve to eighteen inches tall. The northern maidenhair has pairs of dark green, wing-shaped leaflets that become progressively shorter toward the tips of the fronds. This plant grows eighteen to twenty-four inches tall. Both types of maidenhair emerge in the spring as red fiddleheads.

Faery Folklore

According to legend, faeries wore crowns of maidenhair fern for important festive occasions. If a rock crevice served as the entrance to a faery home, tufts of maidenhair fronds were used to drape and conceal it. These ferns were also used as pillows by the faeries.

Magical Workings

Powers and attributes: Abundance, banish, concentration/focus, defense, divination, family and home, healing, hexes (break, protect from), love, luck, peace, prosperity/money, protection, psychic abilities, release (let go, move on), security

Items to purchase when the plant is not available: Cut, dried leaves; powdered leaves

Grow maidenhair in your garden or as a houseplant to attract faeries. To promote peace and security in your life, place the plant or a picture of one in a prominent location in your home. To invite abundance and prosperity into your home, place a handful of dried leaves in a jar on a shelf in the kitchen. When sending healing energy to someone, sprinkle powdered leaves on a large plate and write the person's name or initials with your finger. Leave it in place on your altar for three days.

When preparing for divination sessions or psychic work, place a picture of a maidenhair fern on your altar to help focus your mind and energy. For protection spells, incorporate a picture or a couple of dried fronds. As a protective charm, place a picture or dried fronds where the energy is needed. To enhance defensive magic, carry a small pouch with dried or powdered leaves. Maidenhair fern is also instrumental for banishing anything unwanted from your life.

Also see the profiles for Bracken and Moonwort.

Mallow
Common Mallow, High Mallow, Blue Mallow (Malva sylvestris)
Dwarf Mallow, Common Mallow (M. neglecta)
Folk names: Buttonweed, cheese plant, fairy cheese

Common mallow is an erect, bushy plant with leaves that have three to seven shallow lobes. The five-petaled flowers are notched and range from rosy pink to purplish pink with darker streaks radiating out from their centers. Dwarf mallow is a low, spreading plant. Its five-petaled flowers are also notched and range from white, to pinkish, to lilac with darker streaks. The round, lobed fruit of both mallows has a circular indentation in the center and looks like a little wheel of cheese.

Faery Folklore
In County Limerick, Ireland, lightly striking a person with the stem of a mallow plant purportedly kept them from being controlled by faeries. In England,

the mallow fruits were regarded as faery food; however, human children play-ing in the fields enjoyed eating them, too. In Germany, mallows were used in ointments to counteract spells.

Magical Workings

Powers and attributes: Banish, bind, challenges/obstacles (overcome), deter-mination/endurance, dream work, fertility, healing, hexes (break, protect from), love, nightmares, peace, protection, sex/sexuality, spirit guides/spir-its, spirituality

Items to purchase when the plant is not available: Flower essence is made from the common mallow; blue mallow flower tea; dried flowers; powdered flowers

Gather a few mallow fruit to place on your outdoor altar for faeries and nature spirits to enjoy. Because they are round like the moon, use them in esbat rituals to foster lunar energy and boost your endeavors. When dealing with hexes or any type of negative magic and for banishing spells, burn a couple of leaves in your cauldron. For protective magic, grow mallow at the four corners of your property or, if you live in an apartment, place a dried fruit in each of the cardinal directions. Place them where they will not be seen, such as behind books or in a box.

To attract love, infuse oil with the flowers or use the flower essence and dab a little behind your ears. Wear a sprig of mallow during a handfasting ritual as a symbol of love. To enhance dream work, place a sachet of dried flowers or leaves next to your pillow. Sprinkle dried leaves or flowers on your altar to increase your ability to communicate with spirits.

Maple
Field Maple, Hedge Maple (Acer campestre)
Sugar Maple (A. saccharum)

These maple trees have gray bark and leaves with three to five lobes. In the spring, they produce clusters of small, greenish-yellow flowers. Pairs of winged seeds called *samaras* and *keys* mature in the autumn. Well-known for its fiery autumn colors, the sugar maple can grow quite large. The field maple is smaller; its leaves turn yellow in the autumn.

Faery Folklore

According to legend, maple leaves turn red in the autumn because the faery that lives in the tree paints them. Faeries were also said to sit along maple branches to watch the human activity below. In Germany, a type of fae called *wood folk* were believed to have skin like maple bark and wear clothes made from moss that grew around the roots of maple trees. Wood folk were also known as moss people.

Magical Workings

Powers and attributes: Abundance, balance/harmony, communication, creativity, divination, dream work, loss/sorrow (ease, recover from), love, prophecy, prosperity/money, relationships, release (let go, move on), support (provide, receive), wisdom

Items to purchase when the plant is not available: Maple syrup; flower essence is made from the sugar maple

Use red leaves to work with the faery realm. To boost creativity, press a variety of colored leaves in a book, and then place them on your desk or workspace. Maple is also helpful to hone communication skills. Place a few leaves or seeds in the kitchen to invite abundance into your home. To attract prosperity, place a green leaf under a green candle on your altar as part of a spell. Scatter dried, red leaves on your altar as part of a spell to attract or rekindle love.

To foster prophetic dreams, place a few winged maple seeds and dried leaves in a sachet and hang it on a bedpost. Burn a couple of dried leaves to symbolically release whatever you no longer want in your life. The energy of maple is instrumental for support during divination sessions and when seeking wisdom. For esbat rituals, use seeds to make a circle on your altar with the seed ends touching and the wings pointing outward. Look for fallen maple branches, as they make excellent wands.

Marigold
Common Marigold, English Marigold (Calendula officinalis)
Folk name: Pot marigold

This marigold is a daisy-like flower with a central disk and rays of petals that have a yellow-orange-reddish color. A single flower grows on a stem that reaches from eight to twenty inches tall. The oblong leaves have tapering tips. Don't confuse this flower with plants in the *Tagetes* genus, which are also known as marigolds.

Faery Folklore
In Scotland, a hoop made with butterwort, dandelion, milkwort, and marigold was placed under a milk pail to protect the contents from faery meddling. Growing marigolds in the garden was believed to attract faeries. According to legend, people normally could not see faeries even if they were dancing around their feet, but holding a bouquet of marigolds made the fae visible. Similarly, marigold flowers were one of the ingredients in a recipe that not only made faeries visible, but also aided in conjuring a certain faery named Elaby Gathon.

See the profile on Hollyhock for further details.

Magical Workings
Powers and attributes: Abundance, awareness (expand, heighten), clarity (enhance, foster), communication, creativity, determination/endurance, divination, dream work, happiness, inspiration, justice/legal matters, manifest (desires, dreams, will), negativity (remove, ward off), nightmares, prophecy, prosperity/money, protection, psychic ability, relationships, see faeries, spirit guides/spirits, success, wisdom

Items to purchase when the plant is not available: Flower essence; dried flower petals; seeds

Marigolds can help clarify your purpose in a divination session. Hold a couple of leaves between your hands to center your energy, and then place them on your altar while you proceed with your reading. Also do this to aid in developing and honing psychic skills. Associated with success, marigold leaves can be an aid in legal matters by supporting a determined mind and strong will to put things right. Use flowers and leaves in spells to attract abundance and prosperity. To enhance prophetic dreaming, make a dream pillow and stuff it with dried flower petals. The dream pillow can be placed under the bed to ease nightmares, too. Marigolds are especially helpful when working with the faery realm.

Marsh Marigold

Marsh Marigold (Caltha palustris)
Folk names: Fairy bubbles, goblin flower, kingcup

Unrelated to other flowers commonly known as marigolds, marsh marigold has shiny, deep yellow flowers that resemble large buttercups. The flowers have five to nine petals and grow in clusters on stems that reach between twelve and eighteen inches tall. The rounded base leaves are often seven inches wide. Leaves on the upper stems are smaller and heart- or kidney-shaped.

Faery Folklore

In Ireland, marsh marigold was collected on May Eve or before dawn on Beltane for protection from faeries. The flowers were hung in houses and barns, placed in windows, strewn on doorsteps, and woven into garlands. These garlands were often placed around the necks of cattle to protect them, too. This was also done in Scotland to protect milk. In addition to garlands, marsh marigold was rubbed on the udders of cows after they gave birth to protect the milk.

In less rural areas of Ireland, marsh marigold was collected by children before nightfall on May Eve, and then pushed through the letterboxes of people's houses to keep mischievous faeries from entering. Throughout the month of May, marsh marigold was used for protection, and on the Isle of Man it was carried as a charm.

Magical Workings

Powers and attributes: Clarity (enhance, foster), growth, healing, inspiration, negativity (remove, ward off), prosperity/money, protection, renewal, secrets, spirit guides/spirits, strength

Items to purchase when the plant is not available: Flower essence; seeds

Fresh flowers enhance visualization and aid in making contact with the spirit realm. The flowers also help to create a deeper connection with spirit guides.

When the flowers are not available, prepare a candle with the flower essence and burn it during your sessions.

When dealing with an unwanted spirit, put several dried leaves in a pouch. During the dark phase of the moon, place the pouch in the area where you sense the spirit. On the full moon, scatter the leaves outside as you invite the spirit to move on.

Meadowsweet
Meadowsweet (Filipendula ulmaria syn. Spiraea ulmaria)
Folk names: Meadwort, queen of the meadow

Meadowsweet grows in clumps that usually reach three to four feet tall. The dark green leaves consist of oval, toothed leaflets with prominent veins and whitish down on their undersides. The tiny, five-petaled flowers are creamy white and grow in loose, branching clusters atop the stems. While the flowers have a sweet, almond-like fragrance, the leaves have a sharp, slightly wintergreen scent.

Faery Folklore
In County Galway, Ireland, meadowsweet was placed under the bed to cure a person who had been stricken by any type fairy stroke (enchantment or illness). However, it seems that faeries like meadowsweet, as they were said to hide and dance among it. In Celtic myth, Áine was traditionally crowned with meadowsweet and reputedly gave the flowers their pleasant scent. Originally of the Tuathe Dé Danann, she became known as the faery queen of Munster.

Magical Workings
Powers and attributes: Balance/harmony, creativity, divination, family and home, fertility, happiness, healing, inspiration, love, luck, peace, relationships, security, strength

Items to purchase when the plant is not available: Flower essence; cut, dried flowers; cut, dried leaves; cut, dried leaves and flowers (also powdered) is marketed as meadowsweet herb; flower extract; seeds

To strengthen love and foster a successful marriage, use fresh-cut meadowsweet as a strewing herb at a handfasting ritual. Include meadowsweet in a bridal bouquet or in a chaplet of flowers for blessings of the Goddess on your marriage.

When used around the home, meadowsweet promotes feelings of harmony and security. Meditate with a flower in each palm to bring your energy into alignment or when seeking inspiration. Make an infusion for a pre-ritual bath or use dried flowers to scent ritual clothing. Grow meadowsweet in your garden or sprinkle the powdered herb around your altar to delight the fae. In tribute to Áine, prepare a candle with the flower essence and light it in her honor.

Milkwort
Common Milkwort (Polygala vulgaris syn. *P. oxyptera)*
Dwarf Milkwort (P. amarella)
Folk names: Fairy soap (common milkwort), self-heal (common milkwort)

Usually found in grassy areas, milkwort was named for it milky, white sap. Common milkwort reaches four to ten inches tall and has narrow, lance-shaped leaves. Growing in clusters, the flowers are usually blue, but can also be bluish violet, rosy red, or white. They look like they have wings with two sepals (a specialize type of petal) attached to the base of the tubular flower. Dwarf milkwort is a smaller version of the plant that grows two to six inches tall. The flowers are usually blue, but can also be rosy red or white.

Faery Folklore
According to legend in Ireland, the roots and leaves were used by faeries for a lather to wash their hands after a picnic. In Scotland, a hoop made with milkwort, butterwort, dandelion, and marigold placed under a milk pail protected the contents from faery meddling. A tea of milkwort was given to sick children if it was thought they might have been fairy-struck. It was also used during childbirth to keep faeries from taking the infant.

Magical Workings
Powers and attributes: Abundance, balance/harmony, clarity (enhance, foster), concentrate/focus, consecrate/bless, family and home, healing, protection, renewal

Items to use when the plant is not available: Cut, dried leaves and flowers is marketed as milkwort herb; dried flower tops; seeds

Whenever possible, include a few milkwort leaves when you leave food for the faeries. To invite abundance into your home, keep a jar of dried milkwort on the highest shelf in your kitchen. Place a little of the dried plant in a decorative container in the family or living room to foster harmony, especially when dealing with problems. Burn a pinch of it in your cauldron before ritual to prepare sacred space. When you need help focusing on a task or when studying, place a picture of milkwort on your desk. Hold a picture of it during meditation to bring clarity.

Mistletoe
American Mistletoe (Phoradendron leucarpum syn. *P. flavescens)*
European Mistletoe, Common Mistletoe (Viscum album)
Folk names: All-heal, golden bough

Mistletoe is a semi-parasitic evergreen shrub that grows in clumps on tree limbs. It has thick, leathery leaves and small, white or greenish-white flowers. The berries are white or yellowish and grow in small clusters. While its roots tap into the host tree's circulatory system for water and minerals, these two species of mistletoe contain chlorophyll and produce their own food.

Caution: All parts of mistletoe are toxic and should not be ingested.

Faery Folklore
Mistletoe was used for protection against mischievous faeries. It was hung in the home for protection during the winter fairy rade (procession) at Samhain when the fae were said to move to their winter quarters. Mistletoe was placed on top of babies' cradles to prevent faeries from substituting a changeling. According to one legend, if a faery tried to take the life force of a baby, the mistletoe would absorb the energy until it could be safely returned to the child. Other legends note that children are protected by faeries wherever mistletoe grows.

Magical Workings
Powers and attributes: Banish, challenges/obstacles (overcome), changes/transitions, consecrate/bless, creativity, defense, divination, dream work, family and home, fertility, healing, love, luck, negativity (remove, ward off),

nightmares, peace, prosperity/money, protection, purification, renewal, secrets, security, sex/sexuality, spirit guides/spirits, success

Items to purchase when the plant is not available: Cut, dried European mistletoe is marketed as mistletoe herb

Neither a tree nor shrub and growing between heaven and earth, mistletoe is a plant that is betwixt and between and especially powerful for working with faeries and nature spirits. Before divination and dream work, hold a sprig between your palms to enhance your experience. Hang a small sprig over your altar when facing challenges or dealing with change. Make a ring of mistletoe berries around the base of a green candle for fertility spells and for dealing with any issue related to sex. Use mistletoe leaves for spells to attract love and romance.

To provide protection, hang a large sprig in an area of your home where it will not be easily seen. Allow it to dry and stay in place all year, and then burn it at Yule. Burn a few mistletoe leaves to remove negative energy or as part of a banishing spell. Smoke from the leaves can be used to purify and consecrate ritual space.

Moonwort

Common Moonwort (Botrychium lunaria syn. *Osmunda lunaria)*
Folk name: Moon fern

Moonwort is not what most of us envision as a fern. Growing up to seven inches tall, it sprouts a single shoot that separates into two stems. One stem has up to nine pairs of fan- or half-moon-shaped leaves that often overlap, except when growing in deep shade. The leaves are progressively smaller toward the top of the stalk. The other fruiting stem sprouts branches ladened with round seed capsules. The seed capsules turn yellow when they mature.

Caution: Moonwort is endangered or threatened in many areas.

Faery Folklore
Like ragwort, faeries were said to transform moonwort into horses for riding to their nightly revels. According to some legends, rather than turning the plant into a horse, a pair of moonwort leaves was used as a saddle. Because moonwort

was believed to have the power to open locks, faeries reputedly used it to enter people's homes.

Magical Workings
Powers and attributes: Banish, concentration/focus, defense, divination, hexes (break, protect from), knowledge (seek, acquire), love, luck, prosperity/money, protection, psychic abilities, purification, release (let go, move on), secrets, security, spirit guides/spirits

Items to purchase when the plant is not available: Because of moonwort's status in the wild, use photographs to work with this plant.

To invite faeries into your home, place a photograph of moonwort on your altar. Cut out a sufficient number of leaves from a picture to arrange in a circle on your altar for esbat rituals and spells involving lunar magic. Hold a picture between your hands before divination sessions to focus your mind. This is also helpful when developing psychic skills, especially clairvoyance.

Gaze at a picture of moonwort before meditation when seeking knowledge and a deeper understanding of your path in life. Carry a picture in your pocket or wallet when you feel the need to increase defensive energy. If you happen to find moonwort in the wild, project loving energy toward it and call on the faeries and nature spirits for help in protecting it.

Also see the profiles for Bracken and Maidenhair Fern.

Morning Glory
Common Morning Glory, Tall Morning Glory
(Ipomoea purpurea syn. *Convolvulus purpureus)*

Morning glory has heart-shaped leaves and two-inch wide flowers that can be blue, pink, red, white, or purplish-blue. These trumpet-shaped flowers have white throats. They open in the morning and close at night or in the rain. The vines can grow six to ten feet long. There are many species of morning glories.

Caution: All parts of this plant are poisonous if ingested.

Faery Folklore
Morning glory is associated with faeries but with mixed opinions. According to some people it attracts faeries; others note that it repels them. I have found that

they enjoy morning glories, especially when grown with moonflowers (*I. alba*) because there is always something in bloom day and night. Communicate with the fae and nature spirits in your area before growing these flowers.

Magical Workings
Powers and attributes: Awareness (expand, heighten), balance/harmony, banish, bind, changes/transitions, divination, dream work, family and home, happiness, loss/sorrow (ease, recover from), peace, security, strength, success

Items to purchase when the plant is not available: Flower essence; seeds

To aid in raising awareness before a divination session, use morning glory seeds to make a circle around the base of a candle. To enhance dream work, sprinkle a little of the flower essence on your pillow. For a binding spell, on the night of a new moon, write what you want to bind or secure on a piece of paper, and then roll it into a scroll. Use a piece of vine, stripped of its leaves and flowers, and wrap it around the scroll three times as you say:

> *Morning glory, morning flower,*
> *Help me with your fragrant power.*
> *As I wrap these words of mine,*
> *Make it so with your vine.*

Continue by holding it between your hands as you send your energy into it and visualize your goal. Afterward, take it outside and bury it in the ground as you repeat the incantation.

Mugwort
Common Mugwort, Wild Wormwood (Artemisia vulgaris syn. *Absinthium spicatum)*
Folk names: Motherwort, muggert, silver leaf

Ranging from two to six feet tall, mugwort is a shrubby plant with reddish or purplish-brown stems. Its deeply lobed leaves are dark green on top and slightly silvery with a covering of woolly hairs underneath. The leaves have a sage-like smell that borders on the odor of marijuana when burned. Small, greenish-yellow to reddish-brown flowers grow in clusters along the stems.

Faery Folklore

In Scotland on Midsummer's Eve, mugwort was placed in cowsheds for protection from faery meddling. For protection on the Isle of Man, people wore chaplets of mugwort and attached leafy stems to the horns of their cattle. In medieval England, it was believed that elves could not live in a house where there was mugwort. This plant was reputedly used by faeries for travel spells.

Magical Workings

Powers and attributes: Authority/leadership, awareness (expand, heighten), banish, consecrate/bless, defense, divination, dream work, family and home, fertility, happiness, love, luck, negativity (remove, ward off), peace, protection, psychic abilities, purification, release (let go, move on), skills, spirit guides/spirits, strength

Items to purchase when the plant is not available: Essential oil; flower essence; cut, dried leaves and stems are marketed as mugwort herb; dried stalks

Mugwort is instrumental in honing divination skills, especially scrying, and for purifying or consecrating divination tools. Make a cup of tea with mugwort leaves, let it cool, and then strain it. Use the tea to cleanse scrying balls and other tools. For items such as tarot decks that you do not want to get wet, make a sachet with dried leaves and wrap it in a cloth with your tools when not in use. Alternatively, burn a few leaves and pass your tools through the smoke.

With strong defensive powers, mugwort guards against dark magic and provides excellent protection for the home. Make a wreath with several stalks of leaves and flowers to hang on your front door or over your altar and visualize it repelling all forms of negativity. To enhance the energy of full or dark moon rituals, place fresh leaves and flowers on your altar.

Mullein

Common Mullein, Great Mullein (Verbascum thapsus)
Folk names: Candlewick, flannel leaf

Mullein (rhymes with sullen) is a biennial plant that consists only of a rosette of base leaves during the first year. The large, blue-green leaves are oval-shaped. They are soft and velvety to the touch. A stalk develops in the second year and reaches six to eight feet tall. The leaves taper down in size the higher they grow on the stalk. Densely packed at the top of the stalks, the yellow, five-petaled flowers open a few at a time starting at the lower end of the flower head.

Faery Folklore

According to legend, mullein placed under an infant's cradle would prevent the child from being taken by the faeries. Used as a charm to see faeries, mullein also functioned as an amulet to return children who were either abducted or enchanted by them. Other legends note that the fae used mullein leaves as blankets and bed curtains when sleeping.

Magical Workings

Powers and attributes: Authority/leadership, awareness (expand, heighten), balance/harmony, banish, courage, defense, determination/endurance, divination, healing, hexes (break, protect from), love, negativity (remove, ward off), nightmares, protection, psychic ability, purification, release (let go, move on), security, see faeries, spirit guides/spirits, support (provide, receive)

Items to purchase when the plant is not available: Flower essence; cut, dried flowers; cut, dried leaves; powdered leaves; seeds

Grow mullein on your property to delight the faeries. For protection against negative forces, grow one at each corner of your property to create the corners of an energy fence. To remove negativity from your home, crumble a dried leaf and throw it out the back door as you visualize whatever is undesirable leaving and evaporating. For help in connecting with ancient wisdom, hold a leaf while meditating. Fresh flowers are effective for love charms.

To banish nightmares, place a sachet of dried leaves or flowers under your pillow. To make a walking stick, cut down a flower spike at the end of the season and let it dry out. Make any needed adjustments to the length. A mullein walking stick will provide magical protection as you ramble through woods or across fields. It can also serve as a faery staff.

Mushroom

Fairy Ring Mushroom, Scotch Bonnet (Marasmius oreades)
Field Mushroom, Meadow Mushroom (Agaricus campestris)
Common Puffball (Lycoperdon perlatum)
Folk names: Fairy stool, fairy table, pixy puff, pixy stool

These three types of mushrooms commonly form rings. The cap of the fairy ring mushroom is bell-shaped but can become somewhat flattened with a central bump. Although sometimes white, it is usually buff to tan or reddish tan. On the underside it has white or buff-colored gills, most of which are attached to the stem, which is whitish or the same color as the cap. The field mushroom is stocky and has a white cap that can be convex to nearly flat. The gills, which start out pink and then turn brown, are not attached to the stem. The stem is about as tall as the cap is wide. The puffball is creamy white to tan before turning brown as it matures. It has a spherical cap and pointy warts that leave a net-like pattern on the cap when they wear off. It has a white stem. The spores are released in what looks like a brown puff of smoke.

Caution: While these mushrooms are edible, as with any type of fungus, never eat it unless a qualified expert has identified it.

Faery Folklore

Forever linked with the fae, fairy rings were said to mark the place where they danced in the moonlight. Like fairy circles of grass, some stories note that it is okay to walk through or stand inside the circle but it is unlucky to walk or run around the perimeter because that is a fairy path reserved for them. According to other stories, running around a fairy ring on the first night of a full moon makes the subterranean revels of faeries and elves audible.

In Ireland, mushrooms are associated with faeries in general and, more specifically, with leprechauns. In Scotland, it was said that faeries used them as tables for their feasts. *Bocán* is the Scots Gaelic word for mushroom, which also means "hobgoblin" or "sprite."[73] According to legend, it was unwise to plow through or damage a fairy ring because the penalty was death. Like the grass

---

73. Mac Coitir, *Ireland's Wild Plants*, 293.

circle, a fairy ring of mushrooms was regarded as a lucky place to make a wish. In parts of Europe, mushrooms were regarded as gnome houses.

Magical Workings

Powers and attributes: Awareness (expand, heighten), creativity, divination, fertility, happiness, psychic abilities, secrets, spirit guides/spirits, strength

Items to purchase when the plant is not available: Dried mushrooms; figurines

Whenever you find a ring of mushrooms, make a wish and thank the faeries. As part of a fertility spell, string three dried mushroom caps together and hang them on your bedpost. To increase awareness for a divination session, hold a mushroom between your palms as you ground and center your energy. This is also helpful before any type of psychic work and when contacting spirit guides.

Also see the profiles for Fly Agaric and Jelly Fungus.

Nettle
Common Nettle (Urtica dioica)
Folk name: Stinging nettle

Nettle reaches about six feet tall and forms dense colonies. The lance-shaped leaves are heavily veined and toothed. Tiny, white or green flowers grow in whorls at the stem tips and at the base of the leaves. The stems and leaves are covered with bristly hairs that release an irritant when brushed against.

Caution: The irritant in the bristly hairs causes a burning, itching sensation that can last from a few minutes to twelve hours.

Faery Folklore

In Denmark, nettles were said to grow where elves live. In addition to being a deterrent to house trolls from meddling with milk, nettles were also used to ward off bewitchment by them. In the British Isles, a nettle sting was believed to protect a person against faery mischief. The Anglo-Saxons used nettles in charms to soothe the effects of elf shot.

Magical Workings

Powers and attributes: Abundance, banish, challenges/obstacles (overcome), communication, courage, defense, divination, emotions (deal with, support), family and home, healing, hexes (break, protect from), justice/legal matters, luck, negativity (remove, ward off), peace, protection, psychic abilities, purification, release (let go, move on), security, sex/sexuality

Items to purchase when the plant is not available: Flower essence; cut, dried leaves; nettle leaf tea

If you are nervous about a public speaking engagement, drink a little nettle leaf tea beforehand or put a dab of nettle-infused oil on the bottoms of your feet. It will aid in bolstering your courage, support your communication skills, and keep you grounded. If you feel negativity from a neighbor, sprinkle dried leaves around your property to deflect the energy. When dealing with emotional upsets, dab a little of the flower essence on your third-eye chakra (between and slightly above the eyebrows), your throat, and stomach, and then sit quietly while you simply focus on your breath. Carry a dried leaf for luck when going to court for any type of legal issue.

Oak

Black Oak (Quercus velutina)
English Oak, Common Oak (Q. robur)
White Oak (Q. alba)

The oak leaf has deep indentations with five to seven lobes that can have multiple points at the ends. The black oak leaves have pointed lobes tipped with tiny bristles; white oak leaves are rounded and smooth. The leaves of the English oak have rounded lobes with a pair of smaller ones at the base. The oak nut, or acorn, has a woody cap.

Faery Folklore

Along with ash and hawthorn, the oak was part of the Celtic triad of powerful faery trees. In many countries, oak woods were known as faery places. In parts of England, faeries were said to inhabit oaks. A hole created by a branch that had fallen off was known as a fairy door. It was believed that touching a fairy door could heal disease. In Scotland, a circle drawn with a branch from an oak sapling reputedly provided protection from faeries.

Pilgrimages to sacred wells and springs during the month of May were common in England. Rags were tied to nearby oaks for protection against sorcery and as a tribute to any fae that frequented the well. In Ireland, a solitary oak is regarded as a lone bush. (See the profile for Lone Bush.) The *Dindshenchas of Slige Dála*, a collection of prose and poems from oral tradition and ancient manuscripts, notes that the faery folk passed along the lore of Samhain to humans during meetings in oak woods.[74] Dwarf-like faeries known as oak men are the guardians of forest creatures.

Magical Workings

Powers and attributes: Abundance, ancestors, authority/leadership, awareness (expand, heighten), challenges/obstacles (overcome), consecrate/bless, courage, defense, determination/endurance, family and home, fertility, growth, healing, inspiration, justice/legal matters, knowledge (seek, acquire), loyalty/fidelity, luck, manifest (desires, dreams, will), negativity (remove, ward off), prophecy, prosperity/money, protection, purification, renewal, secrets, security, sex/sexuality, spirit guides/spirits, strength, success, wisdom

Items to purchase when the tree is not available: Pieces of powdered bark from the white oak; flower essence is made from the English oak

Use several acorn caps as cups to place on your outdoor altar with food or gifts for the faeries. Make a row with three acorn cups on a kitchen windowsill and ask for abundance, blessings, and love for your home and family. An acorn on your altar during ritual or meditation aids in connecting with ancient wisdom. To clear away negative energy, burn a dried oak leaf. For healing or when seeking wisdom, hold a piece of bark between your hands and visualize your desired outcome. Also use a piece of bark to help ground energy after ritual. Leaves placed under the bed aid fertility and virility. Use an acorn in spells to manifest what you need. Carry one as a protective amulet.

---

74. *Dindshenchas* is the lore of places and Slige Dála is one of the five legendary roads from Tara. This manuscript is included in the twelfth century *Book of Leinster*.

Pansy

Garden Pansy (Viola x wittrockiana)
Wild Pansy, Field Pansy (V. tricolor)
Folk names: Heartease, Johnny-jump-up

Garden pansies are viola hybrids developed from the wild pansy. The flowers are single- or multicolored and with or without markings. The most common types of pansy have a dark center called a *face*. The wild pansy is smaller than its garden cousin and often has thin, black lines known as whiskers radiating from the center of its face. The leaves are oblong to lance-shaped and are gently lobed. Pansies are cousins to violets (*Viola* spp.).

Faery Folklore

Shakespeare's use of the pansy for faery love spells in *A Midsummer Night's Dream* may have come from the Celtic practice of brewing a love potion with pansy leaves or from other earlier lore that is now lost. At any rate, the pansy has become associated with faeries.

Magical Workings

Powers and attributes: Attraction, clarity (enhance, foster), concentration/ focus, courage, divination, healing, inspiration, loss/sorrow (ease, recover from), love, negativity (remove, ward off), peace, renewal

Items to purchase when the plant is not available: Flower essence; dried flowers and leaves; wild pansy is sometimes marketed as heartsease herb; garden pansy seeds

Because pansies are most fragrant in the early morning and at dusk, use them during these times of day to communicate with nature spirits and faeries. Dawn and dusk are in-between times that support magical energy and give access to other realms. Place wild pansy flowers on your altar when engaging in divination to bring clarity. Hold a few flowers or a potted plant in your hands to deepen meditation or to focus your mind.

Sprinkle flower petals in your bathwater to aid in attracting love. In the Victorian period, pansies were given as a token with the intention of being remembered. With this same intention, give a potted bowl of garden pansies to your lover or someone whose attention you would like to attract. If that is too bold for the situation or not possible, pick a flower and tape or clip it to a picture of him or her as you say:

> *Pansy dear, pansy sweet,*
> *May this be my love to meet.*
> *Send a sign if this be so;*
> *Let true love bloom and grow.*

Peach and Nectarine
Common Peach (Prunus persica syn. *Amygdalus persica)*
Nectarine (P. persica var. *nucipersica)*

Reaching fifteen to twenty-five feet tall, the peach tree has drooping, lance-shaped leaves and pink, five-petaled flowers that grow singly or in pairs. The green fruit ripens to reddish orange and has fuzzy skin. Inside it is fleshy with a large, hard seed that is known as a pit or stone. A nectarine is a peach with smooth skin. It is so genetically similar to the peach that nectarines often show up on peach trees and vice versa.

Faery Folklore
Peach and nectarine are associated with faeries. Although peaches are not mentioned in direct connection with the fae, in Chinese legend they are noted

as growing in the garden of Hsi Wang Mu, the Mother of the West, who lived with her faery legions in the sacred Kunlun Mountains.

Magical Workings

Powers and attributes: Banish, fertility, happiness, healing, hexes (break, protect from), love, loyalty/fidelity, luck, manifest (desires, dreams, will), negativity (remove, ward off), renewal, wisdom, wishes

Items to purchase when the plant is not available: Fresh or dried fruit; peach juice; flower essence; peach kernel oil; dried leaves are marketed as peach leaf tea

For love spells, prepare a candle with peach kernel oil or flower essence. For a fertility charm, place a dried peach blossom in an organza bag and hang it in your bedroom. To boost fidelity and passion, sensually eat a peach or nectarine with your lover. Use a leafy twig in ritual to manifest your dreams. To foster happiness, hang a picture of three peaches in your kitchen. Hold a dried peach pit during meditation when seeking wisdom.

To release pent-up emotions, drink a cup of peach leaf tea. To break a hex, crush a dried pit and throw the pieces in a river or fast-moving stream. If such water is not available, bury it in the ground. Burn a couple of dried leaves to remove any type of negativity or to symbolically banish something you no longer want in your life.

Pear
Common Pear, Wild Pear (Pyrus communis)

The pear tree grows to a height of twenty-five to forty feet. It has glossy, dark green leaves that turn various shades of red and yellow in the autumn. The fragrant, five-petaled flowers are creamy white and sometimes tinged with pink. The fruit is somewhat teardrop-shaped.

Faery Folklore

The pear is associated with faeries.

Magical Workings

Powers and attributes: Bind, consecrate/bless, creativity, healing, justice/legal matters, love, luck, manifest (desires, dreams, will), prosperity/money, protection, sex/sexuality, success, wisdom, wishes

Items to purchase when the plant is not available: Fresh or dried fruit; pear juice; pear wine; perry pear cider (*perry* refers to a type of pear and not the Persian *peri*); flower essence

Use a fresh pear in spells to attract love or heighten passion. Use the juice or flower essence to prepare a candle for meditation when dealing with sexual issues. To consecrate an altar or ritual space, sprinkle a handful of blossoms or burn a couple of dried leaves as you cast a circle. To stoke creativity, place a pear or hang a picture of one in your workspace; eating a pear also helps. Place a branch on your altar for wisdom when seeking justice. Hold a branch during ritual or meditation to aid in manifesting your dreams. Hang a branch over your front door for protection. The fruit is also effective in binding spells and healing circles.

Pearlwort
Trailing Pearlwort, Birdeye Pearlwort (Sagina procumbens)
Folk names: Beads, bird's eyes

Pearlwort is a sprawling, mat-forming plant. It has a base rosette of leaves from which bright-green stems sprout and grow in a crisscrossed pattern. Pairs of narrow leaves merge and wrap around the stems. Individual or clusters of tiny, white flowers grow at the tips of the stems. The flowers have four white petals and four slightly larger green sepals, which are specialized leaves that protect and support the petals. The white seed capsules contain several small, dark seeds. The flower buds and seed capsules resemble beads.

Faery Folklore

Pearlwort was hung over doorways in homes to thwart faery mischief and for general luck. Hung above an exterior door, it reputedly prevented faeries from entering a home. Pearlwort was used during childbirth to prevent the infant or mother from being taken by faeries. Placing a sprig in a milk pail or butter churn ensured that its nutritional essence was not removed. It was also believed that a faery that drank milk with pearlwort in it could not have power over a human. Around the time of Beltane, cows were given pearlwort to eat to protect them from faery meddling. This protection was passed along to anyone who drank the milk or ate butter or cheese made from it.

Magical Workings

Powers and attributes: Banish, bind, hexes (break, protect from), loss/sorrow, love, luck, negativity (remove, ward off), protection

Items to purchase when the plant is not available: There are no products from this plant.

When recovering from the loss of a loved one, place a picture of pearlwort beside a white candle upon which you have written the person's name. Light the candle and recall your memories of the person. Afterward, place the picture on your altar whenever you want to honor your loved one.

Knot several stems together to use in a binding spell for protection against a negative person. Write the person's initials on a small piece of paper and then roll it into a little scroll. Tie it closed with the pearlwort, and then hold it between your hands as you visualize the person's energy unable to reach you. Because pearlwort is associated with protection and love, think of binding the person with positive energy to counteract their negativity. When the situation improves, burn the paper and pearlwort.

Peony

Common Peony, Garden Peony (Paeonia officinalis)
Wild Peony, English Peony (P. mascula)

Peonies are erect, shrubby plants that grow up to three feet tall. They have lance-shaped leaves that are prominently veined. The bowl-shaped flowers have five to ten petals. As the flowers fade, clusters of wedge-shaped seedpods form. The seeds are dark purple to black. The common peony has red flowers and dark green leaves. There are many cultivars of different colors. The roots are round tubers joined together with root strings. The wild peony flowers are rose-pink to deep purplish red and the leaves are light to bluish green. Its roots look like small carrots.

Faery Folklore

A carved peony root was worn around the neck as an amulet to protect from enchantment by faeries and goblins.

Magical Workings

Powers and attributes: Balance/harmony, banish, dream work, family and home, happiness, healing, hexes (break, protect from), loss/sorrow (ease, recover from), luck, negativity (remove, ward off), nightmares, peace, prosperity/money, protection, release (let go, move on), spirit guides/ spirits, success

Items to purchase when the plant is not available: Flower essence is made from the Chinese peony (*P. lactiflora*); whole dried flowers; dried petals; seeds

Peonies in the garden will attract faeries and nature spirits to your property. A sachet of dried petals on the bedside table invites faeries into your dreams; it will also dispel bad dreams or negative thoughts that keep you from falling asleep. Place a vase of flowers near the front door of your house to invite prosperity inside. To balance your energy and foster a deep-rooted sense of peace, hold a flower or place a picture of one on your altar during meditation. Dry and polish a piece of root to carry with you as a good luck charm and to aid in achieving your goals.

To get rid of negative spirits, dry a small piece of root, burn it outdoors, and waft a little smoke around the exterior of your house as you say:

> *Whoever is present in this place,*
> *It's time to leave without a trace.*
> *With the power of this root I now burn,*
> *Leave my home and never return.*

Set your cauldron or other vessel used for burning in a safe place until the ashes cool, and then scatter them to the wind as you repeat the incantation.

Periwinkle

Lesser Periwinkle, Common Periwinkle (Vinca minor)
Greater Periwinkle, Big Leaf Periwinkle (V. major)
Folk names: Fairy paintbrush, sorcerer's violet

Lesser periwinkle reaches only six inches tall and forms a ground cover with its trailing stems. It has shiny, oblong leaves and tubular flowers that are light blue to violet-blue. The five, slightly asymmetrical petals give the flower a pinwheel appearance. Greater periwinkle grows to eighteen inches tall. Its leaves are rounded to somewhat heart-shaped.

Faery Folklore

In Somerset, England, the word *sorcerer* was used as a reference to faeries. In other areas of Britain, periwinkle was known to be a plant favored by the fae and used by them to make charms. According to legend, a part inside the flower (the pistil/stamen) served as a paintbrush for faeries.

Magical Workings

Powers and attributes: Abundance, awareness (expand, heighten), bind, clarity (enhance, foster), divination, healing, hexes (break, protect from), knowledge (seek, acquire), love, loyalty/fidelity, manifest (desires, dreams, will), nightmares, peace, prosperity/money, protection, psychic ability, relationships, security, spirit guides/spirits

Items to purchase when the plant is not available: Flower essence is made from greater periwinkle; cut, dried leaves and stems of lesser periwinkle are marketed as periwinkle herb; pressed, dried flowers; seeds

If you grow periwinkle in your garden, carefully remove the petals of several flowers to find the "paintbrush," and then leave them on your outdoor altar as a gift for faeries. The trailing stems of periwinkle are perfect for making garlands and wreaths. Make a circlet to wear on your head during divination sessions to increase levels of awareness and bring clarity to your readings. To aid in dispelling bad dreams, make a small wreath to hang on a bedpost or place on your bedside table. When seeking deeper knowledge about yourself, prepare a candle with flower essence before meditation. Use periwinkle flowers to strengthen love charms. Sprinkle dried leaves to cast a protective circle when contacting spirits.

Pignut

Pignut, Earthnut (Conopodium majus syn. *C. denudatum)*
Folk name: Fairy potato

Growing only about a foot tall, pignut has hollow stems and feathery leaves that resemble carrot foliage. It has tiny, white flowers that grow in umbrella-like clusters. The root, which is an irregularly round tuber, is edible and has a nutty flavor that is often compared to chestnuts. After blooming in early summer, the flower heads die back and the plant leaves almost no trace above ground. The tubers become as illusive as faeries. If you find a plant, unearthing the tubers can be a challenge that requires patience.

Faery Folklore
Pignut was regarded as a faery plant that they used as food. According to Irish legend, leprechauns favored the tubers roasted. Pignut is most often found at woodland edges and in fairy pastures, small grassy clearings where sunlight reaches the forest floor.[75]

Magical Workings
Powers and attributes: Abundance, challenges/obstacles (overcome), determination/endurance, family and home, luck, prosperity/money, protection, secrets, sex/sexuality

Items to purchase when the plant is not available: Seeds (in the UK and Europe)

Because pignut is difficult to find, it is easier to work with pictures. Place one in your kitchen to draw abundance to your home, or keep a picture with your checkbook to foster prosperity. As you do this, say:

> *Pignut, earthnut, fairy potato,*
> *May abundance to my family flow.*
> *Pignut, earthnut, blessed faery fare,*
> *May we have what we need and some to share.*

---

75. Miller, *Common Wayside Flowers*, 168.

The elusiveness of this plant encourages us to hold secrets when bidden. Write a keyword on a picture of pignut flowers and keep it where you will see it often to be reminded of your promise. When dealing with sexuality issues, place a few seeds in your bedroom, where their energy can aid the situation. To help ground energy after ritual and spellwork, hold a picture of the root between your hands as you visualize your energy connecting with the earth star.

Pine
White Pine, Eastern White Pine (Pinus strobus)
Scots Pine (P. sylvestris)

Pine trees are cone-bearing evergreens with needles that grow in clusters. The cones have rigid, woody scales and hang underneath the branches. The white pine has smooth, gray bark that breaks into small plates as the tree matures. The soft, flexible needles are dark green. Scots pine has distinctive flaking, reddish-brown bark. Its needles are blue-green and the cones are gray or light brown.

Faery Folklore
Throughout Europe and the British Isles, elves, faeries, and pixies were said to live in or gather around pine trees. According to legends in India and Pakistan, faeries made their homes in pine tree trunks during the winter.

Magical Workings
Powers and attributes: Abundance, balance/harmony, banish, bind, changes/transitions, communication, concentration/focus, consecrate/bless, courage, creativity, defense, determination/endurance, emotions (deal with, support), family and home, fertility, growth, happiness, healing, hexes (break, protect from), inspiration, intuition, justice/legal matters, knowledge (seek, acquire), manifest (desires, dreams, will), negativity (remove, ward off), peace, protection, psychic abilities, purification, release (let go, move on), renewal, spirit guides/spirits, spirituality, strength, support (provide, receive), wisdom

Items to purchase when the plant is not available: Dried pine cones; essential oil is made from the needles and twigs of the Scots pine; flower essence is made from the Scots pine; pine nuts

The pine tree is well-known for its purification properties and for dispelling negative energy. It is especially effective in public spaces. The same qualities also make it an ally in defensive magic and for protection from hexes, especially for the home. Burn a few dried needles for these purposes. Use the cones to represent blessings and to attract abundance. Also use them for spells that banish or bind.

The scent of pine can steady and focus the mind for psychic work and for communication with spirits. Also use the scent to stimulate the energy around you during visualizations. On a spiritual level, pine aids in healing, inspiration, and access to ancient wisdom. Carry a few scales from a pine cone for confidence and courage, especially when dealing with legal matters.

Plantain
Broadleaf Plantain, Greater Plantain (Plantago major)
Narrow-leaf Plantain, Ribwort Plantain (P. lanceolata)

Broadleaf plantain has a base rosette of wide, ribbed leaves with wavy edges that grow close to the ground. The upright stalk has a long, cylindrical flower spike that is green to purplish green. As expected, the narrow-leaf plantain has narrow, lance-shaped leaves. Most of the leaves are upright. Each tall, thin stalk holds a short, dense flower spike that is brownish green. These plants are not related to the banana of the same name.

Faery Folklore
Plantain is associated with faeries.

Magical Workings
Powers and attributes: Courage, determination/endurance, divination, dream work, family and home, healing, negativity (remove, ward off), nightmares, protection, purification, sex/sexuality, strength, success, truth
Items to purchase when the plant is not available: Cut, dried leaves

The Anglo-Saxons regarded plantain as sacred and magical; use it in charms to enhance magical power. As you gather plantain, state what you want to achieve to set forth your magical purpose. The root can be dried and carried as an amulet to repel negativity and subdue fears. To ward off bad dreams, place a piece of plantain under your bed. All parts of the plant can aid in grounding energy after ritual or magic work. To surround yourself with the healing energy of plantain, place dried leaves or roots in a mesh bag and hang it under the faucet when drawing a bath.

Primrose

English Primrose, Common Primrose (Primula vulgaris syn. *P. acaulis)*
Polyanthus Primrose (P. x polyantha)
Folk names: Butter rose, fairy cups, key flower

Primrose's six-petaled flowers grow in clusters that rise on short stems from the rosette base of crinkled, green leaves. The English primrose flowers are pale yellow with deep yellow centers that grow on individual stalks. The polyanthus primrose encompasses a group of natural hybrids with flower colors that can be blue, orange, pink, purple, white, or yellow. Multiple flowers grow on each stalk.

Faery Folklore

For centuries, the primrose has been regarded as a magical plant associated with faeries and nature spirits. In Wales and Ireland, it is regarded as a faery plant. Like other faery plants, it was believed to provide protection from them. In Celtic myth, this flower was a symbol of otherworldly beauty. In Ireland, children gathered primroses before dusk on May Eve or before dawn on Beltane to make posies. These were placed on doorsteps and near wells to invite faery blessings. Touching a rock near a ring fort with the right number of primroses in a posy was said to open the way into the faery realm.

Loose flowers were scattered around cowsheds to prevent faeries from helping themselves to the milk; this was reputedly effective for a year. Eating a flower was said to enable a person to see faeries. Like its cousin the cowslip, the primrose was known as the key flower in Germany and it had the power to unlock the door to an enchanted castle or secret place, as well as faery treasure.

Magical Workings

Powers and attributes: Balance/harmony, banish, concentrate/focus, consecrate/bless, dream work, family and home, fertility, growth, healing, knowledge (seek, acquire), loss/sorrow (ease, recover from), love, peace, protection, relationships, see faeries, sex/sexuality, spirituality

Items to purchase when the plant is not available: Flower essence—do not confuse it with evening primrose (*Oenothera biennis*); dried flowers

Planting primroses by your front door will invite the faeries to bless your home. Planting them in the garden will also attract nature spirits to your property. Carrying a primrose flower attracts love. Infuse oil with the flowers to use in a love charm. Prepare a candle with the oil for meditation when recovering from a broken relationship. Hang a sachet of dried flowers and leaves by your bed to enhance and deepen dream work. To banish anything unwanted from your life, burn a couple of dried leaves, and then toss the dried ashes to the wind.

Quince

Japanese Flowering Quince (Chaenomeles japonica syn. *Cydonia japonica, Pyrus japonica)*
Folk name: Fairies' fire

This low-growing shrub has a dense tangle of branches. Its bright, orange-red flowers have five overlapping petals and appear in late winter on thorny branches before the leaves emerge. The flowers bloom in profusion for a few weeks. The oval, dark green leaves are coarsely serrated. The fragrant, greenish-yellow fruit is only about two inches in diameter. Like other types of quince, it is edible, but bitter when eaten raw.

Faery Folklore

While I have not found this plant in my folklore sources, it likely exists somewhere, as it is mentioned in two nineteenth-century poems, both of which are entitled *Fairies' Fire*. Louisa Anne Twamley wrote the earliest one in 1836; Lide Meriwether picked up the theme in 1883.[76] The gist of the poems is that the brilliant, fire-colored flowers that stand in stark contrast to the winter landscape must involve some type of faery magic. Appearing in late winter, the blossoms reputedly melted away the snow and put out a call to every type of elf and faery to come dance around the bush.

Magical Workings

Powers and attributes: Balance/harmony, fertility, growth, love, luck, negativity (remove, ward off), peace, prosperity/money, protection, renewal

Items to purchase when the plant is not available: Flower essence; jam and jelly; seeds

To attract faeries and nature spirits into your home, cut a branch in late winter when the buds appear and put it in water to bloom indoors. As part of a handfasting ceremony, exchange gifts of quince to symbolize love and harmony in the marriage. Also place them in the bedroom on the first night of marriage. To boost fertility spells, include the fruit or leaves in your magic work. Carry several dried seeds in a pouch for protective energy. To remove any form of negativity from your life, burn a small twig or several dried leaves. Create a peaceful atmosphere among family members by placing a picture of this tree in an area of your home that everyone uses.

---

76. Twamley, *The Romance of Nature*, 18; French and Meriwether, *One or Two?*, 163.

Ragwort

Common Ragwort, Tansy Ragwort (Senecio jacobaea syn. *Jacobaea vulgaris)*
Folk name: Fairy horse

Growing three to five feet tall, ragwort has deeply lobed leaves with uneven edges that range from light to dark green. The leaves have an unpleasant odor when crushed. The main flower stem is red at the base and branches at the top with a spray of flowers. The daisy-like flowers are yellow and grow in clusters. Ragwort's seeds have downy, white hairs that carry them on the wind. Do not confuse this plant with tansy (*Tanacetum vulgare*) or the hay fever inducer ragweed (*Ambrosia artemisiifolia*).

Caution: All parts of the plant are toxic when ingested.

Faery Folklore

In Ireland, ragwort is a plant dedicated to the faeries. With a magic word, the fae were said to turn ragwort into golden horses so they could gallop to their midnight revels. Samhain was a favorite time to ride. In the Hebrides of Scotland, ragwort was considered sacred to the fae, who used it to ride between the islands.

According to other legends, ragwort and St. John's wort are daytime disguises for fairy horses. Stepping on one of these plants after sunset reputedly causes the horse to rear up and gallop off with the unsuspecting human on its back. At dawn they will be left far from home with a sprig of ragwort in their hands. Faeries were believed to take shelter from the rain under ragwort, especially on stormy nights.

Magical Workings

Powers and attributes: Courage, divination, hexes (break, protect from), negativity (remove, ward off), prosperity/money, protection

Items to purchase when the plant is not available: Flower essence

As part of a spell to attract wealth and prosperity, place dried flowers in a sachet and keep it with your financial papers. For divination, place several sprigs of flowers and leaves on your altar to boost the energy. Cut long stems of flowers and position them wherever you need to dispel negativity. Counteract any spells sent your way by dabbing a little ragwort flower essence on an amulet. When working with the fae, visualize swaying stems of ragwort as golden horses preparing to carry you to faeryland.

Red Campion

Red Campion (Silene dioica syn. Lychnis dioica, Melandrium rubrum)
Folk names: Bachelor's buttons, fairies' pinks, Robin

Growing between two and three feet tall, the upper part of the branching stem is dark, reddish brown. While the leaves on the lower part of the plant have long stalks, the upper leaves have none. The flowers are a distinctive pinkish-red color and have five, deeply notched petals. The flowers have a long, tubular base surrounded by a protective, purple-brown sheath. The fuzzy, barrel-shaped seed capsules are open at the top to disperse the round, black seeds.

Faery Folklore

On the Isle of Man, it was thought unwise to pick red campion because it was a faery plant. This may be due to legends about faeries storing their honey in the flowers. It was also considered a faery flower in England and associated with Robin Goodfellow, a British nature spirit. He became known as Puck in medieval England and by Elizabethan times he was regarded more as a mischievous brownie or hobgoblin.

Magical Workings

Powers and attributes: Attraction, challenges/obstacles (overcome), clarity (enhance, foster), concentration/focus, courage, creativity, determination/ endurance, healing, inspiration, knowledge (seek, acquire), love, manifest (desires, dreams, will), protection, support (provide, receive), wisdom

Items to purchase when the plant is not available: Flower essence; seedpods; seeds

When working to overcome any type of problem, write a keyword or two on a picture of red campion flowers and hold it between your hands as you visualize a resolution to the problem. Keep the picture in a dresser drawer until the situation has been remedied.

To stoke ideas for a creative project, place a small jar of seeds on your desk or in your work area. When seeking wisdom and clarity in your life, prepare a candle with the flower essence to use during meditation. Hang dried seedpods in your home for protective energy, or carry one with you for support in difficult endeavors.

Reed, Rush, and Cattail
Common Cattail, Great Reed Mace (Typha latifolia)
Common Reed (Phragmites australis syn. Phragmites communis)
Common Rush, Bog Rush, Mat Rush (Juncus effuses)
Folk names: Fairy pipe (reed), fairy woman's spindle (cattail)

The common rush is a grass that reaches two to four feet tall and grows in dense, V-shaped clumps. In summer, tiny florets form on the sides of the round stems and develop into brown seed capsules. Cattail usually grows four to eight feet tall and has flat, blade-like leaves. Its brown, cylindrical flower spikes stay on the plant until autumn before breaking up into downy white fluff. Common reed has long, bluish-green leaves that are flat and blade-like. Plume-like flowers with tufts of silky hair grow on little spikelets. After the leaves break away in autumn, a bare stem is left standing through the winter.

Faery Folklore

Faeries were said to turn rushes into beautiful horses with a magical word and ride them to gatherings. In Welsh legend, faeries liked to dance across the tops of rushes. In Scotland, when the gray fairy horse known as the *kelpie* took human form, it could be identified by the pieces of rush or reed tangled in its hair if it came from fresh water. (Ocean kelpies had seaweed in their hair.) Green rushes were reputedly used to make faery kilts and hats. They were also used to break a faery spell on milk. For protection in Ireland, a green rush was thrown in the direction of a fairy wind when it passed by. The faeries used the hollow stems of reeds for whistles. In Ireland, cattail is regarded as a faery plant.

Magical Workings

Powers and attributes: Abundance, ancestors, awareness (expand, heighten), balance/harmony, concentration/focus, determination/endurance, family and home, growth, healing, inspiration, loyalty/fidelity, prophecy, protection, security, sex/sexuality, spirit guides/spirits, spirituality, support (provide, receive)

Items to purchase when the plants are not available: Dried cattails; rush mats. Check carefully if you buy reed baskets, as they are often made from other types of plants.

Braid a short length of green rush stems to place on your altar for the fae. To aid in connecting with your ancestors, place a couple of long stalks of rush or cattail beside your altar on Samhain. Burn a piece of reed to honor any household spirit, as well as to bring unity and loyalty to your family. Use any of these plants for meditation when seeking personal growth or to foster healing energy.

Pull a cattail flower spike apart to make a protective amulet to wear during journeys to other realms. It will also help to increase awareness of your surroundings. Hang a stalk of one of these plants above your altar to strengthen concentration and focus and to boost the energy of magic work. To enhance passion and sex, especially if there are issues in a relationship, place several long stalks of cattail in a vase in your bedroom.

Rose

Dog Rose (Rosa canina)
Sweet Briar Rose, Briar Rose (R. rubiginosa syn. R. eglanteria)
Folk names: Beach rose (dog rose), wild briar (dog rose)

Unlike the commercial florist roses, these have simple flowers with five petals. The flowers of the dog rose are white to pale pink; the sweet briar flowers are pink with white centers. Sweet briar's leaves have an apple-like scent. Both plants are thicket-forming shrubs. Their arching stems are studded with thorns that help them cling onto and climb up anything nearby.

Faery Folklore
Enamored with roses in general, faeries are said to enjoy cavorting in dog rose thickets. The rose hip from a dog rosebush is known as a pixy pear. In Scandinavia and Germany, roses were believed to be under the protection of elves and dwarves. During the Middle Ages, a dried rose hip was carried as a charm against certain diseases and for protection against enchantment or sorcery. A brush-like tangle of branches on a rosebush was known as elf rod.

Magical Workings
Powers and attributes: Attraction, balance/harmony, banish, bind, challenges/obstacles (overcome), clarity (enhance, foster), communication, consecrate/bless, courage, divination, dream work, emotions (deal with, support), family and home, happiness, healing, hexes (break, protect from), love, loyalty/fidelity, luck, manifest (desires, dreams, will), peace, prophecy, protection, psychic abilities, relationships, secrets, sex/sexuality, spirit guides/spirits, spirituality, strength, trust, wisdom

Items to purchase when the plant is not available: Rose hip tea; rose hip seed oil; rose water; flower essence is made from the dog rose and usually marketed as wild rose

Plant one of these roses to invite faeries and nature spirits into your garden. To help ground and center your energy before a divination session, hold a rose leaf or flower petal between your hands. Also do this before bed to encourage prophetic dreams. Alternatively, drink a cup of rose hip tea. Sprinkle rose water around your home to foster peace and aid in dealing with family issues.

Rose is also instrumental in turning your dreams into reality. Use rose hip seed oil or rose water to consecrate amulets and charms and to prepare candles for spellwork.

Place a rose on your altar when engaging in clairvoyance, communicating with spirits, and psychic work in general to enhance your experience. Use dried and crumbled rose hips to break hexes and in spells to banish unwanted things from your life. Carry a dried rose hip to attract luck. With a heavy-duty needle and darning thread, string rose hips together to make a circlet. Make it large enough to place things within it on your altar for magic and ritual. Make a smaller circlet to wear as a bracelet when engaging in divination or psychic work. Use three thorns or make a small circle with a rose cane to use in protection spells.

Rosemary
Rosemary (Rosmarinus officinalis)
Folk name: Elf leaf

Rosemary is a shrubby, evergreen herb that can grow as tall as six feet. It has short, stiff, needle-like leaves that grow along the stems that become woody as they mature. Its tubular flowers are pale blue and grow in small clusters of two or three.

Faery Folklore
In Mediterranean countries and throughout Europe, rosemary was regarded as a faery plant. Favored by the fae in Sicily, the flowers were reputedly used as cradles for baby faeries; youngsters reputedly slept under the plant disguised as snakes. In Portugal, rosemary was dedicated to the fae and called *Alecrim*, which was derived from *Ellegrim*, a word of Scandinavian origin meaning "elfin plant."[77] In the Netherlands, rosemary was believed to mark a place where elves gathered. The Flemish name for rosemary is *Elfenblad*, "elf leaf."[78]

---

77. Folkard, *Plant Lore, Legends & Lyrics*, 526.
78. De Cleene and Lejeune, *Compendium of Symbolic and Ritual Plants in Europe: Herbs*, 651.

Magical Workings

Powers and attributes: Attraction, awareness (expand, heighten), banish, bind, clarity (enhance, foster), communication, concentration/focus, consecrate/bless, courage, creativity, defense, determination/endurance, dream work, emotions (deal with, support), healing, hexes (break, protect from), inspiration, intuition, knowledge (seek, acquire), love, loyalty/fidelity, negativity (remove, ward off), nightmares, protection, psychic abilities, purification, relationships, release (let go, move on), renewal, spirit guides/spirits, wisdom

Items to purchase when the plant is not available: Flower essence; essential oil; dried leaves; dried sprigs; infused oil

Rosemary can be counted on to attract nature spirits and faeries to your garden. As an alternative to growing it, sprinkle a few leaves around your outdoor area or under the doormat if you live in an apartment. Rosemary is helpful for remembering dreams; hang a sachet of dried flowers from the headboard of your bed. Its cleansing properties make it useful for clearing negativity before ritual, magic, or healing work. Also use it to consecrate charms and amulets.

Because it reduces the intensity of strong emotions, rosemary is helpful in balancing relationships and engendering fidelity between lovers. Also use it in binding spells or to banish what you no longer need in your life. Rosemary is instrumental in defensive magic to remove and protect against hexes. This plant provides focus and clarity for all forms of communication, as well as inspiration for creative pursuits.

Rowan
American Mountain Ash (Sorbus americana)
European Mountain Ash, Common Mountain Ash (S. aucuparia)
Folk names: Quickbeam (European), roan tree (European), sorb apple (European)

These elegant trees have lance-shaped leaflets and dense, flattened clusters of white flowers. Their orange-red berries grow in large clusters and ripen in late summer. The American tree has dark green leaves that turn yellow in the autumn. The leaves of the European tree are light to medium green and turn yellow to reddish purple.

Caution: Rowanberries are only safe to eat when cooked.

Faery Folklore

According to some legends, this tree originated in the faery realm and the berries served as food for the Tuatha Dé Danann. Other legends note that faeries have an aversion to rowan and planting one near a house or barn deters them. A Scottish story tells of a man who was able to enter a faery fort and take a drinking horn because he carried a stick of rowan. Also in Scotland, a changeling was dealt with by burning rowan. The suspect infant would be held in the smoke and if it were a substitute, the changeling would disappear up the chimney. The real infant would be returned shortly afterward.

Although a person is said to be invisible when stuck dancing in a faery ring, it was believed that they could be pulled back to the human realm after a year and a day using a rowan stick. A rowan branch hung in the home enabled people to see a fairy rade (procession).

In County Limerick, Ireland, this tree is noted to be home to good faeries. A sprig of rowan was often worn on a hat to keep bad faeries away. Faeries were reputedly kind to children who carried rowanberries in their pockets. In Ireland, a solitary rowan is regarded as a lone bush and fairy bush. (See the profile for Lone Bush.) If rowan grows on your property you will be blessed by faeries and guarded against bad luck.

Magical Workings

Powers and attributes: Authority/leadership, balance/harmony, bind, challenges/obstacles (overcome), consecrate/bless, creativity, defense, divination, family and home, fertility, healing, hexes (break, protect from), inspiration, knowledge (seek, acquire), luck, peace, prophecy, protection, psychic abilities, secrets, security, see faeries, skills, spirit guides/spirits, strength, success, wisdom

Items to purchase when the tree is not available: Dried berries; flower essence is made from the European mountain ash

If you have a rowan tree on your property, leave gifts and food for faeries underneath it. Rowan is a powerful ally for divination and when working with spirits. Hold a rowan branch to connect with your spirit guides, especially when seeking their advice. Also do this when seeking help from faeries and nature spirits. Burn a small piece of bark or twig to enhance psychic abilities. Place a cluster of berries on your altar to boost the energy of autumn rituals or in spells to remove hexes. Draw the faery star on four leaflets and place them in the cardinal directions on your property to invite harmony and peace to your home. To raise energy for healing rituals, include a picture of the tree on your altar. To attract success, carry a dried rowanberry as an amulet.

Rue

Common Rue, Wild Rue (Ruta graveolens)
Folk names: Herb of grace, herbgrass

Rue is a shrubby plant that reaches between two to three feet tall and wide. Its oblong leaflets are bluish green. They give off a pungent odor when bruised. The flowers are dull yellow or greenish yellow and grow in small clusters. They have four to five stemmed petals.

Caution: May cause dermatitis and photosensitize the skin; it is unsafe to burn the plant.

Faery Folklore

As mentioned in chapter 3, this plant is potent against faeries and genies when you need to end a relationship and keep them away. In Italy, a sprig of rue was called *cimaruta*, from *cima di ruta*, meaning "a piece of rue."[79] The sprig was worn as a protective amulet against faeries, witches, and anything deemed dangerous. According to lore in the Middle East, rue was used to ward off abduction by jinn or to escape from them. On the island of Jersey and throughout the British Isles, rue was believed to foster second sight and the ability to see faeries.

Magical Workings

Powers and attributes: Banish, clarity (enhance, foster), consecrate/bless, defense, divination, emotions (deal with, support), healing, hexes (break, protect from), inspiration, love, luck, negativity (remove, ward off), nightmares, protection, purification, relationships, release (let go, move on), see faeries, spirit guides/spirits, wisdom

---

79. Watts, *Elsevier's Dictionary of Plant Lore*, 74.

Items to purchase when the plant is not available: Cut, dried stems and leaves are marketed as rue herb

Rue is a plant of opposites that can be used to help and bless or to harm and curse. Other than severing ties with a faery, this is a plant to avoid growing or using if you want to work with the fae and nature spirits.

St. John's Wort
St. John's Wort (Hypericum perforatum)
Folk names: Penny-John, rosin rose

St. John's wort is a shrubby plant that reaches two to three feet in height. Its oblong leaves are pale green. Its star-shaped flowers are bright yellow and grow in clusters at the ends of the branches. The flowers have a light, lemon-like scent. The flowers and buds ooze a red liquid when they are squeezed or bruised.

Faery Folklore
According to legend, faeries held a great feast on Midsummer's Eve during which they danced around St. John's wort plants and splashed them with cowslip wine. Although it was believed to be a plant protected by faeries, it was also used as a charm against them. In Scotland, a piece of St. John's wort was carried as a charm; however, it was regarded as effective only if the plant had

been found accidentally. On the Hebrides Islands, it was carried to ward off enchantment and second sight. However, to gain second sight, the juice of St. John's wort, dill, and vervain were combined in an ointment and applied to the eyelids for three days.

Because of faery activity on Midsummer's Eve, bundles of Saint John's wort and rowan were tied together with ribbons and tossed onto the bonfire to raise protective energy. Like ragwort, St. John's wort is reputedly a daytime disguise for fairy horses. If the plant is stepped on after sunset, the horse will rear up from the roots and gallop off. At dawn the unsuspecting person will be left far from home.

Magical Workings

Powers and attributes: Abundance, banish, consecrate/bless, courage, defense, divination, dream work, fertility, happiness, healing, justice/legal matters, love, luck, negativity (remove, ward off), nightmares, peace, prosperity/money, protection, psychic abilities, purification, release (let go, move on), renewal, security, see faeries, spirit guides/spirits, spirituality, strength

Items to purchase when the plant is not available: Essential oil; flower essence; infused oil; extract; cut, dried leaves; powdered leaves; dried flowers; seeds

Grow St. John's wort near your front door or hang a sprig over it to repel negativity and to invite abundance into your home. Of course, it will also be an invitation for faeries. Burn a few dried leaves in a fireplace or cauldron and let its pungent smoke purify your house and ritual area. Also burn a few leaves to clear away any type of negativity. To counteract nightmares, sprinkle a little essential oil on your pillow and bed sheets. Infuse oil with the flowers (it will turn red), and then use it in love charms and in spells to aid fertility. When dealing with legal matters, draw the faery star on a piece of paper, sprinkle it with a little essential oil or infused oil, and keep it with you.

Scarlet Elf Cup

Scarlet Elf Cup, Scarlet Elf Cap (Sarcoscypha coccinea syn. *Peziza coccinea)*
Scarlet Elf Cup, Scarlet Cup (S. austriaca syn. *P. austriaca)*
Folk names: Elf cup, fairy bath, fairy goblet, fairy purse, ruby elf cup

These two species have the same common name and are superficially identical; it takes an expert to tell them apart. Usually a little over an inch tall, these fungi are shaped like a cup with rolled-in rims. The outer surface has a downy texture. The interior of the cup is brilliant red and contrasts with the lighter exterior. Scarlet elf cup can be found on damp mossy branches, buried under leaf litter, or in the soil.

Caution: Although not poisonous, sources vary as to whether these fungi are edible. As with any type of fungus, never eat it unless identified by a qualified expert.

Faery Folklore

Legends throughout Europe note that wood elves used these fungi as cups to drink the morning dew. Because scarlet elf cup resembles old-fashioned purses, it was reputedly used as such by faeries.

Magical Workings

Powers and attributes: Balance/harmony, banish, healing, hexes (break, protect from), luck, negativity (remove, ward off), peace, prosperity/ money, spirit guides/spirits, support (provide, receive)

Items to purchase when the plant is not available: There are no products from this plant.

If you find a scarlet elf cup while walking in the woods, pour a little water into it as an offering to faeries and nature spirits. Food or other small gifts can be placed beside the cups. Gather a few to take home to place on your indoor altar or put them outdoors in your faery garden.

Dry an elf cup by allowing it to sit for about a week, out of sunlight, where air can freely circulate around it. Use it for dealing with an unwanted spirit by crumbling it into a small bowl as you say:

The power of this plant should bring fear
To any spirit not welcomed here.

You cannot stay, leave you must,
As this elf cup I crumble to dust.

Continue by taking the bowl outside and burying the pieces of elf cup in the ground.

Seaweed
Knotted Wrack, Bottle Kelp (Ascophyllum nodosum)
Slender Wart Weed (Gracilaria gracilis)
Folk names: Fairy bottle (knotted wrack), fairy laces (slender wart weed)

While these are but two of many species of seaweed, they fit the folklore more closely than others. Knotted wrack is a common type of brown seaweed with long, strap-like fronds. It has large, egg-shaped air bladders that make a popping sound when squeezed open. With fronds that can grow up to six feet long, it attaches to shoreline rocks or just floats around in the surf. Resembling shoestrings, slender wart weed has cylindrical fronds that are purplish red. The fronds are usually less than twenty inches long. They attach to rocks in clumps.

Faery Folklore
In Ireland, seaweed was associated with faeries. According to legends in Scotland, the gray fairy horse known as a kelpie was covered with seaweed. When it came ashore and manifested into human form, it usually had seaweed tangled in its hair. (Freshwater kelpies had pieces of reeds or rushes in their hair.) Another type of faerie being known as *korrigans* in Brittany, France and Cornwall, England, reputedly danced on the sand dunes and sailed in boats constructed of seaweed.

While on the topic of the ocean, the terms *fairy fleet* and *fairy light* were names given to the phosphorescent effects of bioluminescent plankton that create eerie, blue lights like small neon dots in the waves.

Magical Workings
Powers and attributes: Awareness (expand, heighten), balance/harmony, banish, fertility, negativity (remove, ward off), peace, prosperity/money, protection, psychic abilities, skills, spirit guides/spirits, truth

Items to purchase when the plant is not available: Many varieties of dried and fresh seaweed can be found in stores and online.

Inhabiting the magical in-between place of shoreline and ocean, seaweed is especially powerful for working with faeries. If you live near the ocean, collect loose seaweed from the beach to place in your garden for the fae. Your plants will thank you, too. As part of a money spell, wrap a long strand of seaweed around a dollar bill as you think of drawing prosperity into your life.

Foster a sense of peace and harmony by visualizing long strands of seaweed attached to the ocean floor and gently swaying in the currents. To aid in developing psychic skills, crumble a handful of dried seaweed and sprinkle it in a ring on your altar or wherever you are working.

Sesame

Sesame (Sesamum indicum)
Folk name: Benne

The sesame plant reaches between two and nine feet tall. Flowers grow individually or in clusters of three at the base of the leaves, which are oval and veined. The flowers have a tubular shape and are usually pinkish purple, but they can be white or light pink, too. The lower lip of the flower has a middle lobe that is longer than the others and often marked with a deep purple or reddish blotch at the tip. Long, narrow seedpods hold fifty to one hundred seeds and form inside the flowers as they fade. The seeds range from white to black and have a flattened, pear shape.

Faery Folklore
Sesame is forever linked with the story of Ali Baba and his magical phrase "open sesame." According to folklore in the Hindu Kush region of northern Pakistan, sesame was cultivated by the mountain faeries that were known by their Persian and Sanskrit names of *peri* and *apsaras*, respectively.

Magical Workings
Powers and attributes: Balance/harmony, banish, changes/transitions, consecrate/bless, defense, fertility, healing, justice/legal matters, negativity

(remove, ward off), prosperity/money, protection, purification, release (let go, move on), renewal, secrets, sex/sexuality, spirit guides/spirits, truth

Items to purchase when the plant is not available: Seeds; oil made from the seeds; tahini or sesame paste; sesame seed milk

When you need to surround yourself with defensive energy, carry a pouch with a pinch of seeds. Also carry a pouch with seeds when going to court or meeting with your lawyer. Sesame's powers of purification can be used to consecrate magic space, to remove negative energy, or to release a lover by burning a few seeds and wafting the scent where you need it. To cast out a negative spirit, prepare a candle with sesame seed oil for a banishing ritual. If you have difficulty keeping a secret, eat a spoonful of tahini each time you think of telling it to someone. Leave a little sesame seed milk on your altar for faeries to enjoy.

Silverweed

Common Silverweed, Silverweed Cinquefoil (Potentilla anserina syn. *Argentina anserina)*
Folk names: Goose grass, silver fern

Silverweed grows to about twelve inches tall and has spreading, strawberry-like runners. Its leaflets grow in rows along the stem and have a silvery appearance. The flowers are bright yellow and have five petals. The flowers and leaves grow on separate stalks. Silverweed was cultivated and its roots used extensively for food in Ireland before the potato was introduced.

Faery Folklore
In Ireland, silverweed roots were made into loafs, which served as food for humans and faeries. After the spring plowing, farmers left some of the roots in the fields for the fae.

Magical Workings
Powers and attributes: Authority/leadership, balance/harmony, challenges/
  obstacles (overcome), communication, consecrate/bless, defense, divination,
  dream work, emotions (deal with, support), healing, hexes (break, protect from), inspiration, justice/legal matters, love, luck, manifest (desires,

dreams, will), nightmares, prosperity/money, protection, spirit guides/spirits, strength, success, wisdom

Items to purchase when the plant is not available: Flower essence; cut, dried leaves and flowers are marketed as silverweed herb; seeds

If you grow silverweed in your garden, place a few roots on your outdoor altar or sprinkle some of the dried herb on a plate for the faeries. For emotional support, burn a candle after consecrating it with the flower essence or infused oil that you prepared. For inspiration of any kind, place dried leaves and flowers in a decorative jar and keep it in your workspace or on your meditation altar.

To help strengthen communication skills, draw the faery star on a picture of a silverweed flower and keep it underneath your computer keyboard. For protection, hang a sprig of leaves over your front door or place them under the doormat. Place a couple of dried flowers and a sprig of leaves in a sachet to hang on your bedpost to soothe or ward off nightmares.

Also see the profile for Cinquefoil.

Snowdrop
Common Snowdrop (Galanthus nivalis)
Folk names: Fair maids, white bells, white queen

One of the earliest flowers to peek out of the barren landscape in early spring, the snowdrop's drooping, white blossoms often come up through a blanket of snow. The snowdrop has narrow, grass-like leaves surrounding the flower stems. The pendulous flowers are white with three inner and three outer petals. The inner petals have a touch of green at the tips. Like many popular garden plants, the snowdrop has a number of species and hybrids.

Faery Folklore
It is easy to see why snowdrop has become associated with faeries, as a cluster of opened blossoms can resemble tiny fae dancing across the snow.

Magical Workings
Powers and attributes: Adaptability, challenges/obstacles (overcome), changes/transitions, courage, determination/endurance, family and home,

happiness, loss/sorrow (ease, recover from), negativity (remove, ward off), purification, release (let go, move on), trust, wishes

Items to purchase when the plant is not available: Flower essence; dried flowers; bulbs

When you see the first snowdrop of the season, make a wish, but do not pick it; otherwise your wish won't come true. If you grow these flowers in your garden, place an offering among them to let faeries and nature spirits know that you want to make contact with them. Burn dried leaves in spells and rituals to build resolve when you are faced with difficult issues. Also burn a leaf or two for support when you need to persevere in a situation. To bolster bravery and dispel fear, carry a sachet of dried flowers with you or dab a little flower essence behind your ears.

Sorrel
Wood Sorrel, Common Wood Sorrel (Oxalis acetosella)
Sheep Sorrel, Red Sorrel (Rumex acetosella)
Folk names: Evening twilight (wood sorrel), fairy bells (wood sorrel),
fairy money (sheep sorrel), shamrock (wood sorrel)

While these two plants are not related, they share a species and common name that means "sour."[80] Only two to four inches tall, wood sorrel creates a soft carpet of color. Its white, five-petaled flowers sometimes have a blush of pink and are lightly veined with purple or lilac. While the flowers are shaped more like a cup, their drooping posture as they close at night resembles bells. The three heart-shaped leaflets fold up at night and when it rains. After blooming, wood sorrel produces a second type of flower that is bud-like and stays hidden under the leaves.

Red sorrel has a rosette of base leaves and arrow-shaped leaves on the lower stems. Reaching up to two feet tall, the flower stalks have reddish ridges. This sorrel produces two types of flowers: red (female) and yellowish green (male). It has three-sided, red seeds.

---

80. Eastman, *Wildflowers of the Eastern United States*, 135.

Faery Folklore

A large patch of wood sorrel in a forest reputedly indicates a special place for nature spirits, faeries, and elves. According to Welsh legend, the flowers were rung like bells at midnight to call faeries to dance. A wood sorrel leaf placed in a shoe was said to enable the wearer to see faeries. Wood sorrel was also used to deter mischievous elves.

Magical Workings

Powers and attributes: Defense, happiness, healing, luck, peace, prosperity/money, protection, secrets, see faeries

Items to purchase when the plant is not available: Wood sorrel flower essence; cut, dried leaves are marketed as sheep sorrel herb tea; sheep sorrel seeds

If you find a spot in the woods where wood sorrel is growing, spend time in meditation to reach out to nature spirits and faeries. You may find the energy especially strong and contact easy to establish. Place wood sorrel leaves on your altar when honoring triple goddesses. Carry a leaf with you for luck. Use sheep sorrel seeds in prosperity spells by making a circle with them around the base of a green candle upon which you have carved the faery star. Dry a handful of leaves from either type of sorrel, and then crumble and sprinkle them around the perimeter of your property to raise defensive energy.

Southernwood

Southernwood (Artemisia abrotanum)
Folk names: Lad's love, muggons, sweet Benjamin

Strongly aromatic, southernwood is a close cousin to mugwort. It grows in an erect, bushy mound that can measure up to four feet tall and three feet wide. The plant releases a pleasant, woodsy-citrus fragrance whenever it is brushed against or touched. The fern-like, gray-green leaves retain fragrance after drying and give off scent when burned. Although it rarely flowers, when it does, the flowers look like small, yellow buttons that fade to brownish cream.

Faery Folklore

According to legend, southernwood could cure any type of faery-inflicted illness that occurred after participating in their revels or eating their food. This plant was also used for protection against spells.

Magical Workings

Powers and attributes: Attraction, challenges/obstacles (overcome), divination, fertility, healing, hexes (break, protect from), love, loyalty/fidelity, luck, negativity (remove, ward off), protection, purification, renewal, sex/sexuality, strength

Items to purchase when the plant is not available: Cut, dried leaves and stems are marketed as southernwood herb

Because of its fragrance and light, airy appearance, southernwood is a delightful plant for attracting faeries and nature spirits to the garden. Place a few sprigs on your indoor altar when working with them. To scent ritual clothes, hang a sachet of dried leaves in the closet. Also place a sprig with your magic tools and other gear to aid in purifying them. As part of a ceremony to renew marriage vows, wrap a long stem around your wrists as you join hands. Tuck a few sprigs under the mattress to boost pleasure in the bedroom.

For luck, place a pinch of dried leaves in a pouch to keep with you, especially when dealing with any type of problem in your life. Burn a few dried leaves before a divination session to clear the energy and enhance your skills. Place a picture of southernwood or a few leaves anywhere in the home to dispel negativity or to get energy moving.

Stitchwort

Greater Stitchwort (Stellaria holostea syn. *Rabelera holostea)*
Lesser Stitchwort, Common Stitchwort (S. graminea syn. *Alsine graminea)*
Folk names: Piskie flower (lesser stitchwort), moon flower,
morning stars, satin flower, star grass, starwort

Both types of stitchwort have grass-like leaves and delicate, white flowers. The flowers have five petals with deep notches that make them appear to be ten petals. Growing to about a foot tall, greater stitchwort can be found in hedgerows and at the edge of woodlands and meadows, favorite faery places. Its flowers are about an inch in diameter. Low-growing lesser stitchwort hides its smaller, half-inch wide flowers among meadow grasses.

Faery Folklore

According to legend, stitchwort was under the protection of faeries because they were fond of the flowers and used them to make garlands. When it was growing in hedgerows, pixies reputedly hid among the flowers and popped their heads out of the foliage for a look around. According to legend, pixies guard the plant so it cannot be used in charms against them. Children were told not to pick the flowers because they would be pixie-led into a thicket or swamp.

Magical Workings

Powers and attributes: Adaptability, clarity (enhance, foster), creativity, determination/endurance, emotions (deal with, support), healing, peace, renewal, strength, support (provide, receive)

Items to purchase when the plant is not available: Flower essence is made from lesser stitchwort

Since it is associated with sight, you can use stitchwort to aid in bringing clarity to your endeavors. Place a few flowers or a picture on your altar as you meditate about the situation for which you seek help. When in need of healing, hold several flowers or a picture between your hands as you visualize white light from the flower surrounding the afflicted area of your body. Take the picture with you when you visit your doctor or other health-care provider for support.

Because of its color and the folk name *moon flower*, stitchwort can be included in esbat rituals. Carefully tie long stems with flowers into a garland for your faery altar or to wear as a coronel when contacting nature spirits.

Strawberry
Cultivated Strawberry (Fragaria x ananassa)
Wild Strawberry (F. vesca)

The strawberry plant has short, woody stems and a base rosette of leaves from which rooting runners grow horizontally and form new plants. The leaves consist of three toothed leaflets. The white, five-petaled flowers grow on separate stems. Growing six inches tall, the garden strawberry is a cultivated hybrid of several wild species. The wild strawberry looks like a smaller version of the garden plant. It can be found on moist ground in fields, meadows, and along the edge of woods.

Faery Folklore
In Germany, it was well known that elves were fond of strawberries, and they were believed to protect the plants. The Bavarians tied small baskets filled with strawberries between the horns of their cows so the elves would bless them with abundant milk. According to other legends, it was important to be mindful when walking among wild strawberries on a warm, sunny day because brownies reputedly hid under the leaves to keep cool.

Magical Workings
Powers and attributes: Abundance, adaptability, attraction, balance/harmony, divination, happiness, love, luck, manifest (desires, dreams, will), peace, relationships, sex/sexuality

Items to purchase when the plant is not available: Fresh, dried, or frozen fruit; flower essence; cut, dried leaves; jam and preserve; wine

Leave a small bowl of strawberries in milk as a treat for the faeries and nature spirits in your garden. For a good luck spell, write what you desire on a piece of paper and sprinkle crumbled, dried strawberry leaves on it. Fold up the paper and hold it between your hands as you visualize what you want. When an image is clear, burn the paper and leaves in your cauldron or other safe place. When cool, sprinkle the ashes outside.

To stimulate love interest, write your intended's name on a red candle. Place it on your altar along with several strawberries. Light the candle and slowly eat the fruit. Close your eyes and visualize making love with that person.

Sweet Woodruff

Sweet Woodruff (Galium odoratum syn. *Asperula odorata)*
Folk name: Sweet-scented bedstraw

Sweet woodruff grows in clumps with stems eight to fifteen inches tall. Whorls of six to eight leaves grow around the stems. Growing in small clusters, its dainty, white flowers are funnel-shaped with petals that splay open at the ends. While the flowers seem to have little or no fragrance, they develop a strong, sweet, hay-like scent after they are dried. The scent can linger for several years. The dried leaves smell sweet, like new-mown hay or vanilla.

Faery Folklore
Sweet woodruff is associated with faeries.

Magical Workings
Powers and attributes: Adaptability, balance/harmony, changes/transitions, clarity (enhance, foster), communication, consecrate/bless, divination, dream work, healing, negativity (remove, ward off), peace, prophecy, prosperity/money, protection, purification, relationships, skills, success
Items to purchase when the plant is not available: Cut, dried leaves; seeds

Because the fragrance of sweet woodruff is stronger when dried or crushed, use it as a strewing herb on a porch, patio, or outdoor ritual area. This will scent the air and dispel negative energy. Also infuse the leaves and flowers in water, and then sprinkle it around the home to purify and bless it. Burning dried leaves or flowers as incense works, too. Drink sweet woodruff tea before bed to foster prophetic dreams, or place a sachet of dried leaves under your pillow. Have a question on your mind before going to sleep, and paper and pen or smart phone handy at your bedside to take notes when you wake up.

Thistle

Scottish Thistle, Cotton Thistle (Onopordum acanthium)
Spear Thistle, Common Thistle (Cirsium vulgare syn. *Carduus lanceolatus)*
Folk name: Pixy gloves

Thistles are spiny plants with stems covered in dense hairs. The base of each leaf has spiny projections that extend downward along the stem. The flower head consists of long, tubular florets surrounded by prickly bracts (modified leaves) that curl outward at the base. Toward the end of the growing season, the flowers are replaced with tufts of white hairs, known as thistledown, that carry the seeds on the wind.

The Scottish thistle can grow up to eight feet tall. Its stem has flat, spiny wings along its length. The silvery green leaves have large, toothed lobes with wavy edges. The flowers are dark pink to violet. The spear thistle grows up to six feet tall. Its lance-shaped leaves have widely spaced lobes that narrow to long, sharp spines. The flowers are purplish pink to purple.

Faery Folklore

In Ireland, thistles are regarded as faery plants. After casting a travel spell, faeries were said to ride home to faeryland on thistledown. Pixies reputedly use thistle spines as swords.

Magical Workings

Powers and attributes: Banish, challenges/obstacles (overcome), clarity (enhance, foster), courage, defense, determination/endurance, healing, hexes (break, protect from), negativity (remove, ward off), nightmares, protection, purification, release (let go, move on), renewal, spirit guides/spirits, strength, trust

Items to purchase when the plant is not available: Flower essence; dried flower heads; seeds

To release something unwanted from your life, such as a fear or anxiety, collect a handful of thistledown. Hold it between your hands as you think about what you want to let go of, and then open your hands and blow the thistledown to the wind. Close your eyes for a moment to feel the freedom.

When working with spirit guides, place a picture of thistles on your altar to strengthen your connection with them. Use the spines in defensive protection spells or to break a hex. Place a flower head at each corner of your bed to ward off bad dreams.

Thyme
Common Thyme, Garden Thyme (Thymus vulgaris)
Wild Thyme, Creeping Thyme (T. serpyllum)
Folk names: Mother-thyme (wild thyme), shepherd's thyme (wild thyme)

Growing up to fifteen inches tall, common thyme has oval, gray-green leaves and small, pink to lilac or bluish-purple flowers that grow in little clusters. Wild thyme is a smaller ground cover plant that only reaches two to four inches tall. The base stem of both plants becomes woody with age.

Faery Folklore

In some parts of England, thyme was said to be a favorite of the faeries, and brushing a sprig of it across the eyes allowed a person to see them. According to some stories, a person needed to lie on a faery mound with a handful of thyme over their eyes; others note that the thyme sprigs needed to be gathered at a certain time of day.

An area where wild thyme grows often indicates a favored stomping ground for the fae. Although according to one legend, faeries did not like it when people took thyme indoors, sprinkling it on the doorstep to your home is an invitation for faeries to enter. The flower tops of thyme were one of the ingredients in a recipe that not only made faeries visible, but also aided in conjuring a certain faery named Elaby Gathon. See the profile on Hollyhock for further details.

Magical Workings

Powers and attributes: Adaptability, authority/leadership, awareness (expand, heighten), consecrate/bless, courage, divination, dream work, family and home, growth, happiness, healing, loss/sorrow (ease, recover from), love, luck, negativity (remove, ward off), nightmares, peace, prosperity/money, protection, psychic abilities, purification, renewal, see faeries, skills, strength

Items to purchase when the plant is not available: Dried leaves; dried flowers; fresh or dried bunches; essential oil and flower essence are made from common thyme

Wear a sprig when making contact with nature spirits and faeries to increase awareness. Sprinkle dried leaves on your altar to stimulate energy for divination and psychic work as well as any type of work involving the faery realm. Thyme is well known for its purification properties, making it ideal for preparing ritual space and consecrating altars. Also use thyme to clear negative energy in general. Use dried leaves in a sachet to increase the effectiveness of spells involving love, luck, and money. Stuff a little dream pillow with thyme leaves and flowers to help remember and interpret your dreams.

Tulip

Common Garden Tulip, Didier's Tulip (Tulipa gesneriana)

This popular tulip is one of about a hundred natural root species from which thousands of cultivars and hybrids have been created. Growing from the base of the plant, the broad, gray-green leaves have a tendency to flop over rather than stand upright. Growing on leafless stems, the large, cup-shaped flowers range from white and many shades of pinks and reds to oranges and yellows.

Faery Folklore

According to legends, faeries lulled their babies to sleep in tulips before going dancing in the meadows. After the revelries, they retrieved the little ones at dawn. Any tulip that seemed to live longer than other flowers in a garden was reputedly a faery baby cradle. Tulips were favored by faeries and elves that were said to cultivate and protect them.

Magical Workings

Powers and attributes: Abundance, attraction, banish, courage, divination, dream work, fertility, happiness, love, loyalty/fidelity, luck, peace, prosperity/money, protection, release (let go, move on), sex/sexuality

Items to purchase when the plant is not available: Flower essence is made from many varieties and sometimes marked by color; dried petals; bulbs

Grow tulips in your garden to attract faeries and nature spirits, or place potted plants outside or inside your home. Carry a bulb as an amulet for luck, or place a vase of flowers in your kitchen to invite abundance into your home. Sprinkle the flower essence on a picture of tulips, and then burn it in your cauldron as part of a banishing ritual. Dispose of the ashes by casting them to the wind.

Meditate with a picture of a white tulip to foster a sense of peace. Associated with love, the color of a tulip can be employed for different purposes: pink can help kindle flirting and romance, red for passion, and white for fertility. Place a few pink or red petals in a sachet under your pillow to dream of romance or of your lover. To enhance passion and sex, place a handful of petals underneath your bed.

Vervain

Vervain, Verbena (Verbena officinalis)
Folk names: Enchanter's weed

Vervain is a sprawling, branching plant that grows between one to three feet tall and wide. The deeply lobed leaves are heavily veined and toothed. Small lavender or pinkish, five-petaled flowers grow on delicate spikes.

Faery Folklore

In Sussex, England, dry leaves were sewn into children's clothing to keep faeries away. For adults, drinking a cup of vervain tea provided protection from faeries and their spells. In Wales, the powdered root was worn in a sachet around the neck as an amulet. Some sources indicate that the plant material had to be tied with a white ribbon or carried in a black silk bag. In other areas, it was carried in the pocket for protection against fairy stroke (enchantment or illness). To gain second sight, the juice of vervain, St. John's wort, and dill were combined in an ointment and applied to the eyelids for three days.

Magical Workings

Powers and attributes: Abundance, balance/harmony, banish, challenges/obstacles (overcome), consecrate/bless, creativity, defense, determination/endurance, divination, dream work, family and home, fertility, healing, hexes (break, protect from), inspiration, justice/legal matters, loyalty/fidelity, luck, manifest (desires, dreams, will), negativity (remove, ward off), nightmares, peace, prophecy, prosperity/money, protection, purification, relationships, release (let go, move on), see faeries, spirit guides/spirits, success, support (provide, receive)

Items to purchase when the plant is not available: Flower essence; essential oil; cut, dried leaves and stems are marketed as vervain herb; extract

For aid in communicating with nature spirits and faeries, hold a small bundle of leaves and flowers. This also aids in seeing them. Use long stems of vervain to sweep your ritual and magic space or in other areas to remove any form of negativity. Place leaves on your altar to bless the space and empower your rituals. To consecrate ritual and divination tools, make an infusion of the leaves and sprinkle a little over your magical gear.

Place a sachet of dried flowers under your pillow to aid in dream work. This will also encourage dreams of prophecy and help banish nightmares. If you believe someone has used negative magic against you, sprinkle a circle of dried leaves on the ground, and sit or stand in the center as you work a spell for defense and protection. Grow vervain or scatter dried leaves on your property to attract abundance.

Vetchling
Bitter Vetch, Bitter Vetchling (Lathyrus linifolius)
Broad Bean, Broad Vetch, Fava Bean (Vicia faba)
Sweet Pea, Wild Pea (Lathyrus odoratus)
Folk names: Bell bean (broad bean), fairies' corn (bitter vetch), heath pea (bitter vetch)

Also known as peavines, vetchlings are slender, bushy or climbing plants in the genus *Lathyrus*. The flowers have two upright petals and two lower petals that form a structure that looks like the keel of a boat. These plants are winged, meaning that they have protrusions along the sides of the stems. Bitter vetch has pairs of pointed leaflets. Growing in clusters of up to six, the veined flowers are pink to red or purple and turn blue as they age. The peapods turn black as they mature. This plant should not be confused with *Vicia ervilia*, which is also known as bitter vetch. Sweet pea has tendrils that allow it to climb. Its oblong leaflets grow in pairs. The highly fragrant flowers grow in clusters. They can be white, pink, purple, blue, violet, red, lavender, or orange. The peapods turn brownish yellow when they mature.

While technically not a vetchling, the broad bean is a related wild legume in the *Vicia* genus. Growing up to six feet tall, the broad bean has a coarse, square stem. The leaves consist of three to seven oval leaflets. The fragrant, pea-like flowers are white to purplish and grow in clusters. Their lower petals have dark brown blotches and the upper petals are streaked. The cylindrical, oblong seedpod contains up to six seeds that range in color from reddish to brown to green.

Caution: All parts of bitter vetch are toxic, especially the seeds; sweet pea seeds are poisonous.

Faery Folklore

According to legend, the small tubers of bitter vetch and the beans of the broad bean served as faery food. The fragrant sweet pea flowers were reputedly favored by faeries.

Magical Workings

Powers and attributes: Attraction, balance/harmony, courage, creativity, emotions (deal with, support), family and home, happiness, love, loyalty/fidelity, negativity (remove, ward off), peace, psychic abilities, relationships, skills, spirituality, strength, truth, wisdom

Items to purchase when the plant is not available: Flower essences are made from bitter vetch and sweet pea and marketed as sweet pea; they are sometimes marketed according to flower color; flower essence is also made from the broad bean; fresh or dried broad beans; sweet pea seeds

When dealing with emotional upheaval, place a circle of vetchling flowers or a picture of them on your altar, and then visualize your energy connecting with the earth star to keep you centered. After moving into a new home, place pictures or sweet pea seeds in various locations around the house to foster a sense of belonging. When developing new skills, especially psychic ones, place a picture of one of these plants where you will see it as you practice. When seeking the truth in a situation, hold a couple of flowers in your upturned palms as you meditate. Sweet peas are a lovely addition to any garden, which will please the fae. They can be grown in a flowerpot.

Violet

Common Blue Violet, Meadow Violet (Viola sororia)
Sweet Violet, English Violet (V. odorata)

Cousins to pansies, violets form clumps that can be four inches tall and six inches wide. Their leaves and flowers grow on separate stems directly from the rhizome (root). The flowers consist of five rounded petals: two upper, two out to the sides, and one lower petal. Violet leaves are wide, oval to heart-shaped, and gently serrated. The flowers of the common blue violet are bluish violet or white with purple veining. Adored for their fragrance, the flowers of the sweet violet are dark purple but occasionally white.

Faery Folklore

According to legend, faeries used violets for various types of spells including ones to protect themselves. Like many plants used by the fae, violets were also used for protection against them.

Magical Workings

Powers and attributes: Banish, changes/transitions, communication, divination, dream work, emotions (deal with, support), family and home, fertility, happiness, healing, hexes (break, protect from), justice/legal matters, love, loyalty/fidelity, luck, manifest (desires, dreams, will), negativity (remove, ward off), nightmares, peace, protection, psychic abilities, relationships, sex/sexuality, wishes

Items to purchase when the plant is not available: Flower essence; dried violet leaves; dried flowers; seeds

Violets are helpful for making contact with faeries and nature spirits. When the plants begin to sprout in the early spring, use a stick to draw a circle around each clump to signal that your garden is a safe and welcoming place for them. When seeking changes in your life and to help your dreams come true, place a handful of flowers in a small vase on your altar. Hang a picture in your home where your family gathers to invite happiness and peace inside.

Burn a small amount of dried leaves and waft the smoke in areas where you sense negative energy. Sprinkle a little flower essence before a divination session to enhance your psychic skills. Violets are associated with sleep and support dream work. Place a picture of white violets under your pillow as you say three times:

Violet flowers, scent so sweet,
Aid my dreams as I sleep.

Walnut
Black Walnut (Juglans nigra)
English Walnut, Persian Walnut (J. regia)

Walnut trees have lance-shaped leaves that turn dull yellow in the autumn. The long, slender male catkins hang from the branches while the female catkins grow on short spikes near the ends of the branches. The round nuts of the black walnut are encased in yellow-green husks. The English walnut tree produces the familiar brown nuts sold in stores.

Faery Folklore
Walnut is associated with elves.

Magical Workings
Powers and attributes: Changes/transitions, clarity (enhance, foster), con-secrate/bless, fertility, healing, inspiration, love, luck, manifest (desires,

dreams, will), prophecy, prosperity/money, protection, purification, sex/sexuality, spirit guides/spirits, success, wishes

Items to purchase when the plant is not available: Nuts from both trees; flower essence is made from the English walnut; oils are obtained from both trees

Carry a small walnut for luck. Use a walnut in a protection spell, and then place it near the front door of your home. To provide clarity when making decisions, meditate while holding two walnut leaves. To enhance the effectiveness of a healing circle, burn a few dried leaves to prepare and begin the process of raising energy. Just before Yule, wrap enough walnuts in silver paper for each member of the family. On the night of the solstice, each person should hold theirs and make a wish before hanging it on the Yule tree.

As part of a love spell, separate the halves of a walnut and remove the nutmeat. Write your name and the other person's name on small slips of paper and place one in each half of the shell. Tie the shell back together by wrapping red thread around it and keep it where you will see it often.

Water Lily
White Water Lily, White Lotus (Nymphaea alba)
American White Water Lily, Fragrant Water Lily (N. odorata)
Yellow Pond Lily (Nuphar lutea)
Folk name: Rabhagach (white water lily)

The flowers of the white water lily are bowl-shaped and fragrant. They measure between three to six inches wide and have twenty to thirty petals. The leaves are reddish when young, then turn medium green. They are round and four to twelve inches across. Although it is called *white lotus*, it is not a true lotus. The differences are that the water lily leaf has a cleft or notch and its flower petals are pointed and starlike; lotus flowers are rounded and their leaves have no indentation.

The American white water lily flower is also bowl-shaped. It grows up to eight inches across and usually has twenty petals. Its dark green leaves are round to heart-shaped and four to ten inches across. The yellow pond lily has a waxy, yellow flower that is cup-shaped. It is less than three inches across with fifteen to twenty petals. The green, oval leaves grow up to sixteen inches long.

Caution: The yellow pond lily is toxic if ingested.

Faery Folklore

According to Scottish legend, faeries used water lilies to boost their spells of enchantment, especially over children. The water lily was used to strengthen other types of faery spells, too. The Scottish folk name *rabhagach* means "beware."[81] In Germany, water faeries called *nixies* reputedly played on them and hid from humans underneath the leaves.

Magical Workings

Powers and attributes: Clarity (enhance, foster), communication, courage, growth, happiness, inspiration, love, luck, manifest (desires, dreams, will), peace, protection, psychic abilities, purification

Items to purchase when the plant is not available: Flower essence is made from the American white water lily

Place a picture of a white water lily wherever you need to foster a sense of peace or inspire clear communication. Sprinkle a little flower essence to cleanse your altar for ritual or magic work. Also use it to enhance psychic skills. Use a picture of a water lily to write a keyword or two of something you want to bring into your life. Carry the picture with you from one full moon to the next.

White Dead Nettle
White Dead Nettle, Bee Nettle (Lamium album)
Folk names: Fairy boots, fairy feet

Growing in pairs, white dead nettle leaves are heart-shaped and toothed. They closely resemble nettle. The difference is that white dead nettle leaves are covered in fine hairs and do not sting. Although it is often found growing with stinging nettle, the plants are not related. Dead nettle's tubular flowers grow in whorls around the stem just above a leaf pair. The flower opening has an upper hood and a three-lobed lower lip. The dark ends of the four stamens underneath the upper hood look like little shoes or feet.

Faery Folklore

The flowers were reputedly where faeries stored their dancing shoes. According to one legend, the faeries were tired of centipedes taking their shoes, so they

---

81. Cameron, *Gaelic Names of Plants*, 120.

hid them among the nettles for safekeeping. The fae had to use a spell to avoid getting stung by the nettles when they retrieved their shoes. Another legend notes that white dead nettle flowers were faery houses where they had a custom of leaving their shoes on the doorstep.

Magical Workings

Powers and attributes: Challenges/obstacles (overcome), determination/ endurance, family and home, healing, love, luck, protection, relationships, release (let go, move on), secrets

Items to purchase when the plant is not available: Flower essence; cut, dried leaves; powdered leaves

Plant white dead nettle in an area of your property where you feel the need for protection for your home and family. To invite luck into your home, position it near the main entrance. Use the leaves in spells to increase perseverance and determination when working to overcome obstacles.

Dry a piece of the root to use as a love charm; it will also aid in healing quarrels between lovers.

Carry a dried flower in a sachet to attract love or to promote renewal in a relationship. Place a picture of white dead nettle where you will see it often as a reminder to keep a secret.

Willow

Pussy Willow, American Willow (Salix discolor)
Weeping Willow (S. babylonica)
White Willow, European Willow (S. alba)
Folk names: Sallow (pussy willow), sally (pussy willow), withy (white willow)

These trees have narrow, lance-shaped leaves that are lighter underneath than on top. They turn greenish yellow in the autumn. The silky, white undersides of the white willow's leaves give the tree a whitish appearance. The pussy willow has fuzzy, gray catkins that resemble the soft pads of cats' feet. The weeping willow is widely loved for its long, graceful branches that sweep to the ground.

Faery Folklore

Willow branches were often placed beside or under a butter churn to prevent faeries from removing its nutrition. Usually found near water, willows are linked with sacred and mysterious powers as well as enchantment. In Ireland, the pussy willow is regarded as a lone bush. (See the profile for Lone Bush.) Common throughout folklore, the willow is noted as an entrance to the otherworld and faery realm. In parts of Germany, its often swampy, misty habitat gave the willow an association with the will-o-the-wisp, a sprite carried by or existing as a wisp of light.

Magical Workings

Powers and attributes: Adaptability, bind, communication, consecrate/bless, courage, divination, dream work, fertility, healing, inspiration, intuition, knowledge (seek, acquire), loss/sorrow (ease, recover from), love, prophecy, protection, relationships, sex/sexuality, skills, spirit guides/spirits, strength, wishes

Items to purchase when the tree is not available: Dried bark in pieces or powdered from the white willow; willow baskets; flower essence is made from the golden willow (*S. alba* var. *vitellina*), a cultivar of the white willow

Associated with in-between times and places, a willow is often a good location to make contact with nature spirits and faeries. To aid in raising lunar energy, make a circle with pussy willow catkins and willow leaves on your esbat altar. Long, thin willow branches also work well for knot magic.

To empower love spells or divination sessions, use a thin weeping willow branch, strip off the leaves, and wind it into a circle. Tie short pieces of yarn in several places to keep the circle intact, and then set it on your altar. Draw the faery star on a pink or red candle for love spells or on a white candle for divination, and then place it in the middle of the willow circle. Willow branches work well as the base for any size wreath to which flowers and leaves from other plants can be attached.

Wood Anemone

European Wood Anemone (Anemone nemorosa)
North American Wood Anemone (A. quinquefolia)
Folk names: Fairy windflower, wood windflower

The star-shaped wood anemone flower closes its petals and droops before it rains, on cloudy days, and at night. The petals have delicate veins that look like they were sketched on with a pencil. The European anemone flowers are white inside with a ring of yellow at the center and tinged with pink or purple on the outside. They have six to eight petals. Reaching up to twelve inches tall, each stalk has a solitary flower. The leaves are lobed and grow in a whorl around the stalk. The flower of the North American anemone is white or pink with five to eight petals. The stalks grow up to eight inches tall, with lobed leaves that range from green to purple.

Caution: Toxic if ingested.

Faery Folklore

Wood anemones are reputed to be a great favorite of the faeries. According to legend, the faeries paint the streaks/veins on the flowers in the moonlight. The faeries are also responsible for closing the flowers, using them as a tent when it rains and at night to sleep inside them.

Magical Workings

Powers and attributes: Balance/harmony, courage, determination/endurance, emotions (deal with, support), loss/sorrow (ease, recover from), love, luck, protection, wishes

Items to purchase when the plant is not available: Flower essence is made from the European wood anemone; bulbs

If you are experiencing emotional upheavals or dealing with any type of loss, place a picture of wood anemones on your altar. Gaze at it for several minutes, and then visualize a soft, white light surrounding you and the picture. Let all the emotions that you need to release go into the picture. When you begin to feel that balance is returning to your life, dispose of the picture by burying it outside.

To bolster courage, carry three seeds in your purse or pocket. For luck, blow on the first wood anemone you see in the spring and make a wish. When you see an anemone flower close at dusk, say good night to the faery or nature spirit who may be inside.

Yarrow

Common Yarrow (Achillea millefolium)
Folk names: Thousand leaf, yarra

Growing one to three feet tall, yarrow is a slender, upright plant with branching stems. Its leaves are fern-like and covered with soft hairs. Small, white to pinkish flowers grow in wide umbrella-shaped clusters and bloom from midsummer to autumn. The plant has a pleasant, sweet-herby fragrance.

Faery Folklore

In Scotland, yarrow was boiled in water and given to cows to protect them from faery meddling. It was used to remove fairy stroke (enchantment or illness) in humans. According to belief in the Hebrides, holding a leaf against your eyes would result in second sight and the ability to see faeries. However, in order for this to work, the plant had to be pulled up while reciting the proper incantation.

Magical Workings

Powers and attributes: Attraction, authority/leadership, balance/harmony, banish, challenges/obstacles (overcome), consecrate/bless, defense, divination, dream work, emotions (deal with, support), fertility, happiness, healing, hexes (break, protect from), intuition, loyalty/fidelity, luck, negativity (remove, ward off), peace, protection, psychic abilities, purification, relationships, release (let go, move on), secrets, see faeries, skills, spirit guides/spirits, spirituality, strength, success

Items to purchase when the plant is not available: Essential oil; flower essence; cut, dried leaves and flowers; dried flower bunches; seeds

Use yarrow to purify ritual space by scattering leaves or flowers on your altar or on the floor as you cast a circle. Consecrate magic and ritual tools by storing a few yarrow flowers with them. A bouquet of fresh flowers or a bowl of dried ones aids in stimulating intuition for divination. Place a drop of yarrow essential oil or flower essence on your third-eye chakra to support and stimulate psychic abilities, especially clairvoyance. Place several dried leaves in a small pouch to keep with you when learning new skills, especially when beginning a leadership role. Draw the faery star on a picture of yarrow and put it wherever you feel the need for protective energy or to dispel negativity.

Yellow Iris

Yellow Iris (Iris pseudacorus)
Folk names: Flag, sword lily, yellow flag

Reaching up to four inches wide, the bright-yellow iris flowers grow atop stems in groups of two or three. The stems can reach three feet tall. The iris flower has three upright petals called *standards* and three lower petals called *falls*. The falls of the yellow iris have brown or violet veining. The flat, gray-green leaves are sword-shaped.

Caution: The sap can cause skin irritation; all parts of the plant are toxic if ingested.

Faery Folklore

In Ireland, a method for determining whether an infant was a faery changeling was to throw it into a river or other body of water. If it was a changeling, it would turn into a clump of yellow iris or fern fronds. Needless to say, if the child wasn't a changeling, the event would have been an unconscionable tragedy. In Celtic legends, faeries were often described as having hair the color of yellow iris. In England, faeries were said to nestle in the flowers during the day.

Magical Workings

Powers and attributes: Adaptability, authority/leadership, awareness (expand, heighten), clarity (enhance, foster), communication, concentration/focus, creativity, defense, determination/endurance, family and home, healing, inspiration, knowledge (seek, acquire), love, luck, protection, psychic abilities, purification, release (let go, move on), success, wisdom

Items to purchase when the plant is not available: Flower essence

Growing yellow iris in the garden or placing a vase of cut flowers in a prominent place in the home invites domestic bliss. When you need to raise healing energy, place a couple of iris flowers or a picture of them on your altar. Keep a picture of yellow iris on your desk or in your workspace to act as a muse for creative inspiration. Burn a dried flower in a spell to bring success. Use a piece of dried rhizome in sachets for love magic or as an amulet for protection. For meditation when seeking wisdom, prepare a candle with the flower essence.

Yew
American Yew, Canada Yew (Taxus canadensis)
English Yew, Common Yew (T. baccata)

Yews are evergreen trees with multiple trunks and reddish bark. The American yew reaches about six feet tall; the English yew can grow to almost fifty feet. Both have dark green, needle-like leaves that are glossy on top and gray to pale green underneath. The red, cup-shaped berry contains seeds, which ripen in the autumn.

Caution: The seeds and foliage are toxic if ingested.

Faery Folklore

According to legend, in Wales, faeries could be seen when they were under a yew tree. In Scotland, they were said to often live under them. Near the village of Llanwrin in northern Wales, a magical yew was said to grow at the center of the woods known as the Forest of the Yew. While there were reputedly a number of fairy circles in the forest, the one under this great yew was known as the Dancing Place of the Goblin. It was associated with legends of people being whisked into faeryland. In Inverness, Scotland, Tomnahurich Hill, also known as Hill of the Yew Trees, is said to be a faery mound and the resting place of Thomas the Rhymer.

Scotsman Thomas Learmont or Thomas of Erceldoune (c. 1220–c. 1297/8) was known for his prophecy, poetry, and supernatural powers. According to legend, he met the faerie queen, spent seven years in faeryland, returned home for seven, and then disappeared. He is believed to have returned to faeryland. His legend is told in the *Ballad of Tam Lin*. Other versions of his story note that Thomas met the faery queen under a hawthorn or broom bush.

Magical Workings

Powers and attributes: Adaptability, ancestors, changes/transitions, communication, divination, dream work, hexes (break, protect from), justice/legal matters, knowledge (seek, acquire), loss/sorrow (ease, recover from), negativity (remove, ward off), nightmares, protection, psychic abilities, renewal, see faeries, skills, spirit guides/spirits, strength

Items to purchase when the plant is not available: Boxes and other small objects are made from yew wood; flower essence is made from the English yew

To invite faeries and nature spirits to your garden, grow yew or place yew sprigs on your outdoor altar. Hang a sachet of dried berries on a bedpost or place it on a bedside table to soothe bad dreams. A picture of a yew tree on your altar during divination sessions helps to heighten psychic abilities.

If you have a spirit in your house that troubles you, hang sachets with yew leaves and berries or sprigs of yew in active areas on the dark moon. As you do this, suggest that the spirit follow the energy of the yew to find peace and rest in the otherworld. On the full moon, take the sprigs or sachets down.

Conclusion

We are attracted by the mystery and the hope of discovery when we sense the fleeting presence of faeries and nature spirits. They seem to call to us from the shadows at the edge of our awareness. When we open our hearts and minds, they step into the light—in their own way, of course.

When we contact and find common ground with them, our own world grows larger and we take on the responsibility that goes with interacting with these beings from another realm. It is a privilege and greatly soul-felt experience when they touch our lives. While this is serious business, remember that faeries and nature spirits like to play and dance, so have fun, too. We have so much to learn from them, but most importantly we can learn how to abide in concert with the natural world and discover how to live our everyday lives in magic.

Spend time outside. Put your bare feet in the grass or in the dirt, but remember that even within the most densely populated city, the realm of the faery and nature spirit can be found. Draw on your energy and breath and attune to the seven directions. Know that you are a part of the magical mystery of this earth.

Appendix A
Powers and Attributes

This listing provides a quick reference to help you find the plants to suit your purposes.

Abundance
Apple, birch, blackberry, bracken, buttercup, cedar, chamomile, cherry, clover, crab apple, dill, elder, fairy flax, gooseberry, gorse, grape, grass, harebell, hazel, hollyhock, horse chestnut, honeysuckle, jasmine, juniper, laurel, maidenhair fern, maple, marigold, milkwort, nettle, oak, periwinkle, pignut, pine, reed rush and cattail, St. John's wort, strawberry, tulip, vervain

Adaptability
Bog myrtle, buttercup, butterwort, forget-me-not, heather and heath, honeysuckle, lilac, snowdrop, stitchwort, strawberry, sweet woodruff, thyme, willow, yellow iris, yew

Ancestors
Apple, boxwood, crab apple, cypress, hawthorn, oak, reed rush and cattail, yew

Attraction
Apple, chamomile, cherry, daisy, elm, honeysuckle, ivy, jasmine, lavender, lilac, linden, pansy, red campion, rose, rosemary, southernwood, strawberry, tulip, vetchling, yarrow

Authority/Leadership
Alder, blackthorn, cedar, cinquefoil, daisy, dandelion, heather and heath, honeysuckle, mugwort, mullein, oak, rowan, silverweed, thyme, yarrow, yellow iris

Awareness (Expand, Heighten)
Ash, birch, blackberry, butterwort, cherry, cypress, daisy, dandelion, fairy flax, fir, fly agaric, forget-me-not, foxglove, hazel, heather and heath, honeysuckle, lady's mantle, laurel, lavender, marigold, morning glory, mugwort, mullein, mushroom, oak, periwinkle, reed rush and cattail, rosemary, seaweed, thyme, yellow iris

Balance/Harmony
Agrimony, angelica, apple, ash, blackberry, broom, burdock and bitter dock, cedar, chamomile, cherry, clover, columbine, coriander, cow parsley, daisy, dandelion, dill, evening primrose, fairy flax, fir, forget-me-not, forsythia, foxglove, geranium, grape, harebell, hazel, holly, ivy, jasmine, jelly fungus, juniper, lady's mantle, lavender, lily, lily of the valley, maple, meadowsweet, milkwort, morning glory, mullein, peony, pine, primrose, quince, reed rush and cattail, rose, rowan, scarlet elf cup, seaweed, sesame, silverweed, strawberry, sweet woodruff, vervain, vetchling, wood anemone, yarrow

Banish
Agrimony, alder, angelica, birch, blackthorn, bracken, broom, burdock and bitter dock, cedar, clover, crocus, cypress, elder, evening primrose, fairy wand, fly agaric, gorse, hazel, hemlock, holly, hollyhock, horse chestnut, juniper, laurel, lilac, maidenhair fern, mallow, mistletoe, moonwort, morning glory, mugwort, mullein, nettle, peach and nectarine, pearlwort, peony, pine, primrose, rose, rosemary, rue, St. John's wort, scarlet elf cup, seaweed, sesame, thistle, tulip, vervain, violet, yarrow

Bind
Angelica, apple, cypress, fairy flax, forget-me-not, grape, honeysuckle, ivy, jasmine, mallow, morning glory, pear, pearlwort, periwinkle, pine, rose, rosemary, rowan, willow

Challenges/Obstacles (Overcome)

Angelica, birch, blackberry, blackthorn, bluebell, broom, butterwort, cedar, chamomile, cherry, cinquefoil, daisy, dill, elder, foxglove, gooseberry, grass, harebell, hawthorn, hazel, ivy, jasmine, juniper, lady's mantle, laurel, lavender, lilac, lily of the valley, mallow, mistletoe, nettle, oak, pignut, red campion, rose, rowan, silverweed, snowdrop, southernwood, thistle, vervain, white dead nettle, yarrow

Changes/Transitions

Alder, ash, birch, coriander, cypress, dill, elder, elm, evening primrose, fairy flax, fir, forsythia, grape, hawthorn, hazel, heather and heath, hollyhock, honeysuckle, hyssop, jasmine, lady's mantle, lily, linden, mistletoe, morning glory, pine, sesame, snowdrop, sweet woodruff, violet, walnut, yew

Clarity (Enhance, Foster)

Alder, birch, cedar, chamomile, cypress, daffodil, dandelion, fir, forget-me-not, harebell, heather and heath, honeysuckle, hyssop, jasmine, laurel, lavender, lily of the valley, marigold, marsh marigold, milkwort, pansy, periwinkle, red campion, rose, rosemary, rue, stitchwort, sweet woodruff, thistle, walnut, water lily, yellow iris

Communication

Ash, blackberry, broom, cedar, chamomile, cinquefoil, daisy, dandelion, elecampane, fir, forget-me-not, foxglove, geranium, grass, hazel, jasmine, lavender, lily, linden, maple, marigold, nettle, pine, rose, rosemary, silverweed, sweet woodruff, violet, water lily, willow, yellow iris, yew

Concentration/Focus

Ash, birch, bog myrtle, bracken, broom, cedar, cypress, forget-me-not, geranium, honeysuckle, lady's mantle, lavender, lilac, maidenhair fern, milkwort, moonwort, pansy, pine, primrose, red campion, reed rush and cattail, rosemary, yellow iris

Consecrate/Bless

Angelica, apple, birch, cedar, chamomile, cinquefoil, columbine, coriander, cypress, daffodil, daisy, elder, fairy wand, grape, hawthorn, holly, horse chestnut, hyssop, jasmine, lily, lily of the valley, milkwort, mistletoe, mugwort, oak, pear, pine, primrose, rose, rosemary, rowan, rue, St. John's wort, sesame, silverweed, sweet woodruff, thyme, vervain, walnut, willow, yarrow

Courage

Angelica, cedar, columbine, cow parsley, forsythia, geranium, holly, lady's mantle, laurel, lavender, lily of the valley, mullein, nettle, oak, pansy, pine, plantain, ragwort, red campion, rose, rosemary, St. John's wort, snowdrop, thistle, thyme, tulip, vetchling, water lily, willow, wood anemone

Creativity

Apple, ash, birch, broom, chamomile, cherry, columbine, daisy, dill, elder, evening primrose, fir, fly agaric, foxglove, geranium, grape, hawthorn, hazel, honeysuckle, hyssop, jasmine, laurel, lavender, lilac, lily, maple, marigold, meadowsweet, mistletoe, mushroom, pear, pine, red campion, rosemary, rowan, stitchwort, vervain, vetchling, yellow iris

Defense

Angelica, blackthorn, bog myrtle, boxwood, bracken, burdock and bitter dock, cinquefoil, cypress, dill, elder, fir, globeflower, gorse, hawthorn, hazel, heather and heath, hemlock, holly, jasmine, juniper, laurel, lilac, lily of the valley, linden, maidenhair fern, mistletoe, moonwort, mugwort, mullein, nettle, oak, pine, rosemary, rowan, rue, St. John's wort, sesame, silverweed, sorrel, thistle, vervain, yarrow, yellow iris

Determination/Endurance

Bog myrtle, broom, butterwort, cedar, chamomile, elm, gorse, laurel, mallow, marigold, mullein, oak, pignut, pine, plantain, red campion, reed rush and cattail, rosemary, snowdrop, stitchwort, thistle, vervain, white dead nettle, wood anemone, yellow iris

Divination

Alder, angelica, apple, ash, birch, boxwood, bracken, broom, burdock and bitter dock, buttercup, cedar, chamomile, cherry, cinquefoil, coriander, cowslip, crab apple, crocus, cypress, daisy, dandelion, dill, elecampane, elm, fir, fairy flax, fly agaric, gorse, grape, hazel, heather and heath, holly, honeysuckle, horse chestnut, hyssop, ivy, jasmine, juniper, lady's mantle, lady's smock, laurel, lavender, lilac, linden, maidenhair fern, maple, marigold, meadowsweet, mistletoe, moonwort, morning glory, mugwort, mullein, mushroom, nettle, pansy, periwinkle, plantain, ragwort, rose, rowan, rue, St. John's wort, silverweed, southernwood, strawberry, sweet woodruff, thyme, tulip, vervain, violet, willow, yarrow, yew

Dream Work

Agrimony, alder, angelica, apple, ash, bilberry, bog myrtle, buttercup, butterwort, cedar, chamomile, cinquefoil, clover, coriander, crocus, daisy, dandelion, elder, elm, fly agaric, heather and heath, holly, honeysuckle, jasmine, juniper, laurel, lavender, lilac, linden, mallow, maple, marigold, mistletoe, morning glory, mugwort, peony, plantain, primrose, rose, rosemary, St. John's wort, silverweed, sweet woodruff, thyme, tulip, vervain, violet, willow, yarrow, yew

Emotions (Deal With, Support)

Buttercup, cedar, chamomile, cinquefoil, columbine, coriander, cow parsley, crocus, cypress, dandelion, fairy wand, fir, forsythia, foxglove, geranium, hawthorn, hollyhock, juniper, lavender, lilac, lily, lily of the valley, nettle, pine, rose, rosemary, rue, silverweed, stitchwort, vetchling, violet, wood anemone, yarrow

Family and Home

Agrimony, bilberry, broom, butterwort, cedar, columbine, coriander, cow parsley, crocus, daffodil, daisy, dill, evening primrose, fairy flax, forsythia, gorse, hawthorn, heather and heath, holly, hollyhock, horse chestnut, juniper, laurel, lilac, maidenhair fern, meadowsweet, milkwort, mistletoe, morning glory, mugwort, nettle, oak, peony, pignut, pine, plantain, primrose, reed rush and cattail, rose, rowan, snowdrop, thyme, vervain, vetchling, violet, white dead nettle, yellow iris

Fertility
Apple, ash, birch, blackberry, boxwood, broom, cedar, chamomile, cherry, coriander, crab apple, crocus, daisy, fairy wand, fly agaric, forsythia, geranium, gooseberry, gorse, grape, hawthorn, hazel, hogweed, hyssop, ivy, jasmine, juniper, lady's mantle, lady's smock, mallow, meadowsweet, mistletoe, mugwort, mushroom, oak, peach and nectarine, pine, primrose, quince, rowan, St. John's wort, seaweed, sesame, southernwood, tulip, vervain, violet, walnut, willow, yarrow

Growth
Angelica, ash, blackberry, cedar, chamomile, cypress, dill, fir, forsythia, geranium, grape, hawthorn, heather and heath, hyssop, ivy, jasmine, juniper, marsh marigold, oak, pine, primrose, quince, reed rush and cattail, thyme, water lily

Happiness
Apple, blackberry, boxwood, buttercup, cherry, coriander, crab apple, crocus, elecampane, fir, forsythia, grape, grass, hawthorn, hollyhock, honeysuckle, jasmine, juniper, lady's mantle, lilac, lily, lily of the valley, linden, marigold, meadowsweet, morning glory, mugwort, mushroom, peach and nectarine, peony, pine, rose, St. John's wort, snowdrop, sorrel, strawberry, thyme, tulip, vetchling, violet, water lily, yarrow

Healing
Agrimony, alder, angelica, apple, ash, bilberry, birch, blackberry, broom, burdock and bitter dock, butterwort, cedar, chamomile, cinquefoil, clover, coriander, cow parsley, cowslip, crab apple, crocus, cypress, daisy, dandelion, elder, elecampane, elm, evening primrose, fairy wand, fir, forsythia, foxglove, gooseberry, grape, hazel, heather and heath, hogweed, holly, honeysuckle, horse chestnut, hyssop, ivy, jasmine, jelly fungus, juniper, lady's mantle, lady's smock, larch, laurel, lavender, lily of the valley, maidenhair fern, mallow, marsh marigold, meadowsweet, milkwort, mistletoe, mullein, nettle, oak, pansy, peach and nectarine, pear, peony, periwinkle, pine, plantain, primrose, red campion, reed rush and cattail, rose, rosemary, rowan, rue, St. John's wort, scarlet elf cup, sesame, silverweed, sorrel, southernwood, stitchwort, sweet woodruff, thistle, thyme, vervain, violet, walnut, white dead nettle, willow, yarrow, yellow iris

Hexes (Break, Protect From)

Agrimony, angelica, ash, bilberry, blackthorn, boxwood, bracken, butterwort, cedar, chamomile, cinquefoil, clover, cow parsley, dill, elder, fir, geranium, globeflower, gorse, grass, hemlock, hogweed, holly, honeysuckle, horse chestnut, hyssop, jelly fungus, juniper, laurel, lilac, maidenhair fern, mallow, moonwort, mullein, nettle, peach and nectarine, pearlwort, peony, periwinkle, pine, ragwort, rose, rosemary, rowan, rue, scarlet elf cup, silverweed, southernwood, thistle, vervain, violet, yarrow, yew

Inspiration

Angelica, ash, birch, bog myrtle, cedar, chamomile, cinquefoil, columbine, fairy wand, fir, gorse, grape, hazel, honeysuckle, ivy, jasmine, laurel, lavender, lilac, lily of the valley, marigold, marsh marigold, meadowsweet, oak, pansy, pine, red campion, reed rush and cattail, rosemary, rowan, rue, silverweed, vervain, walnut, water lily, willow, yellow iris

Intuition

Alder, ash, birch, blackberry, broom, chamomile, clover, elecampane, elm, foxglove, hazel, holly, honeysuckle, jasmine, larch, laurel, lavender, pine, rosemary, willow, yarrow

Justice/Legal Matters

Cedar, chamomile, cinquefoil, cypress, dill, elm, honeysuckle, horse chestnut, jasmine, larch, laurel, linden, marigold, nettle, oak, pear, pine, St. John's wort, sesame, silverweed, vervain, violet, yew

Knowledge (Seek, Acquire)

Alder, angelica, apple, ash, birch, blackberry, cherry, crab apple, cypress, dill, elder, fly agaric, hazel, heather and heath, ivy, juniper, larch, moonwort, oak, periwinkle, pine, primrose, red campion, rosemary, rowan, willow, yellow iris, yew

Loss/Sorrow (Ease, Recover From)

Angelica, cinquefoil, cypress, fairy wand, fir, forget-me-not, geranium, harebell, hazel, lavender, maple, morning glory, pansy, pearlwort, peony, primrose, snowdrop, thyme, willow, wood anemone, yew

Love

Apple, ash, bilberry, birch, bluebell, boxwood, bracken, burdock and bitter dock, buttercup, butterwort, cedar, chamomile, cherry, cinquefoil, clover, columbine, cow parsley, coriander, cowslip, crab apple, crocus, daffodil, daisy, dandelion, dill, elder, elecampane, elm, fairy wand, forget-me-not, geranium, gorse, grape, harebell, hawthorn, heather and heath, honeysuckle, horse chestnut, ivy, jasmine, juniper, lady's mantle, lady's smock, lavender, lilac, lily, lily of the valley, linden, maidenhair fern, mallow, maple, meadowsweet, mistletoe, moonwort, mugwort, mullein, pansy, peach and nectarine, pear, pearlwort, periwinkle, primrose, quince, red campion, rose, rosemary, rue, St. John's wort, silverweed, southernwood, strawberry, thyme, tulip, vetchling, violet, walnut, white dead nettle, water lily, willow, wood anemone, yellow iris

Loyalty/Fidelity

Blackthorn, bluebell, cedar, clover, coriander, daisy, elder, elm, fairy wand, forget-me-not, harebell, honeysuckle, ivy, laurel, lavender, linden, oak, peach and nectarine, periwinkle, reed rush and cattail, rose, rosemary, southernwood, tulip, vervain, vetchling, violet, yarrow

Luck

Alder, apple, ash, bilberry, blackberry, bog myrtle, boxwood, bracken, butterwort, cedar, chamomile, cherry, cinquefoil, clover (four-leaf), daffodil, daisy, dandelion, dill, elecampane, fly agaric, forget-me-not, grass, hawthorn, hazel, heather and heath, holly, honeysuckle, horse chestnut, ivy, jasmine, jelly fungus, lady's mantle, larch, lavender, lilac, lily of the valley, linden, maidenhair fern, meadowsweet, mistletoe, moonwort, mugwort, nettle, oak, peach and nectarine, pear, pearlwort, peony, pignut, quince, rose, rowan, rue, St. John's wort, scarlet elf cup, silverweed, sorrel, southernwood, strawberry, thyme, tulip, vervain, violet, walnut, water lily, white dead nettle, wood anemone, yarrow, yellow iris

Manifest (Desires, Dreams, Will)

Angelica, bilberry, bluebell, buttercup, chamomile, cherry, cinquefoil, crocus, dandelion, elm, grass, hawthorn, hazel, heather and heath, holly, hyssop, juniper, laurel, lavender, lily, marigold, oak, peach and nectarine, pear, periwinkle, pine, red campion, rose, silverweed, strawberry, vervain, violet, walnut, water lily

Negativity (Remove, Ward Off)
Agrimony, alder, angelica, ash, birch, blackthorn, bracken, broom, burdock and bitter dock, butterwort, cedar, chamomile, columbine, cow parsley, daffodil, dandelion, elm, globeflower, gorse, grass, harebell, hawthorn, hemlock, hogweed, hyssop, ivy, jelly fungus, juniper, laurel, lavender, lilac, lily, linden, marigold, marsh marigold, mistletoe, mugwort, mullein, nettle, oak, pansy, peach and nectarine, pearlwort, peony, pine, plantain, quince, ragwort, rosemary, rue, St. John's wort, scarlet elf cup, seaweed, sesame, snowdrop, southernwood, sweet woodruff, thistle, thyme, vervain, vetchling, violet, yarrow, yew

Nightmares
Bluebell, chamomile, cinquefoil, crocus, daffodil, dill, evening primrose, mallow, marigold, mistletoe, mullein, peony, periwinkle, plantain, rosemary, rue, St. John's wort, silverweed, thistle, thyme, vervain, violet, yew

Peace
Angelica, apple, ash, bog myrtle, broom, burdock and bitter dock, cedar, chamomile, cherry, columbine, coriander, cow parsley, cowslip, crocus, cypress, daffodil, dandelion, dill, elecampane, fir, foxglove, gooseberry, harebell, hawthorn, heather and heath, honeysuckle, horse chestnut, hyssop, jasmine, jelly fungus, lady's mantle, laurel, lavender, lilac, lily, lily of the valley, linden, maidenhair fern, mallow, meadowsweet, mistletoe, morning glory, mugwort, nettle, pansy, peony, periwinkle, pine, primrose, quince, rose, rowan, St. John's wort, scarlet elf cup, seaweed, sorrel, stitchwort, strawberry, sweet woodruff, thyme, tulip, vervain, vetchling, violet, water lily, yarrow

Prophecy
Alder, apple, ash, bilberry, boxwood, broom, butterwort, crab apple, dandelion, dill, elm, fly agaric, grape, ivy, laurel, lilac, linden, maple, marigold, oak, reed rush and cattail, rose, rowan, sweet woodruff, vervain, walnut, willow

Prosperity/Money

Apple, ash, bilberry, blackberry, bog myrtle, boxwood, bracken, broom, buttercup, cedar, chamomile, cinquefoil, clover, cowslip, crab apple, crocus, dandelion, dill, elder, fairy flax, fir, gorse, grape, hawthorn, hazel, hollyhock, honeysuckle, horse chestnut, hyssop, jasmine, juniper, laurel, lily, maidenhair fern, maple, marigold, marsh marigold, mistletoe, moonwort, oak, pear, peony, periwinkle, pignut, quince, ragwort, St. John's wort, scarlet elf cup, seaweed, sesame, silverweed, sorrel, sweet woodruff, thyme, tulip, vervain, walnut

Protection

Agrimony, alder, angelica, ash, bilberry, birch, blackberry, blackthorn, bog myrtle, boxwood, bracken, broom, burdock and bitter dock, butterwort, cedar, chamomile, cinquefoil, clover, cow parsley, coriander, cowslip, crab apple, crocus, cypress, daffodil, daisy, dandelion, dill, elder, elecampane, elm, evening primrose, fairy flax, fairy wand, fir, fly agaric, forget-me-not, foxglove, geranium, gorse, grass, hawthorn, hazel, heather and heath, hemlock, holly, honeysuckle, horse chestnut, hyssop, ivy, jasmine, juniper, larch, laurel, lavender, lilac, lily, lily of the valley, linden, maidenhair fern, mallow, milkwort, marigold, marsh marigold, mistletoe, moonwort, mugwort, mullein, nettle, oak, pear, pearlwort, peony, periwinkle, pignut, pine, plantain, primrose, quince, ragwort, red campion, reed rush and cattail, rose, rosemary, rowan, rue, St. John's wort, seaweed, sesame, silverweed, sorrel, southernwood, sweet woodruff, thistle, thyme, tulip, vervain, violet, walnut, white dead nettle, water lily, willow, wood anemone, yarrow, yellow iris, yew

Psychic Abilities

Bracken, cedar, chamomile, coriander, crocus, dandelion, elecampane, elm, fairy flax, fir, fly agaric, geranium, grape, grass, hazel, heather and heath, honeysuckle, hyssop, jasmine, juniper, laurel, lavender, lilac, maidenhair fern, marigold, moonwort, mugwort, mullein, mushroom, nettle, periwinkle, pine, rose, rosemary, rowan, St. John's wort, seaweed, thyme, violet, vetchling, water lily, yarrow, yellow iris, yew

Purification
Agrimony, ash, angelica, birch, blackberry, blackthorn, bog myrtle, bracken, broom, burdock and bitter dock, cedar, chamomile, columbine, dandelion, dill, elder, elecampane, evening primrose, fairy wand, fir, gorse, hawthorn, heather and heath, hemlock, hyssop, jasmine, juniper, lady's mantle, laurel, lavender, lilac, mistletoe, moonwort, mugwort, mullein, nettle, oak, pine, plantain, rosemary, rue, St. John's wort, sesame, snowdrop, southernwood, sweet woodruff, thistle, thyme, vervain, walnut, water lily, yarrow, yellow iris

Relationships
Apple, bog myrtle, clover, coriander, crocus, daffodil, elecampane, forget-me-not, foxglove, geranium, hawthorn, jasmine, lady's mantle, lavender, lily, maple, marigold, meadowsweet, periwinkle, primrose, rose, rosemary, rue, strawberry, sweet woodruff, vervain, vetchling, violet, white dead nettle, willow, yarrow

Release (Let Go, Move On)
Agrimony, birch, bracken, burdock and bitter dock, cedar, clover, columbine, cypress, elder, foxglove, hazel, hemlock, hollyhock, honeysuckle, juniper, laurel, lavender, lilac, maidenhair fern, maple, moonwort, mugwort, mullein, nettle, peony, pine, rosemary, rue, St. John's wort, sesame, snowdrop, thistle, tulip, vervain, white dead nettle, yarrow, yellow iris

Renewal
Alder, angelica, apple, ash, birch, bluebell, boxwood, cedar, cherry, coriander, cypress, daffodil, dill, elder, elm, fairy flax, fir, fly agaric, gorse, hogweed, holly, honeysuckle, ivy, lilac, lily, milkwort, marsh marigold, mistletoe, oak, pansy, peach and nectarine, pine, quince, rosemary, St. John's wort, sesame, southernwood, stitchwort, thistle, thyme, yew

Secrets
Angelica, coriander, cowslip, elecampane, fairy flax, fly agaric, forget-me-not, globeflower, hazel, honeysuckle, ivy, juniper, lily, marsh marigold, mistletoe, moonwort, mushroom, oak, pignut, rose, rowan, sesame, sorrel, white dead nettle, yarrow

Security

Angelica, apple, bracken, broom, cedar, cinquefoil, coriander, cypress, daffodil, dill, elder, evening primrose, fir, hawthorn, hazel, holly, ivy, juniper, lilac, maidenhair fern, meadowsweet, mistletoe, moonwort, morning glory, mullein, nettle, oak, periwinkle, reed rush and cattail, rowan, St. John's wort

See Faeries

Alder, ash, bluebell, clover (four-leaf), dill, elder, grass, harebell, hawthorn, hazel, hollyhock, lavender, marigold, mullein, primrose, rowan, rue, sorrel, St. John's wort, vervain, thyme, yarrow, yew

Sex/Sexuality

Apple, chamomile, coriander, crocus, elecampane, fairy flax, fairy wand, geranium, grape, hawthorn, hogweed, hyssop, jasmine, lady's smock, mallow, mistletoe, nettle, oak, pear, pignut, plantain, primrose, reed rush and cattail, rose, sesame, southernwood, strawberry, tulip, violet, walnut, willow

Skills

Crocus, daisy, dandelion, fairy flax, honeysuckle, lily of the valley, mugwort, rowan, seaweed, sweet woodruff, thyme, vetchling, willow, yarrow, yew

Spirit Guides/Spirits

Agrimony, alder, apple, ash, birch, blackberry, bracken, cedar, cinquefoil, cowslip, crab apple, daffodil, dandelion, dill, elecampane, fir, fly agaric, grass, harebell, heather and heath, holly, hyssop, jasmine, jelly fungus, juniper, lavender, lilac, lily, mallow, marigold, marsh marigold, mistletoe, moonwort, mugwort, mullein, mushroom, oak, peony, periwinkle, pine, reed rush and cattail, rose, rosemary, rowan, rue, St. John's wort, scarlet elf cup, seaweed, sesame, silverweed, thistle, vervain, walnut, willow, yarrow, yew

Spirituality

Angelica, buttercup, cedar, chamomile, cherry, columbine, dandelion, elder, fir, forsythia, geranium, heather and heath, holly, hyssop, ivy, jasmine, juniper, lady's mantle, larch, laurel, lavender, lilac, lily of the valley, mallow, pine, primrose, reed rush and cattail, rose, St. John's wort, vetchling, yarrow

Strength
Alder, angelica, apple, ash, blackthorn, broom, cedar, cinquefoil, cow parsley, cowslip, crocus, cypress, daisy, fairy flax, fir, forget-me-not, geranium, hazel, hogweed, holly, honeysuckle, horse chestnut, juniper, laurel, lily, linden, marsh marigold, meadowsweet, morning glory, mugwort, mushroom, oak, pine, plantain, rose, rowan, St. John's wort, silverweed, southernwood, stitchwort, thistle, thyme, vetchling, willow, yarrow, yew

Success
Angelica, apple, bilberry, buttercup, cedar, chamomile, cinquefoil, dill, elder, evening primrose, forget-me-not, geranium, gooseberry, hawthorn, hollyhock, juniper, larch, laurel, lily of the valley, marigold, mistletoe, morning glory, oak, pear, peony, plantain, rowan, silverweed, sweet woodruff, vervain, walnut, yarrow, yellow iris

Support (Provide, Receive)
Angelica, birch, butterwort, columbine, dill, fairy wand, fir, hazel, holly, jasmine, jelly fungus, lavender, linden, maple, mullein, pine, red campion, reed rush and cattail, scarlet elf cup, stitchwort, vervain

Trust
Bracken, columbine, cowslip, heather and heath, rose, snowdrop, thistle

Truth
Blackthorn, bluebell, buttercup, clover, daisy, elecampane, evening primrose, foxglove, harebell, hazel, plantain, seaweed, sesame, vetchling

Wisdom
Apple, ash, birch, broom, buttercup, cedar, cherry, cinquefoil, crab apple, cypress, dill, elder, elm, geranium, hawthorn, hazel, laurel, lilac, maple, marigold, oak, peach and nectarine, pear, pine, red campion, rose, rosemary, rowan, rue, silverweed, vetchling, yellow iris

Wishes
Chamomile, cinquefoil, dandelion, elm, fairy wand, hawthorn, hazel, holly, honeysuckle, horse chestnut, juniper, laurel, lavender, peach and nectarine, pear, snowdrop, violet, walnut, willow, wood anemone

Glossary

Apsaras — A type of faery from ancient Hindu legends that was originally associated only with water and trees but later affiliated with other plants.

Awd Goggie — The faery that guards unripe gooseberries in Scotland.

Bilé ratha — The term for a venerated tree growing in or near a rath, or ancient ring fort. It often refers specifically to a hazel tree.

Brownie — A term used in parts of England and Scotland for a type of household faery.

Caird / card — A tool used to prepare wool for spinning; the process is called *carding*.

Cairn and dolmen — Two types of megalithic tombs that became associated with the fae. These structures are believed to be entrances to faeryland.

Changeling — A deformed or sometimes old faery substituted for a human child.

Cloutie croft — A piece of land left in a wild state and dedicated to the faeries.

Cloutie tree — Usually growing beside or near a sacred well, a cloutie tree was a place to tie a piece of cloth while making a wish or praying for something needed. In Ireland a cloutie tree was also regarded as a faery tree.

Colt pixy — An orchard spirit in the form of a horse that guards apple trees.

Deva — A term from Hinduism and Buddhism referring to a demigod or divine being. It was applied to nature spirits in the late 1800s.

Dryads — Human-like Greek tree nymphs that were originally associated exclusively with the oak, but came to represent the woodland spirits of all trees.

Elaby Gathon/Gathen — A faery commonly called upon by nannies to watch over and protect babies as they slept.

Elf — A magical being from Norse and Germanic mythology that equates with the faeries of the British Isles and elsewhere in Europe.

Elf knots / elf locks — The tangles that pixies make in the manes of colts while riding them. They are often made using the prickly burs of burdock.

Elf rod — A brush-like tangle of branches sometimes found on rosebushes.

Elf shot — An invisible magical weapon used by elves to cause disease. It also refers to the illness itself.

Fairy's broom — A dense tangle of birch branches.

Fairy butter — A type of gelatinous fungus more widely known as jelly fungus.

Fairy bush — A term used for a hawthorn, holly, elder, or rowan that grows on a fairy path.

Fairy chains — A name used for daisy chains in Ireland.

Fairy circle / fairy ring — A circle of grass or mushrooms said to mark a place where elves or faeries danced. Some stories note that it is okay to walk through or stand in the circle but it is unlucky to walk or run around the perimeter because that is a fairy path reserved for them.

Fairy door — A hole created by a branch that has fallen off an oak tree.

Fairy faith / fairy tradition — In addition to believing in faeries and their realm, it includes developing a relationship for working with them.

Fairy fleet / fairy light — Names given to the phosphorescent effects of bioluminescent plankton that create eerie blue lights on the ocean.

Fairy glamour — The art of illusion used by the fae that makes things appear different from what they are.

Fairy horse — Ragwort and St. John's wort were reputedly daytime disguises for fairy horses. Stepping on one of these plants after sunset would cause the horse to rear up and gallop off with the unsuspecting human on its back. Faeries were said to turn rushes into horses with a magical word so they could ride them to revels.

Fairy mead — A mixture of milk and honey with a drop of vanilla extract.

Fairy oil — A special oil created through an elaborate ritual. The ingredients included hollyhock buds, marigold flowers, hazel buds, thyme flowers that had been gathered from a hill where faeries had been, and grass from a faery circle. When anointed to the eyes, the oil made invisible faeries and elves visible. It was also used to conjure the faery Elaby Gathon, while reciting the proper incantation.

Fairy pasture — A small, grassy clearing where sunlight reaches the forest floor.

Fairy path — A line of energy running along a trail frequently used by faeries; it usually connects sites important to them.

Fairy rade — A procession or pageant of display, "rade" being a shortened form for the word *parade*. It is also known as a fairy ride.

Fairy stroke / struck — An illness, paralysis, or enchantment caused by a faery. It is sometimes referred to as a fairy blast.

Fairy sweets — A treat consisting of coriander seeds dipped in powdered sugar.

Fairy thorn — Refers to hawthorn and blackthorn trees.

Fairy wind — A sudden gust of air or a whirlwind that is not created by the weather. In Ireland a whirlwind of dust was regarded as faeries on a journey. Likewise, in Wales, small whirls of dust were believed to conceal faeries. In the Middle East a whirlwind on the desert was often regarded as a flight of jinn.

Fey / fay — Derived from Old French, this term meaning "fairy" emerged in medieval literature.

Ghillie Dhu — A spirit in Scotland that lives in birch woods.

Gooseberry wife — A faery on the Isle of Wight that guards the gooseberries and appears as a huge, hairy caterpillar.

Hamadryads — Whereas the dryad came to be regarded as a more general spirit that dwelled among all the woodland trees in Greek mythology, the hamadryad took on the role of a spirit who lived and died with a particular tree.

Hobgoblin — A type of house faery associated with the hearth in England and parts of Scotland.

Hollen — Faery-like spirits in Germanic/Teutonic areas of Europe that give aid to humans when called upon.

Jinn — A magical being in pre-Islamic Arabian mythology that has many parallels with European faeries. The name was Anglicized to *genie*.

Kelpie — A water faery of Scotland in the form of a gray horse.

Korrigan — A type of faerie being of Brittany, France, and Cornwall, England, that is sometimes described as dwarf-like.

Lieschi — A Russian faerie or genie of the forest that often shape-shifts into animal form. They reputedly favor places where fly agaric grows.

Lone bush — A designation most often applied to a solitary hawthorn, but it can also refer to a blackthorn. In Ireland the term also includes alder, birch, broom, elder, gorse, hazel, holly, oak, pussy willow, and rowan.

Lunantishee — Luna sídhe or moon faeries that are the guardians of blackthorn trees.

Mist gate — A magical gap in the mist or fog that surrounds a faery place.

Moss people — From Germanic mythology, the faery-like beings that lived and died with specific trees. They are also known as the wood folk.

Nixie — A female water faery from Germanic mythology.

Nymphs — Female nature spirits or faeries from Greek mythology.

Oak men — The dwarf-like faeries that are guardians of forest creatures.

Peri / pari — The faery-like beings from Persian mythology ranked between angels and humans. Sometimes depicted with wings, the peri became equated with European faeries.

Perry dancers — A term for the aurora borealis equating it with the magical peri beings of Persia.

Picts — The group of pre-Roman, pre-Celtic tribes of northern Scotland.

Pixie / pixy / piskies — Terms used for small faeries in the southwestern areas of England.

Pixie-led — A term meaning to be led astray to a place where it is difficult to find a way out or to find the way back home.

Pixy paws — A folk name for hawthorn berries, which are usually known as haws.

Pixy pears — A folk name for the rose hips from the dog rose and for hawthorn berries.

Pooka / puca — A type of faery that takes an animal form.

Portunes — Tiny, half-inch tall faeries noted in early medieval writings. In France they were known as Neptunes.

Rath — An ancient hilltop ring fort in Ireland. Faeries are closely associated with these structures, sometimes making their homes in them.

Salgfraulien — A type of female forest spirit or faery dressed in white in the Tyrolean folklore of Austria.

Seliges fräulein — A female faery-like being in Germanic areas of Europe who watches over certain plants. She has similarities to the Salgfraulien.

Sídhe — A term for *faery* in Celtic mythology that is commonly used among Pagans and Wiccans.

Troll — A dwarf-like being or ogre in Scandinavian mythology.

Trow — Faeries of the Scottish Orkney and Shetland Islands.

Tuometar — A type of Finnish tree faery associated with the European bird cherry.

Vila — The beautiful forest faeries in Serbian lore.

Wild Hunt — A spectral cavalcade of the dead that travels across the sky at night during midwinter and usually led by Woden or other powerful huntsman. It is part of Norse and Germanic mythology.

Will-o-the-wisp — A sprite carried by or existing as a wisp of light.

Bibliography

Andrews, Elizabeth. *Ulster Folklore*. New York: E. P. Dutton & Co., 1919.

Arnovick, Leslie K. *Written Reliquaries: The Resonance of Orality in Medieval English Texts*. Philadelphia: John Benjamins Publishing Company, 2006.

Bane, Theresa. *Encyclopedia of Fairies in World Folklore and Mythology*. Jefferson, NC: McFarland & Company, Inc., Publishers, 2013.

Barnhart, Robert K., ed. *The Barnhart Concise Dictionary of Etymology*. New York: HarperCollins, 1995.

Beveridge, Jan. *Children into Swans: Fairy Tales and the Pagan Imagination*. Montreal, Canada: McGill-Queen's University Press, 2014.

Briggs, Katharine. *An Encyclopedia of Fairies: Hobgoblins, Brownies, Bogies, and Other Supernatural Creatures*. New York: Pantheon Books, 1976.

———. *The Fairies in Tradition and Literature*. New York: Routledge Classics, 2002.

Britten, James, and Robert Holland. *A Dictionary of English Plant-Names*. London: Trübner and Co., 1886.

Bruton-Seal, Julie, and Matthew Seal. *The Herbalist's Bible: John Parkinson's Lost Classic Rediscovered*. New York: Skyhorse Publishing, Inc., 2014.

Buzan, Tony. *Mind Mapping: Kick-start Your Creativity and Transform Your Life.* North York, Canada: Pearson Education Canada, 2006.

Cameron, John. *Gaelic Names of Plants (Scottish and Irish).* London: William Blackwood and Sons, 1883.

Campbell, John Gregorson. *Superstitions of the Highlands and Islands of Scotland.* Glasgow, Scotland: James MacLehose and Sons, 1900.

Chainey, Dee Dee. *A Treasury of British Folklore: Maypoles, Mandrakes & Mistletoe.* London: Pavilion Books Company, Ltd., 2018.

Chisholm, Hugh, ed. *The Encyclopaedia Britannica: A Dictionary of Arts, Sciences, Literature and General Information*, vol. 10. 11th ed. New York: Cambridge University Press, 1910–1911.

Clarke, J. Erskine, ed. *Chatterbox, 1876.* New York: The American News Company, 1876.

Connolly, Shane. *The Secret Language of Flowers: Rediscovering Traditional Meanings.* New York: Rizzoli International Publications, 2004.

Coombes, Allen J. *Dictionary of Plant Names.* Portland, OR: Timber Press, Inc., 1985.

Cundall, James. *The Everyday Book of Natural History.* London: Frederick Warne and Company, 1866.

Dalal, Roshen. *The Vedas: An Introduction to Hinduism's Sacred Texts.* New Delhi, India: Penguin Random House India, 2014.

Darwin, Tess. *The Scots Herbal: The Plant Lore of Scotland.* Edinburgh, Scotland: Mercat Press, 1997.

De Cleene, Marcel, and Marie Claire Lejeune. *Compendium of Symbolic and Ritual Plants in Europe: Trees and Shrubs*, vol. 1. Ghent, Belgium: Man & Culture Publishers, 2003.

———. *Compendium of Symbolic and Ritual Plants in Europe: Herbs*, vol. 2. Ghent, Belgium: Man & Culture Publishers, 2003.

Dennys, N. B. *The Folklore of China and Its Affinities with that of the Aryan and Semitic Races.* London: Trübner and Co., 1876.

Dietz, S. Theresa. *The Complete Language of Flowers: A Definitive and Illustrated History*. New York: Wellfleet Press, 2020.

Dinneen, Patrick S., comp., ed. *An Irish-English Dictionary: Being a Thesaurus of the Words, Phrases and Idioms of the Modern Irish Language, with Explanations in English*. Dublin: M. H. Gill & Son, Ltd., 1904.

Eastman, John. *Wild Flowers of the Eastern United States*. Mechanicsburg, PA: Stackpole Books, 2014.

Editorial Staff, *Webster's Third New International Dictionary*, unabridged, vol. 1. Chicago: Encyclopedia Britannica, Inc., 1981.

Editors of Encyclpaedia Britannica, s.v. "Jinni," Encyclopaedia Britannica Online, November 16, 2018. https://www.britannica.com/topic/jinni. Accessed June 3, 2020.

Evans-Wentz, W. Y. *The Fairy Faith in Celtic Countries*. New York: Citadel Press, 1994.

Falconer, Rachel, and Denis Renevey, eds. *Medieval and Early Modern Literature, Science and Medicine*. Tübingen, Germany: Narr Francke Attempto Verlag GmbH, 2013.

Fernie, W. T. *Herbal Simples Approved for Modern Uses of Cure*. 2nd ed. Philadelphia: Boericke & Tafel, 1897.

Finneran, Richard J., ed. *The Yeats Reader: A Portable Compendium of Poetry, Drama, and Prose*, rev. ed. New York: Scribner, 2002.

Folkard, Richard. *Plant Lore, Legends, and Lyrics: Embracing the Myths, Traditions, Superstitions, and Folklore of the Plant Kingdom*. 2nd ed. London: Sampson, Low, Marston & Company, 1892.

Fowler, H. W. *Fowler's Dictionary of Modern English Usage*. 4th ed. Edited by Jeremy Butterfield. Oxford, England: Oxford University Press, 2015.

Fox, Frances Margaret. *Flowers and Their Travels*. New York: The Bobbs-Merrill Company Publishers, 1936.

Franklin, Anna. *The Illustrated Encyclopedia of Fairies*. London: Vega, 2002.

French, Lucy Virginia, and Lide Smith Meriwether. *One or Two?* St. Louis, MO: Meriwether Bros., 1883.

Friend, Hilderic. *Flowers and Flower Lore.* 3rd. ed. London: Swan Sonnenschein, LeBas & Lowrey, 1886.

Furdell, Elizabeth Lane, ed. *Textual Healing: Essays on Medieval and Early Modern Medicine.* Boston: Brill Academic Publishers, 2005.

Gaffin, Dennis. *Running with the Fairies: Towards a Transpersonal Anthropology of Religion.* Newcastle upon Tyne, England: Cambridge Scholars Publishing, 2012.

Gerard, John. *The Herball or Generall Historie of Plantes.* London: John Norton, 1597.

Gesler, Wilbert M. *Healing Places.* Lanham, MD: Rowman & Littlefield Publishers, Inc., 2003.

Gordon, Lesley. *Green Magic: Flowers, Plants & Herbs in Lore & Legend.* New York: The Viking Press, 1977.

Grimm, Jacob. *Teutonic Mythology*, vol. 1. Translated from the fourth edition by James Steven Stallybrass. Mineola, NY: Dover Publications, Inc., 2004.

Gwynn, Edward, trans. *The Metrical Dindshenchas.* Cork, Ireland: CELT: Corpus of Electronic Texts, University College, Cork. Accessed September 10, 2020. https://celt.ucc.ie/published/T106500C.html.

Hart, Henry Chichester. *Flora of the County Donegal, or, List of the Flowering Plants and Ferns with Their Localities and Distribution.* London: David Nutt, 1898.

Heath, Francis George. *Trees and Ferns.* London: Sampson Low, Marston, & Co., 1879.

Henderson, Lizanne, and Edward J. Cowan. *Scottish Fairy Belief: A History.* East Linton, Scotland: Tuckwell Press, 2001.

Hopkins, E. Washburn. *Epic Mythology.* New York: Biblio and Tannen Booksellers and Publishers, Inc., 1969.

Keightley, Thomas. *The Fairy Mythology: Illustrative of the Romance and Super-stition of Various Countries*. London: D. G. Bohn, 1860.

Kear, Katherine. *Flower Wisdom: The Definitive Guidebook to the Myth, Folklore, and Healing Powers of Flowers*. London: Thorsons, 2000.

Kirk, Robert. *The Secret Commonwealth of Elves, Fauns and Fairies*. London: David Nutt, 1893.

Krishna, Nanditha, and M. Amirthalingam. *Sacred Plants of India*. New Delhi, India: Penguin India, 2014.

Lebling, Robert. *Legends of the Fire Spirits: Jinn and Genies from Arabia to Zanzibar*. New York: I. B. Tauris & Co., Ltd., 2010.

Lindow, John. *Norse Mythology: A Guide to the Gods, Heroes, Rituals, and Beliefs*. New York: Oxford University Press, 2002.

Locke, Tony. *Tales of the Irish Hedgerows*. Dublin: The History Press Ireland, 2017.

Mac Coitir, Niall. *Ireland's Trees: Myths, Legends and Folklore*. Wilton, Ireland: The Collins Press, 2015.

———. *Ireland's Wild Plants: Myths, Legends and Folklore*. Wilton, Ireland: The Collins Press, 2015.

MacKillop, James. *Oxford Dictionary of Celtic Mythology*. New York: Oxford University Press, 1998.

MacManus, Dermot. *The Middle Kingdom: The Faerie World of Ireland*. 2nd ed. Gerrards Cross, England: Colin Smythe Ltd., 1973.

MacLeod, Sharon Paice. *Celtic Myth and Religion: A Study of Traditional Belief, with Newly Translated Prayers, Poems and Songs*. Jefferson, NC: McFarland & Company, Inc., 2012.

Mahon, Michael P. *Ireland's Fairy Lore*. Boston: Thomas J. Flynn & Company, 1919.

Martin, Laura C. *Wildflower Folklore*. Charlotte, NC: The East Woods Press, 1984.

———. *The Folklore of Trees & Shrubs*. Chester, CT: The Globe Pequot Press, 1992.

McNeill, F. Marian. *The Silver Bough: Scottish Folk-Lore and Folk-Belief*, vol. 1. New York: Cannongate, 2001.

Miller, Thomas. *Common Wayside Flowers*. New York: George Routledge and Sons, 1873.

Monaghan, Patricia. *The Encyclopedia of Celtic Mythology and Folklore*. New York: Facts On File, Inc., 2004.

Monier-Williams, Monier. *A Sanskrit-English Dictionary*. Delhi, India: Motilal Banarsidass Publishers, 2002.

Moodley, Roy and William West, eds. *Integrating Traditional Healing Practices into Counseling and Psychotherapy*. Thousand Oaks, CA: Sage Publications, Inc., 2005.

Moore, A. W., comp. *A Vocabulary of the Anglo-Manx Dialect*. London: Oxford University Press, 1924.

Moyes, Holley, ed. *Sacred Darkness: A Global Perspective on the Ritual Use of Caves*. Boulder, CO: University Press of Colorado, 2012.

Narváez, Peter, ed. *The Good People: New Fairylore Essays*. Lexington, KY: The University Press of Kentucky, 1997.

Northall, G. F. *English Folk-Rhymes: A Collection of Traditional Verses Relating to Places and Persons, Customs, Superstitions, etc.* London: Kegan Paul, Trench, Trübner & Co., Ltd., 1892.

Oliver, Evelyn Dorothy, and James R. Lewis. *Angels A to Z*. 2nd ed. Detroit, MI: Visible Ink Press, 2008.

Paton, Lucy Allen, trans. *Sir Lancelot of the Lake: A French Prose Romance of the Thirteen Century*. New York: Routledge, 2015.

Phillpotts, Beatrice. *The Faeryland Companion*. New York: Barnes & Noble Books, 1999.

Pogačnik, Marko. *Nature Spirits & Elemental Beings: Working with the Intelligence in Nature*. 2nd. ed. Forres, Scotland: Findhorn Press, 2009.

Porteous, Alexander. *The Forest in Folklore and Mythology.* Mineola, NY: Dover Publications, Inc., 2002.

Quattrocchi, Umberto. *CRC World Dictionary of Medicinal and Poisonous Plants: Common Names, Scientific Names, Eponyms, Synonyms, and Etymology.* Boca Raton, FL: CRC Press, 2012.

Rhys, John. *Celtic Folklore: Welsh and Manx,* vol. 2. Oxford, England: Clarendon Press, 1901.

Rich, Vivian A. *Cursing the Basil and Other Folklore of the Garden.* Victoria, Canada: Horsdal & Schubart Publishers, Ltd., 1998.

Ritson, Joseph. *Fairy Tales, Legends and Romances Illustrating Shakespeare and Other Early English Writers.* London: Frank & William Kerslake, 1875.

Schimmel, Annemarie. *The Mystery of Numbers.* New York: Oxford University Press, 1993.

Shakespeare, William. *A Midsummer Night's Dream.* New York: Simon & Schuster, 2004.

Sharma, Arvind, ed. *Women in World Religions.* Albany, NY: State University of New York Press, 1987.

Sigerist, Henry E., ed. *Four Treatises of Theophrastus von Hohenheim called Paracelsus.* Translated by C. Lilian Temkin, George Rosen, Gregory Zilboorg, and Henry E. Sigerist. Baltimore: The Johns Hopkins University Press, 1996.

Sikes, Wirt. *British Goblins: Welsh Folk-lore, Fairy Mythology, Legends and Traditions.* Boston: James R. Osgood and Company, 1881.

Silver, Carole G. *Strange and Secret Peoples: Fairies and Victorian Consciousness.* New York: Oxford University Press, 1999.

Simpson, Jacqueline, and Stephen Roud. *A Dictionary of English Folklore.* New York: Oxford University Press, 2001.

Skinner, Charles M. *Myths and Legends of Flowers, Trees, Fruits, and Plants, in All Ages and in All Climes.* Philadelphia: J. B. Lippincott Company, 1925.

Spence, Lewis. *The Magic Arts in Celtic Britain*. Mineola, NY: Dover Publications, 2012.

Stevenson, Angus, ed. *Oxford Dictionary of English*. 3rd ed. New York: Oxford University Press, 2010.

Stewart, Amy. *Wicked Plants: The Weed that Killed Lincoln's Mother & Other Botanical Atrocities*. Chapel Hill, NC: Algonquin Books of Chapel Hill, 2009.

Stewart, R. J. *The Living World of Faery*. Glastonbury, England: Gothic Image Publications, 1995.

———. *Earth Light: The Ancient Path to Transformation: Rediscovering the Wisdom of Celtic and Faery Lore*. Lake Toxaway, NC: Mercury Publishing, 1995.

Storms, Godfrid. *Anglo-Saxon Magic*. s-Gravenhage, The Netherlands: Martinus Nijhoff, 1948.

Tarn, William Woodthorpe. *The Treasure of the Isle of Mist*. New York: G. P. Putnam's Sons, 1922.

Thiselton-Dyer, T. F. *The Folk-lore of Plants*. New York: D. Appleton and Company, 1889.

Thomas, W. Jenkyn. *The Welsh Fairy Book*. London: T. Fisher Unwin, 1915.

Tongue, Ruth L. *Forgotten Folk-tales of the English Counties*, vol. 8. New York: Routledge, 2015.

Traill, Catharine Parr. *Pearls & Pebbles*. Edited by Elizabeth Thompson. Toronto, Canada: Natural Heritage/Natural History Inc., 1999.

Turville-Petre, E.O.G. *Myth and Religion of the North: The Religion of Ancient Scandinavia*. New York: Holt, Rinehart and Winston, 1975.

Twamley, Louisa Anne. *The Romance of Nature: or, The Flower-Seasons Illustrated*. 2nd ed. London: Charles Tilt, 1836.

Valk, Ülo, and Daniel Sävborg, eds. *Storied and Supernatural Places: Studies in Spatial and Social Dimensions of Folklore and Sagas*. Helsinki, Finland: Finnish Literature Society, 2018.

Varner, Gary R. *Creatures in the Mist: Little People, Wild Men and Spirit Beings around the World, A Study in Comparative Mythology.* New York: Algora Publishing, 2007.

Vickery, Roy, ed. *Oxford Dictionary of Plant-Lore.* Oxford, England: Oxford University Press, 1997.

———. *Garlands, Conkers and Mother-Die: British and Irish Plant-lore.* New York: Continuum US, 2010.

———. *Vickery's Folk Flora: An A-Z of the Folklore and Uses of British and Irish Plants.* London: Weidenfeld & Nicolson, 2019.

von Marilaun, Anton Kerner. *The Natural History of Plants: Their Forms, Growth, Reproduction and Distribution*, vol. 2. Translated and edited by F. W. Oliver. London: Blackie & Son, Limited, 1902.

Watts, D. C. *Elsevier's Dictionary of Plant Lore.* Burlington, MA: Academic Press, 2007.

Westermarck, Edward. *Ritual and Belief in Morocco*, vol. 1. London: Macmillan and Co., Limited, 1926.

Williams, Rose. *The Book of Fairy: Nature Spirits from Around the World.* Hillsboro, OR: Beyond Words Publishing, Inc., 1997.

Witzel, Michael. "Kalash Religion." *The Vedas: Texts, Language & Ritual.* Edited by Arlo Griffiths and Jan E. M. Houben. Groningen, The Netherlands: Egbert Forsten Publishing, 2004.

Woehrel, Mary L., and William H. Light. *Mushrooms of the Georgia Piedmont and Southern Appalachians: A Reference.* Athens, GA: The University of Georgia Press, 2017.

Wright, Elizabeth Mary. *Rustic Speech and Folk-lore.* 2nd ed. New York: Oxford University Press, 1914.

Zipes, Jack, ed. *The Oxford Companion to Fairy Tales.* New York: Oxford University Press, 2015.

Index

Y

To Write to the Author

If you wish to contact the author or would like more information about this book, please write to the author in care of Llewellyn Worldwide Ltd. and we will forward your request. Both the author and publisher appreciate hearing from you and learning of your enjoyment of this book and how it has helped you. Llewellyn Worldwide Ltd. cannot guarantee that every letter written to the author can be answered, but all will be forwarded. Please write to:

Sandra Kynes
℅ Llewellyn Worldwide
2143 Wooddale Drive
Woodbury, MN 55125-2989
Please enclose a self-addressed stamped envelope for reply,
or $1.00 to cover costs. If outside the U.S.A., enclose
an international postal reply coupon.

Many of Llewellyn's authors have websites with additional information and resources. For more information, please visit our website at
http://www.llewellyn.com